Consulting Techniques

for

Digital Transformation

A Practice Guide for IS Consultants

and

Business Analysts

ISBN: 978-0-646-71804-0

About the Authors

Dr Greg Timbrell

Dr Timbrell is an academic and consultant with over 30 years' experience. He has consulted in the areas of information systems to small and large firms, government agencies, Senate committees and advises on strategy to a Web3 agency, Labrys in an ongoing capacity. More recently Dr Timbrell has been advising on academic governance to private institutes, chairing Academic Boards and sitting on Governing Councils. He has published several academic papers across a range of topics including digital strategy and consulting. While working at an Australian university, Dr Timbrell established and taught an award-winning course on consulting skills, drawing on his early experience working in large international consulting firms.

Dr Elizabeth (Lizzie) Valentine

Dr Valentine is an award-winning researcher, experienced CEO, CIO and organisation transformation consultant. She has led the technical, process and people capability aspects of some of New Zealand and Australia's largest industry and organisation transformations within the public and private sectors. She has served on multiple committees and advisory groups associated with competencies and international standards for digital leadership, and Information and Technology governance. She specialises in practical approaches to strategic capability and competency development for boards and senior leaders in the areas of digital and information and technology transformation strategy and governance.

Since 2013 Dr Valentine has taught Digital Transformation Consulting Practice to undergraduate and master's students in Australian and New Zealand universities and is currently Adjunct Professor of Practice (School of Information Management) and Teaching Fellow at Victoria University of Wellington NZ. Dr Valentine has published several academic and industry papers.

Executive Summary

Mastering the Consulting Techniques outlined in this book will help you win clients. While this book provides some background to Digital Transformation and is primarily aimed at Information Systems (IS) Consultants and Business Analysts (BAs), the techniques described here are essentially universal.

Chapters 1 and 2 introduce Digital Transformation and consider the capabilities and competencies associated with Consultants and Business Analysts. The topic of the Consulting Lifecycle is discussed in Chapter 3. Chapter 4 looks at Engagement in detail and Chapter 5 sets out a structure and techniques to be used in a Client-Consultant Engagement meeting. This is when we introduce the Art of Influence using the Rhetorical Triangle. This powerful model, when used expertly, will help you win project work. Chapter 6 describes common analysis frameworks. Chapter 7 describes the innovative Business Canvas, which develops the information you need to prepare a consulting or BA Proposal while Chapter 8 sets out its structure.

Chapter 9 provides guidance on how to professionally present your proposal to clients. Chapter 10 provides some great negotiation techniques that you can use, not only in the engagement process but also when you are doing the project and in life generally. Chapter 11 considers the implications of Change on the organisation.

What we do in this book is provide steps and checklists, decomposing complex situations for easier practical application. This is the way that Information Systems (IS) Consultants and Business Analysts (BAs) work so we wrote it in this fashion.

We spend a lot of time talking about how people think, feel and make decisions. Again, this is the world of our target audience. IS Consultants and BAs all know that when dealing with digital transformation projects, getting the people right is the central aim. Technology doesn't complain or get stressed when it is changed but people do.

The focus of the book is not so much doing the job but rather *getting the job*. If you are an IS Consultant and no matter how technically talented you are, if you can't land a client, you won't stay in business for long.

While the book sets out lots of frameworks and processes, as individuals you will pick out those that work for you. We use coloured boxes in the book. The light green ones are examples or stories. The dark yellow Top Tip boxes contains our best advice, learnt the hard way in most cases.

We hope you enjoy the book as much as we enjoyed writing it.

Greg and Lizzie.

Table of Contents

Chapter 6- Common Analysis Frameworks and Tools 117

Chapter 7 – Research and Proposal Planning 135

Chapter 1 - A Rapidly Transforming Digital World

Setting the stage for consultants and business analysts

Chapter guide

This chapter provides an overview of the world that organisations - of all types and sizes - operate in. We set the scene for Information Systems Consulting and Business Analyst (BA) practice, from an Information Systems (IS) perspective. We:

- Provide the context within which IS consultants and BAs work – digital (business) transformation;
- Clarify the differences and interdependencies between digital (business) transformation, information transformation and technology transformation;
- Define Information Systems from a practitioner's perspective;
- Highlight seven types of Information Systems commonly used within organisations and by consultants and business analysts as agents of change and improvement.

Digital Transformation – the Context

The digital revolution has forced every organisation to reinvent itself, or at least rethink how it goes about doing business. Most large companies have invested substantial money into what is generally labelled 'digital transformation.' However, these investments are often made without seeing clear benefits or a Return on Investment (ROI).

Underestimating the various steps or stages required to successfully execute a transformation agenda can lead to cost escalations and eventually failure or discontinuation of a program of work. Defining the benefits and / or ROI is often the job of IS Consultants and Business Analysts (BAs).

In practical terms, digital transformation (DT) is the process of replacing traditional business processes with digital technologies, to improve, advance or streamline ways of working.

DT can mean different things for different organisations. It can involve the adoption of new technologies, such as cloud computing, artificial intelligence, blockchain, robotics and the Internet of Things (IoT), to improve business processes and operations.

It can also involve the redesigning of business models, products, and services to better meet customer needs in a digital age. As shown in Figure 1-1 there are three distinct perspectives of digital, information and technology transformation.

By understanding the differences, approaches and priorities, as well as the interdependencies between each perspective, you can better inform your client on a proposed change or transformation approach. These three perspectives are summarized next.

Figure 1-1 Three different goals for digital business transformation

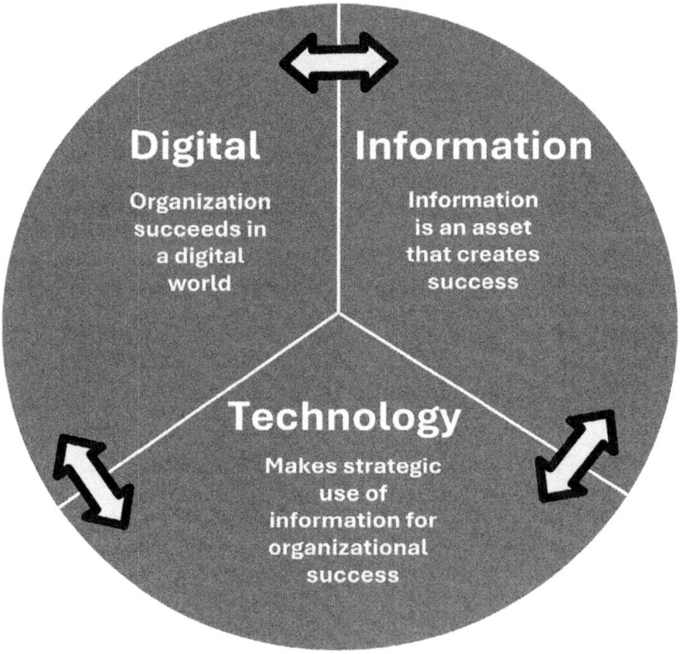

Digital Transformation as a Strategy

The goal of Digital Transformation is for the organisation to survive and preferably thrive in a digital world. In many ways it is better to simply refer to transformation in the digital era as business or organisational transformation.

The scope of transformation in the current era may examine:

- Competitive and market positioning and establishing a new strategic vision that is more relevant to a high tech, automated world;
- New customer experiences and new customer segments;

- New business models and areas for performance improvement;
- The relationship between information and the technology transformation of the organisation; and / or,
- Transformation leadership maturity and capability, and the associated culture in which it resides.

Digital transformation approaches you might recommend include: Products, systems, processes, customer experiences, or innovations – including their costs and time to market; Improving the change agility of the organisation; Channel / marketing innovation strategies; User experience design – for some or all stakeholders; Systems automation; The use of Artificial Intelligence (AI) and Machine Learning (ML); and, Change and transformation leadership capability.

To transform any type of organisation using a digital business strategy requires a complementary analysis of both the information and technology strategies. These two strategies should be reviewed at the same time.

Information Transformation as a Strategy

Information Transformation is a key part of a digital transformation strategy. Information transformation strategy helps organisations increase their agility, efficiency, and competitiveness in the digital age through the intentional capture and use of data. The goals are generally to improve the creation, accessibility, and security of information as an asset, and to support the timeliness and quality of decision-making at all levels of an organisation.

The scope of information transformation can include examining:

- Information strategy, policy and governance;
- Identity management: security;
- Data and analytics capability – whether employees have access to and can analyse data in real time to support decision-making and performance - in all roles;
- Business process improvement to understand and prioritise data sources from current and future digital systems;
- Systems and software architecture alignment with access and reporting;
- Creation, storage and access requirements – exploring your unique needs;
- The interaction between all types of information systems to optimize the secure creation, access, storage, retrieval and use of information/content within/ between systems.

Examples of what an Information Transformation review might potentially recommend: Security and risk management strategy and roadmap; Process /system alignment with data and reporting requirements; Information / data, and records strategy and roadmap; or, Digital identity and access management.

Ultimately the organisation builds the capability to use its information and data as trusted, secure, accessible assets and to improve decision quality and overall agility. This happens through the intentional and ongoing architecture and improvement of Information Systems (as discussed in the next section).

Technology Transformation as a Strategy

The goals of Technology Transformation are to align with strategy and underpin strategic success using computer-enabled technologies. Technology Transformation is a key part of digital strategy. It involves upgrading the company's IT infrastructure, including mobile infrastructure, digital platforms, data lakes and the cloud[1]. The goal of a technology transformation strategy is to provide an accelerated path to delivering on strategic initiatives and enabling teams to thrive. By doing so, companies can adapt to market disruptions, shifting consumer habits, and changing competitive landscapes[2].

The scope of Technology Transformation can include examining:

- Technology innovation relevant to the industry sector and organisation type and size;
- Technology performance gaps and the planned retirement of technical debt;
- Technology solutions, options and architecture – e.g., cloud vs on-premises or hybrid;
- Technology investment priority, policy and governance.

Examples of what a Technology Transformation review might recommend: Technology strategy & roadmap – this relies on the digital capability of board and senior leaders; Architecture that solves business and information problems; or Prioritised investment – balanced investment across Operating Expenditure (Opex), Capital Expenditure (Capex) & Innovation.

Across these three different but interdependent areas of transformation strategy, changes are brought about by designing approaches targeted at solving the underlying problems of the organisation where the effects - impacts and consequences - are most likely to improve implementation success and produce measurable value.

This often means helping organisations adopt new, more agile and innovative ways of working. Choosing where the emphasis needs to be placed in a transformation strategy always depends on the strategic and/or competitive challenge the organisation is trying to overcome, and the priority assigned to fixing existing identified problems.

Even small inroads into each area of transformation requires understanding the role of the organisation's current information systems in the efficient and effective operation of their business and helping them determine priorities as part of a digital business, information and technology transformation.

The Role of Information Systems in Transformation

Information Systems (IS) play a crucial role in the success of businesses of all types and sizes. Knowledge of the types and functions of information systems, and how to transform them, is used by consultants and business analysts alike to help organisations enhance their operations and improve decision-making processes.

Information systems help businesses to manage their data, automate processes, and provide insights into their operations. They can also help businesses to engage with their customers and users, develop valuable insights about who they are, their preferences, needs and priorities. It can identify new opportunities and improve a business's performance and competitive position in the market.

Information Systems Defined

Information systems play a crucial role in business processes by providing a platform for businesses to manage their data and automate their processes.

They help businesses to design and implement efficient processes that can be integrated with other systems. Information systems also help businesses to transform their operations by providing real-time data that can be used to make informed decisions.

Information systems are made up of multiple different components designed (often architected in larger organisations) to include hardware, software, and system connectivity depending on the organisation type and user needs.

Information systems personnel are responsible for sustaining the software, hardware, data storage, and networks and underpinning organisational processes; and the data and information derived from them. Their job is to enable an organisation to create, gather, process, store, and disseminate information securely, ethically and compliantly. Tools such as laptops, tablets, databases, networks and smartphones are part of the information systems landscape.

People and organisations rely on information systems to work efficiently and effectively across all industries and sectors, whether for profit, not-for-profit or government organisations. These systems are used to engage with staff, customers, suppliers and regulatory stakeholders. They help to manage the organisation, perform or support essential business operations, and ultimately achieve the organisation's plans and strategies.

Information Systems enable users to conduct all manner of communications, transact online, look up information via a search engine, analyse data, meet regulatory requirements, make use of artificial intelligence, collaborate or engage in learning at work. Essentially Information Systems underpin every aspect of modern work and life.

The Importance of IS to Consultants and BAs

Information systems are at the heart of the consulting and business analysis fields. They help organisations to process data, which is critical for demonstrating the measurable business value expected from a BA or consulting engagement.

Overall, IS knowledge and skills are essential in the consulting and business analysis fields as they help businesses to make informed decisions, improve their operations, products and services, and reduce costs. The role and competencies of consultants and business analysts are explored in more depth in Chapter 2.

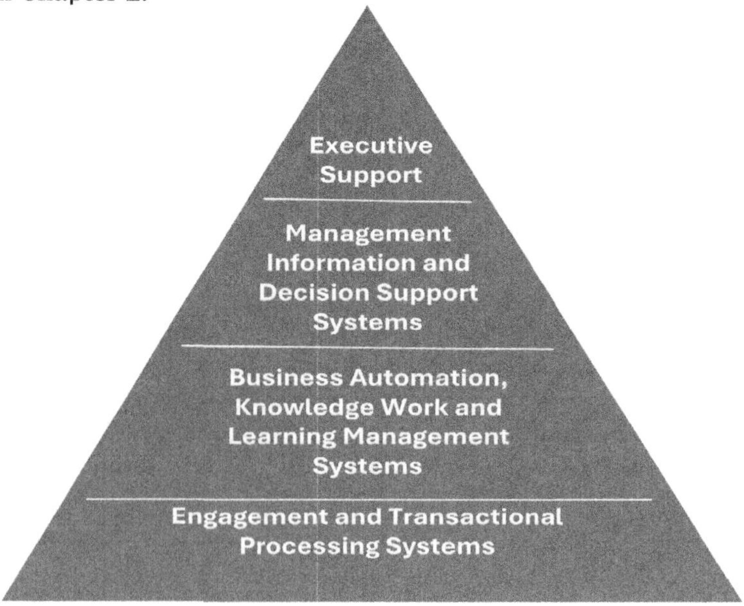

Figure 1-2 Seven information systems used across and between four levels

Seven Major Types of Information Systems

As seen in Figure 1-2, there are seven types of information systems, each supporting outcomes and often used at or between four main different organisational levels.

- First there are the Engagement and Transaction Processing Systems (ETPS) at the operational level;
- Next are the Business Automation Systems (BAS), Knowledge Work Systems (KWS), and the Learning Management System (LMS) - all working at the performance support and service delivery levels;
- Next, the management level has Management Information Systems (MIS) and Decision Support Systems (DSS);
- Finally, the Executive Support Systems (ESS) operate at the executive and governance oversight levels.

Each highlighted system is a candidate for requirements elicitation and analysis by consultants and BAs alike.

Engagement and Transaction Processing System

Engagement and Transaction Processing Systems (ETPS) are essential to helping organisations connect with customers, users, and employees, and perform daily operations. Engagement Systems enable all users to discover information about the organisation, its products, processes and services and make decisions about whether to query or further the contact or purchase a product or service.

Transactions are defined as any activity or event that affects the organisation, and include things like orders, deposits, withdrawals, shipping, billing customers, order entry, and placing orders. Transaction Processing Systems support these business transactions.

Next, we examine Business Automation Systems.

Business Automation Systems

Business Automation Systems (BAS) consist of tools that enable data to move from one system to another automatically and accurately. These tools help organisations collect, locate, manage, and analyse information securely to accomplish everyday tasks and processes at every level in the organisation.

BAs reduce manual effort and store a large amount of data. They not only streamline day-to-day tasks but also speed up information retrieval. Additionally, these tools improve process visibility and help businesses spot bottlenecks easily. BASs save time and money and support improved service experiences. They:

- Reduce manual completion of routine tasks;
- Cut down on manual errors;
- Reduce the processing time for business processes;
- Provide performance insights into process function and efficiency;
- Provide greater process visibility and identify potential bottlenecks; and,
- Support sound business decision-making based on data.

Examples include an organisation's website, online shopping and payment systems, supply-chain and inventory management systems.

Knowledge Work and Learning Management Systems

Knowledge Working Systems (KWS) and Learning Management Systems (LMS) are specialized performance support and improvement systems. Both are multimedia content repositories used to capture and store company information and instructions, policies and procedures as well as learning, training and teaching materials. These systems and Collaboration Platforms such as Microsoft Teams, ensure that the business's technical skills and knowledge are captured, saved, accessible and used for just-in-time performance support and learning and training.

Content can be pages of searchable content that use text and graphics, video or links to external content. They frequently include communications and document management tools. For example: service centre and sales knowledge-based systems such as Service Now© and Salesforce©.

Customer Relationship Management Systems (CRM) capture and access current and potential customer information.

Computer-Aided Design Systems (CAD) automate design creation and revision via computers and graphics software, especially in the manufacturing and tooling processes.

Financial Workstations pull and combine data from many different internal and external sources, covering research reports, market data, and management data. Financial workstations can rapidly analyse huge financial datasets and trading situations.

Virtual Reality (VR) and Small Simulation Systems (Sims) take the CAD systems and automation software to the next level, using interactive graphics utilities to create realistic computer-generated simulations (sims).

VR systems are typically found in scientific, educational, and business circles. Sims are increasingly found in KWS and made available via LMS or a client-facing website. So too are forms of AI and Machine Learning (ML) commonly seen in chat bots and learning support bots contained on websites and within learning and performance support materials. They are increasingly used in automation of recruitment processes.

Management Information Systems

Management Information Systems (MIS) are specially designed to help middle managers, supervisors and team leaders make decisions, plan, and control workflows.

An MIS pulls transactional data from various Business Automation Systems and Transactional Processing Systems, compiling the information, and presenting it in reports and online displays.

Additionally, these reports can be produced monthly, quarterly, or annually, although many MIS can also provide just-in-time performance data and insights.

Decision Support System

A Decision Support System (DSS) is a management-level, interactive computer-based information system that helps managers to make informed, intelligent business decisions. Decision Support Systems use different decision models to analyse or summarize large pieces of data into a form that makes it easier for managers to compare and analyse information. Often, these summaries come in the form of charts and tables comparing past, current and sometimes projected (predictive) models and data.

Executive Support System

The Executive Support System (ESS) is like the MIS but for executive and governance (e.g. board) level decision-making. The decisions involve company-wide matters, so the stakes are higher, demanding deeper insight and judgment.

The ESS, well configured to align with strategy and annual plan achievement, provides wider, more efficient display options than the DSS. In addition, Executive Support Systems help monitor performance and compliance, track competitors, spot opportunities, and forecast future trends.

Before we move past these various systems it is important to understand the concept of technical debt and how this is treated when considering the transformation of any information system, irrespective of whether the priority is information or technology transformation.

What is Technical Debt?

Technical debt describes the consequences of software development actions that intentionally or unintentionally need to be refactored because of poor design, ageing technology or inadequate user requirements, thus incurring more expenditure over time than was ever intended. Technical debt is like financial debt – it entails levels of debt, debt accrual over time and the likely pressure to pay back the debt (by rework or reinvestment) at some point in time.

Practitioners need to know about, and look out for, the costs of technical debt, because its existence often makes it very costly to 'ditch' an old system or software because of high levels of sunk cost. These are key considerations in any transformation, as is consideration of whether, where and how Artificial Intelligence might be integrated into a transformation approach.

The Rapidly Emerging Role of AI

Artificial Intelligence (AI) has been playing an increasingly important role in Information Systems (IS) and is expected to continue to do so in the future. AI can help organisations to improve their decision-making processes, automate routine tasks, and enhance customer experiences. AI can also help organisations to identify patterns and trends in data that can be difficult or impossible for humans to detect. In the near future, AI is expected to enable next-generation consumer and workplace experiences. In their June 2023 report, Info-Tech Research Group state:

AI is no longer the new "flavour of the month." It's time to either start scaling AI across the enterprise or risk being left behind. But to be able to answer questions or discover new relationships, AI needs an underlying architecture that not only describes the data it will operate on, but also takes other factors, such as data volume, velocity, veracity, and variety, into account.

This same research indicates that '84% of executives believe they won't achieve their growth objectives unless they scale AI; and 76% of executives struggle with how to scale AI across the business[3].'

AI based on Large Language Models is emerging as being endowed with the intellectual processes characteristic of humans, such as the ability to reason, discover meaning, generalize, or learn from past experience[4].

AI is the ability of a digital computer or computer-controlled robot to perform tasks commonly associated with intelligent beings. AI applications include advanced web search engines, recommendation systems, understanding human speech, self-driving cars, generative or creative tools, automated decision-making, and competing at the highest level in strategic game systems[5]. There are also concerns about the impact of AI on jobs and society as well as whether AI is being used ethically and safely.

Why do practitioners need to know about AI?

As you will discover in Chapter 2, consultants and BAs share many common capabilities, competencies, and skills. To be able to help clients to improve systems and make changes within their organisations means practitioners are (or at least should be) on a continuous learning journey. This knowledge and skill acquisition covers areas such as understanding and applying new and emerging technology such as the competitive use of AI, and new ways of analysing systems and processes.

Chapter summary

To offer advice and solutions and become a top professional in a digital world, you must thoroughly understand the business context you are operating in, and you must strive to keep up!

In the next chapter we examine the roles of consultants and business analysts and the competencies they need to make a positive contribution with their clients as a professional practitioner.

Endnotes

1. Furr, N., Shipilov, A., Rouillard, D., & Hemon-Laurens, A. (2022). The 4 Pillars of successful digital transformations. Harvard Business Review.
2. Chamorro-Premuzic, T. (2021). The essential components of digital transformation. Harvard Business Review.
3. Info-Tech Research Group, (2023) Create an Architecture for AI Build your target state architecture from predefined best-practice building blocks. go.infotech.com/it-create-an-architecture-for-ai
4. Based on https://www.britannica.com/technology/artificial-intelligence
5. Furr, N., Shipilov, A., Rouillard, D., & Hemon-Laurens, A. (2022). The 4 Pillars of successful digital transformations. Harvard Business Review.

Chapter 2 - The Roles of IS Consultants and Business Analysts

Chapter guide

In this chapter we focus on the current and emerging role of consultants and BAs in change and transformation, and the complementary but different role each of these professional practitioners plays. We:

- Identify how top consultants and BAs view the organisation they work with by taking a systems approach
- Define each role, highlighting the similarities and differences
- Provide comparisons between business and systems analysts
- Compare the core skills required of consultants and business analysis.

How do IS Consultants and BAs see the World?

We all work in an increasingly complex, tech-saturated world. To help understand organisations and how they can survive and thrive into the future, requires a comprehensive approach.

To answer the question, 'How do IS Consultants and BAs see the world?', we first need to consider how top professionals view organisations as whole systems, and how they use this thinking approach (Systems Thinking) to understand the issues and identify the root causes of any problem.

Also, in this chapter and throughout the rest of this book, we explore tools and analysis methods that broaden your understanding of the ways that the parts of a system function, interrelate and work over time.

The study of 'organisations as systems' draws on many disciplines. In practical terms, organisations are man-made systems that are viewed as groups of interrelated, interdependent component parts. These parts vary from organisation to organisation, primarily depending on the organisation's size, the industry and sector of which it is part, and how work is structured within the organisation to achieve results.

As shown in Figure 2-1, all organisational interactions happen within the context of wider systems inside and outside of every organisation.

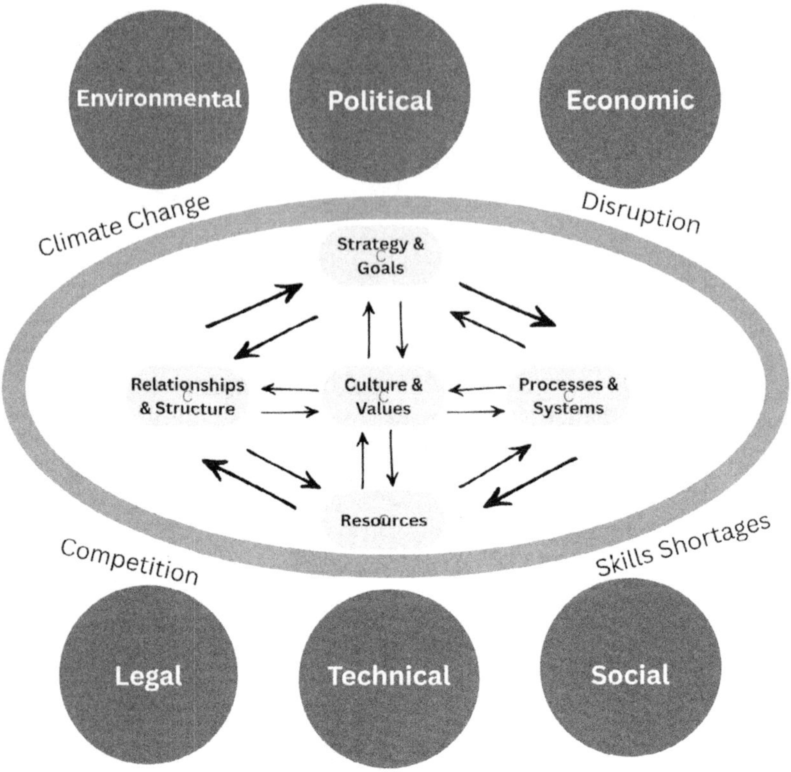

Figure 2-1 Organisations are systems within the wider operating environment

Equally, organisations are considered systems of interconnected, networked and interdependent formal and informal structures applied to producing outcomes.

To understand and change organisations requires a holistic or Systems Thinking approach.

Systems Thinking

In short, Systems Thinking is about investigating what set of factors and interactions are contributing, could contribute to, or could create a barrier to achieving current or desired outcomes.

Consultants and BAs use Systems Thinking to analyse client problems by breaking down the problem into its constituent parts and understanding how they interrelate. This helps them identify the root cause(s) of the problem and develop a solution that addresses the problem and underlying issues.

Systems Thinking is a mindset more than a prescribed practice. It facilitates consideration around how individuals and teams can work together, and thereby creates a foundation for more agile, collaborative ways of operating the business.

Thinking about the impact of any system, as it relates to decision-making, is important to understanding the broader scope of how all the pieces in organisations connect and interact. So, Systems Thinking, along with current state analysis and impact analysis, are amongst the most important core capabilities of both roles. These are explored later in the Dialogue / Diagnose phase of a consulting or BA engagement.

> Elizabeth's father was a very good mechanical engineer. She loved hanging out with her dad in the workshop when he was fixing motors. During these times together, they chatted about fixing or tuning engines.
> He would ask, 'If I adjust this part of the engine, what other part of the engine will be affected?' Without realizing it, Elizabeth's Dad taught her to think about whole systems (such as an engine) and how change in one part can impact and have unintended consequences in another part of the 'system'. He taught her to think like a Systems Thinker.

The Characteristics of Systems Thinking

Holistic, Systems Thinking considers the whole over the parts. When using a Systems Thinking approach, experienced BAs and Consultants may look at:

- A firm's vision, mission and strategy and how work is organised (structured), and jobs designed and described to achieve these;
- How an organisation's performance is monitored and measured and whether this helps or hinders strategy achievement;
- Whether current information and technology systems are optimized to support effective and efficient ways of working and timely decision-making;
- Patterns of x within and across teams or divisions (functional or dysfunctional) and wider organisational culture;
- Stakeholders, both inside and outside the organisation, who might have insights or who might be affected, positively or negatively, by a proposed change.

The question is, how do consultants and BAs obtain this information?

Systems Thinking is a Foundation Approach

Systems Thinking reminds us to always consider the bigger picture thereby providing a broad and complete perspective. Applying a Systems Thinking mindset helps provide clarity around all the different factors that are contributing to a current issue, problem or outcome. Such an approach helps to determine priorities when designing solutions.

By making it a habit to consider and reconsider how systems and roles are connected, whether dependently or interdependently, we need to understand risks and impacts and enhance our ability to mitigate these and deliver quality solutions.

If you just try to fix a problem by focusing on the part that needs fixing and not considering how that part got broken in the first place, or how the 'fix' may impact others, you risk either getting a new problem, getting deep resistance to the proposed solution, or re-creating the same problem again down the track.

The essential thing is that consultants and BAs alike must take a systems approach to eliciting the right information. Multiple analysis approaches rely on one core capability: the art of asking the right questions using a Systems Thinking mindset.

The Art of the 'Killer Question'

Another key characteristic of Systems Thinking is the willingness and confidence to ask the right questions; to ask for the information you need to get to the heart of a problem and identify any systemic issues.

> ***Top Tip***: Learn the art of crafting and asking 'killer questions' – the type of open question that helps the client or practitioner to uncover and agree root causes and get to the heart of challenges and opportunities.

This process starts by clarifying and agreeing the issues and problems, and then considering the factors that might be impacting and causing those issues and problems.

Asking the right questions and considering all possible answers, as well as taking the time to experiment to find the answers rather than guessing at the answers, is key to the effective use of Systems Thinking. Planning a highly effective questioning approach (what we call asking 'killer questions') is key, as is learning to craft questions during a client interaction. We explore questioning technique in detail in Chapter 4.

An example of Systems Thinking

While any team at work or at play is a system, perhaps the biggest system of all is the one with which we're most familiar: the natural environment. There are thousands of different interactions within an ecosystem as it responds to different environmental factors. When one aspect of the ecosystem changes, there is a domino effect on the rest of the system, sometimes in quite unpredictable ways. Consultant and BAs can apply that thinking to organisations within a sector, within a workplace and to a specific role.

Consider this example. The sector is health care, the workplace is a clinic or hospital, and we will use the role of a nurse to illustrate.

Nursing professionals need to have a comprehensive understanding of many different but related systems to do their job. They must know about the human body, the rules and regulations they must comply with, how to access clinical systems and medical equipment, patient records, information systems and access ancillary services within their workplace as well as outside in the community.

Nursing professionals must be able to connect the dots far and wide throughout these different systems to provide the best outcomes for patients throughout their treatment.

Analysis models that provide a Systems View

As we will see throughout the rest of this book, there are many approaches to analysing situations in a holistic, systemic way. While we are focusing on the role and capabilities of consultants and BAs, in this section we provide an example of a useful model that illustrates the difference between a generalist management consultant and an IS Consultant approach to systems analysis.

A Model of Organisational Subsystems

The first model was created by a couple of thought leaders in the 1980s, the decade that saw significant growth in the Information Systems consulting industry. Kast and Rosenzweig (1985) conceived organisations as systems consisting of five subsystems and operating in an environmental supra-system.

The five organisational subsystems listed in Table 2-1 are:

- **Technical**: encompassing the equipment / facilities and the knowledge and techniques used in delivering outputs;
- **Structural**: the tasks, business processes and rules, workflows and procedures;

Table 2-1 Different Organisational Systems

Subsystem	Examples
Technical	These are the Knowledge, Performance and Support systems: they include Engagement and Transaction Processing, Business Automation, Knowledge Work, Learning Management, Management Information and Decision Support, and Executive Support Systems i.e. underlying technology and information systems.
Structural	Structures facilitate how work gets done and include formal and informal roles, workflows, information flows, procedures, policies and rules.
Managerial	Planning, organizing, monitoring, improving, reporting, coaching.
Psychosocial	People deployment, attitudes, team dynamics, leadership and interpersonal relationships; communication.
Goals and values	Focus, culture, philosophy, organisation, group, team and individual goals.,

- **Managerial**: planning, directing, monitoring and coordinating the organisation;
- **Psychosocial**: encompassing issues around human resources, leadership and communications; and,
- **Goals and Values** which concern, organisation strategy, policy, culture, philosophy and values and the goals that the organisation is trying to achieve.

While not exhaustive, this model provides an initial view of the many interconnected and interdependent systems that consultants and BAs must explore in each assignment to ensure they have covered all likely causes and impacts of a problem and proposed solutions.

When taking a systems view, current state and impact analyses are very useful to understand the full implications of the proposed transformation. There are literally dozens of analytical models and frameworks that practitioners can draw on, depending on the situation.

What is important is gaining a fact-based understanding of the current state of each subsystem, identifying root causes, and understanding the impact of recommended changes across the whole system. This is called Current State Analysis.

Current State Analysis

Current state analysis is a crucial process for practitioners to understand the existing conditions of an organisation before implementing any changes. Done well, current state analysis is inherently a holistic, Systems Thinking approach. It involves evaluating the current processes, systems, and structures to identify strengths, weaknesses, and areas for improvement.

Steps to Conduct a Current State Analysis

1. **Define Objectives**: Clearly outline the goals of the analysis. What do you want to achieve? This could include improving efficiency, reducing costs, or enhancing customer satisfaction.
2. **Gather Information:** Collect data through various methods such as interviews, surveys, observations and document reviews. Engage with stakeholders at all levels to get a comprehensive view.
3. **Map Current Processes**: Create detailed process maps to visualise how current workflows operate. This helps in identifying bottlenecks and inefficiencies.
4. **Analyse Data**: Evaluate the collected data to identify patterns, trends, and issues. Use tools like SWOT analysis (Strengths, Weaknesses, Opportunities, Threats) to structure your findings.
5. **Identify Gaps and Issues**: Highlight areas where the current state does not meet the desired performance or where there are significant inefficiencies.
6. **Document Findings**: Prepare a research canvas (see Chapter 6) or if sufficiently advanced through the consulting / BA lifecycle, provide a detailed report or proposal summarizing your findings, including process maps, data analysis, and identified gaps.
7. **Communicate with Stakeholders:** Share your findings with stakeholders and discuss potential solutions. Ensure there is a shared understanding of the current state. (This engagement is commonly carried out with the stakeholders through an engagement meeting (see the Chapters on 'Meetings' and 'Presentations').
8. **Develop Recommendations**: Based on the analysis, propose actionable recommendations to address the identified issues and improve the current state.

Consider this example where a retail company is experiencing declining sales and customer complaints about slow service. The objective is to improve customer satisfaction and increase sales.

To gather the required information, the analyst can conduct interviews with store staff, managers, and customers to review sales data and customer feedback. The analyst would then need to map current processes to capture the relevant sales and customer service workflows.

Having completed the first two steps, they would then analyse the data to identify problems with the checkout process, which is slow. They identify gaps and issues, discovering that the underlying causes are an outdated Point of Sale system and insufficient staff training.

The analyst then documents and communicates the findings, providing a report detailing the slow checkout process and training gaps. This communication with stakeholders involves presenting their findings to store managers and the IT department.

After engaging to check whether there is a shared view of current state problems and underlying causes, the analyst then develops recommendations in a formal proposal, which recommends upgrading the POS system and implementing a comprehensive staff training needs analysis and program.

By conducting a current state analysis, the business analyst helped the company understand the root causes of their issues and provides a clear path to improvement. This process ensures that any changes made are based on a thorough understanding of the existing conditions, leading to more effective and sustainable solutions.

Impact Analysis

Impact analysis is a systematic approach used by business analysts and consultants to identify and evaluate the potential consequences of changes or disruptions to business processes, systems, or projects. It helps in understanding the 'ripple' effects of these changes on various aspects of the organisation, including operations, finances, staff capability and morale, and customer satisfaction.

Steps to conduct an Impact Analysis

1. **Identify the Change or Disruption:** Clearly define the change or disruption that needs to be analysed. This could be a new project, a system upgrade, or an unexpected event like a cyber-attack.
2. **Gather Data:** Collect relevant data about the current state of the business processes, systems, and resources. This includes

financial data, operational metrics, and stakeholder inputs.

3. **Analyse Dependencies:** Identify and analyse the interdependencies among various business components. Understand how changes in one area might affect others.
4. **Assess Impact:** Evaluate the potential impacts on different aspects of the business, such as operations, finances, customer service, and compliance. This involves both qualitative and quantitative analysis.
5. **Prioritise Impacts:** Rank the identified impacts based on their severity and likelihood. Focus on the most critical areas that need immediate attention. This step should identify both impact and urgency.
6. **Develop Mitigation Strategies:** Create strategies to mitigate the negative impacts. This could include contingency plans, resource reallocation, or process adjustments.
7. **Communicate Findings:** Share the results of the impact analysis with stakeholders. Ensure that everyone understands the potential impacts and the proposed mitigation strategies.
8. **Monitor and Review:** Continuously monitor the situation and review the impact analysis as new data becomes available or as the situation evolves. If appropriate, ensure that any elevated risk is recorded informally (for example email) or formally (by formal entry into the organisation's risk register).

Consider this example of Impact Analysis in a Client Organisation where the same retail organisation's planned change is to implement a new inventory management system. The analyst has collected data on current inventory levels, sales patterns, and existing system performance and analysed dependencies to better understand how the new system will interact with other systems like sales, procurement, and logistics. This enabled them to assess the impact, and evaluate the potential impacts on inventory accuracy, order fulfilment times, and customer satisfaction.

Next, they prioritised each for impact and urgency, identifying that the most critical impact is on order fulfilment times, which in turn directly affects customer satisfaction. This enabled the analysts to develop mitigation strategies that included planning for additional training for staff, a phased rollout of the new system, and temporary manual checks for accuracy.

These findings recommendations were then communicated to the management team, highlighting the potential benefits and risks. Management agreed that with customer impacts high on the risk scale, the implementation team would need to continuously monitor and review the system's performance post-implementation and adjust tactics as needed.

By conducting a thorough impact analysis, business analysts and consultants can help organisations anticipate challenges, minimize risks, and ensure smoother transitions during changes or disruptions. Impact analysis also helps ensure that the expected Return on Investment (ROI) is achieved. Both current state and impact analysis models can work well as part of other common analysis frameworks such as TOGAF, which is used for technical analysis.

TOGAF - a technical analysis model

A common technical analysis model used by IS Consultants and BAs is The Open Group Architecture Framework or TOGAF. TOGAF is an interrelated set of methods and models based on four architecture domains: Business, Application, Data and Technical. Whereas the Organisational Sub-system model (in Table 2-1) breaks down the dynamics of the organisation, TOGAF breaks down the information systems sphere into parts. This act of 'breaking down' comes naturally to IS Consultants and BAs, and is called decomposition or reductionism.

Once a system is decomposed, consultants and analysts usually turn their efforts to building a better future for their clients by designing and constructing new systems and processes. So, just as there are models for organisations and systems, so there are models for IS Consulting. Adopting a wide range of models, frameworks and methods is a career-long activity for both roles.

Models and methods such as current state, impact and TOGAF all contribute to the common outcome of IS Consulting and BA roles alike - ***Organisational Change!*** (Chapter 10 explores how to manage the impacts of change in an organisation.)

Consultants and BAs are focused on Client Outcomes!

Both consultants and BAs are professional practitioners who help other professionals. They commonly work with managers and leaders of organisations to improve and transform the people, process and technology aspects of their businesses.

Practitioners gather information and data in a wide variety of ways. They will use a comprehensive model or approach such as illustrated in Table 2-1 to make sure they understand the whole picture. In this process, all practitioners must:

- Understand the required client outcome;
- Identify the issues or problems to be addressed;
- Identify root causes, symptoms or impacts of problems as they present in the current state; and,
- Identify the needs of the client's relating to their short-term or long-term goals and strategies.

The outcomes and goals of the work of BAs and consultants are similar too. They set about building a better future for the client.

Consultants and analysts consider the systems and procedures a company or organisation uses, assessing these for strengths and weaknesses and making recommendations based on their findings.

Another similarity is that both types of professionals compare a company or organisation to its competitors or similar types of organisations within the marketplace. This offers the prospect of finding potential opportunities to help the client organisation to set itself apart from the competition. Additionally, both consultants and analysts create and provide reports and proposals based on their findings for the organisation to help the client make better-informed decisions going forward. So, let's go a little deeper into the roles.

The Role of Consultants

Consultants are hired to offer guidance in the form of solutions, strategies and approaches to identified issues and problems. They are often from firms that are external to their client organisations. They can be specialists in one area within a field and offer advice related to that specific area or they can be generalists. Two common types of consultants are Management Consultants and Information Systems (IS) Consultants.

Management Consultants and IS Consultants

Consultants commonly work as individual specialists, or form client-focused teams to tackle problems depending on the required sub-system improvement/s that will solve client issues.

Traditional management consultants tend to focus on three of the subsystems: Management, Goals and Values, and Psychosocial. These traditional consultants may consider or assess the effect of these three subsystems on the Technical and Structural subsystems if they have some IS skills.

IS Consultants (and systems BAs), have developed many tools to assess, model, diagnose and create artifacts in the Technical and Structural subsystems, which inform the Management subsystem. Naturally, IS

Consultants and BAs must be aware of the effects of their proposals on the other subsystems i.e. taking a systems thinking approach.

Many large consulting firms offer services that are specialised, employing advanced knowledge and skills. These assignments can include strategic reviews such as competitive market analysis, financial strategy and auditing, operations effectiveness, automation and digital, information and technology transformation.

Ultimately, on behalf of their consulting organisation, top consultants are adept at developing and presenting highly polished professional reports and proposals that include a wide range of data and information to help the client decide whether to employ the consulting organisation to undertake an assignment or contract. This is covered in Chapter 8 where we focus on crafting reports and proposals.

What is important to understand is how to help organisations decide what type of consultant (or BA) they need to successfully complete an assignment.

The Role of Business Analysts

Business Analysts are also hired to offer guidance in the form of solutions, strategies and approaches to identified issues and problems. They are more commonly employed within organisations. They can also be specialists in one area within a field and offer advice related to that specific area or they can be generalists.

Table 2-2 Role similarities and differences between Business and Systems Analysts

Business Analyst	Systems Analyst
Focuses on business processes and strategies	Focuses on technical aspects of systems
Identifies business needs and requirements	Identifies technical needs and requirements
Analyses and documents business requirements	Analyses and documents technical requirements
Develops business cases and feasibility studies	Develops user requirements and technical specifications
Communicates with stakeholders to understand business needs	Communicates with stakeholders to understand technical needs
Works with project managers to ensure project success.	Works with project managers to ensure technical success.

As already raised, Business Analysts are agents of change and improvement. However, there are different types of BAs. Another common type of analyst is a Systems Analyst. Business Analysts and System Analysts are technically different roles. Table 2-2 shows the similarities and differences.

While Table 2-2 clearly shows the difference between non-technical (more generalist) BAs and more technical / systems BAs, the table also clearly illustrates that both roles have a shared focus in digital business, information and technology transformation. As technology permeates all facets of business, BAs become more prominent in the professional services landscape and perform similar roles to consultants. Here we suggest that top BAs act as Internal Consultants. The difference is usually the scale and scope of the projects or work undertaken whether specialist or generalist.

However, no BA (or IS consultant) can escape the fact that their work is required to improve the relationship between technology, information and people as shown in Figure 2-2.

In understanding this balancing act, increasingly a main role of consultants and BAs is to integrate organisational activities with technology to create beneficial business outcomes. The trick is to ensure the right people with the right expertise and experience are assigned to the job (or to check that you are the right person to execute it).

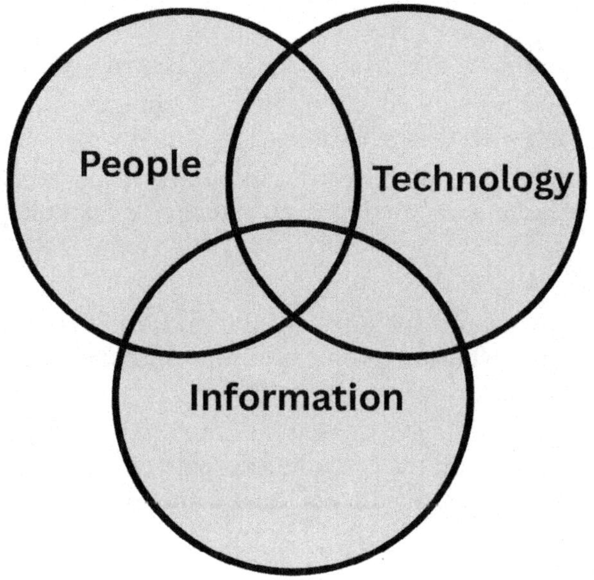

Figure 2-2 The integrated factors of Consulting and Business Analysis

Choosing the right people for the right reasons

There are two common reasons why organisations use consultants - to either **Complement** or **Supplement** an organisation's expertise (capabilities and associated competencies) in the conduct of activities within the client's subsystems.

Complementing organisational capabilities happens when the organisation doesn't possess the necessary competencies, skills or experience amongst existing managers or employees. Rather than hiring a resource, which could be a difficult undertaking if the skills are rare, they 'rent' a resource from a consulting organisation. Further, if the resource is only required for a short¬ term project or a one-off project where the skills will not be used again (e.g., initial configuration of a financial system), then 'renting' the consulting resource on a variable cost basis can be more cost-effective.

Similarly, an organisation may **supplement** the IS workforce during times of increased workload. The way in which consultants complement or supplement organisations varies, as described in the next section. Here, an advanced BA or consultant will consider competencies and capabilities required to facilitate the change they are promoting. An example is when an organisation is implementing a new system. The organisation needs to keep the old system running while they build the new one. Supplementary resources are required to enable these short-term needs.

Schein's Model

In 1978, Edgar Schein[7] created a typology of consultants based on the relationship they had with their clients.

Schein believed that there were two broad categories of consultation: the expert model and the process model. Each category is further split into two.

The Expert Model

In the expert model Schein includes the Purchase of Expertise model in which the client knows what the problem is, and the expert provides specific services that contribute towards its resolution.

The other expert model is the Doctor-Patient model where the client requires a diagnosis of the issues, and the consultant provides a suggested or perhaps prescriptive course of action to address those issues.

The Process Model

In the process model the consultant is either a Catalyst, where the consultant does not know the solution but provides a set of techniques that assists the client in resolving the issues, or a Facilitator, where the consultant provides personal input and ideas towards the resolution of the issue(s). This work on consulting models was extended by David Maister.

Maister's EEE Model

In his 1993 book, Managing the Professional Service Firm, Maister[6] described three types of consulting offerings (see Figure 2-3). The three types are Expertise, Experience and Efficiency, each of which applies to practitioners.

An Expertise practice deals with new and complex issues, requiring innovation and creativity. We sometimes call this 'blank page consulting' because you often start with an ambiguous and ill-defined problem, to which you must bring your own style of reductionism, order and holistic thinking. Expertise practices, because of the rarity of knowledge involved, tend to charge more for their services.

An Efficiency practice, by contrast, deals with well-known issues such as configuration, programming or implementation work. Because the problems are common, there is usually a competitive marketplace for these services, making the work price sensitive.

Somewhere in the middle is the Experience practice. This practice deals with less familiar, or perhaps specialist issues where past experience is required to conduct a successful engagement.

Our own research and practical experiences indicate that almost every experienced IS Consultant has elements of each type of practice in their portfolio of offerings. This is also closely mirrored in the role Business Analysts perform.

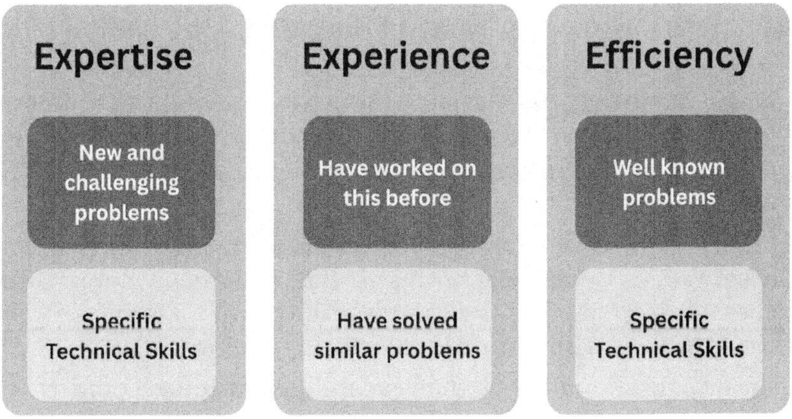

Figure 2-3 Based on Maister's three types of consulting practice.

Capabilities and Competencies

Organisation capabilities are the often intangible, strategic assets that an organisation draws from to get work done. They are at the heart of being able to execute business strategy and meet customer or stakeholder expectations.

As shown in Table 2-3, capabilities and competencies have different levels and are closely related.

It is useful for consultants and analysts to be aware of the differences and distinctions at each level and how to build competencies to enhance your career at every stage.

Let's see how you can use this information. When conducting background research for an assignment (or making career decisions) it's useful to understand the industry and sector, and to gather information about these. This is because all organisations operate in a context as introduced earlier. This is called the external environment.

At a sector or individual capability level, you need to decide whether you are the right consultant or BA for a role or assignment. Here (using Maister's EEE model and Table 2-3) you might consider your direct or relevant experience.

Industry or Sector-level Capabilities

In Table 2-3 we provide a general description of sector and industry capabilities. Often used interchangeably, the terms "sector" and "industry" have different meanings.

Sectors are broad economic segments that contain industries while an industry falls within a sector and breaks down according to more specific companies and their business activities.

An Industry refers to a specific group of similar types of companies, while a sector is a large segment of the economy.

For example, manufacturing is a sector where capabilities differ across multiple different industry types such as automotive, or agriculture supplies. Government capabilities differ across departments based on their different statutory mandates.

Consider this: Let's use the example of manufacturing. At the sector level, the capability set relates to manufacturing. At the industry level, the capability set becomes more refined. For example, Automotive Manufacturing is a category of industries within the Manufacturing Sector.

It is at an organisational level that capabilities become competitive and distinct.

Table 2-3 Capability and competency relationship and levels

Capability or competency	Focus areas	Examples / Comments
Sector / Industry CAPABILITIES	Manufacturing, Government, Forestry, Healthcare, Education, Agriculture, Finance, Professional services, Transportation	For example, manufacturing is a sector where capabilities differ across multiple different industry types such as automotive, or agriculture supplies. Government capabilities differ across departments based on their different statutory mandates.
Organisation UNIQUE CAPABILITIES and CORE COMPETENCIES	Industry-specific CAPABILITIES within a sector i.e., subsectors of each sector or industry, are made up of CORE COMPETENCIES. These competencies are the building blocks of an organisation's strategic capability.	For example: Automotive manufacturing has recently experienced a clear division between ICE (Internal Combustion Engine) and fully BEVs (Battery Electric Vehicles). The goals of organisation capabilities include strategic success, high performance, sustainability, unique competitive advantage, compliance. Unique capabilities are tightly aligned with strategy and clearly defined Core Competencies to create market advantage or best practice in government.
Division or Team COMPETENCIES	Subsector and organisation-specific clusters of competencies.	At this level, capabilities disaggregate into the high-level groups of competencies or JOB FAMILIES which appear within organisation design (Organisational Structure) and job design (Position Descriptions). For example, in Battery Electric Vehicle manufacturing competency areas might include Automotive Software; Battery Technology; Supply Chain Management; Electrical Engineering; Vehicle Engineering; Automation, and Operations.

Capability or competency	Focus areas	Examples / Comments
Individual COMPETENCIES Skills, Knowledge and Experience	Individual job-relevant competencies and associated clusters of skills, knowledge and experience.	At this level, competencies disaggregate into the clusters of skills, knowledge and experience required to deliver business plans and strategies. They can be seen in job description competencies and personal specifications. For example, in BEV manufacturing the competency area 'Technology' might include Automation, Robotics, BEV Software development and the use of AI and Machine learning in Self Driving Vehicles.

Organisational Level Capabilities

As illustrated in Table 2-3, capabilities define an organisation's unique, difficult to replicate (Teece, 1997[8]), mission critical characteristics such as competitive positioning, sustainability, levels of compliance and so on.

Organisation capabilities are acquired and refined internally from multiple interactions and are organisation specific. They can include expertise, activities, information, knowledge, relationships, procedures, processes, skills, systems, technologies, or unique adaptive features.

The strength and alignment of capability assets define a company's identity and differentiate it from competitors. Each organisation develops and integrates these attributes into its culture over time, so capabilities are challenging for others to pinpoint and replicate.

Here, it is essential to understand the role of competencies as the building blocks of capabilities. For example: Automotive Manufacturing competitive capabilities.

Legacy manufacturers of Internal Combustion Engine (ICE) vehicles (think Toyota, Ford, GM, BMW, Mercedes etc) manufacture a wide range of different types and sizes of vehicles with different features available on a per vehicle basis.

Emerging manufacturers of clean energy vehicles powered by electrons (think TESLA and BYD) or other fuels such as hydrogen have disrupted and challenged the competitive positioning and profitability of the ICE vehicle manufacturing industry. ICE manufacturers have had to gain new competencies to compete effectively.

Information Systems Consultants and Business Analysts are two different roles offering both supplementary and complementary capabilities and competencies to clients and their organisations.

Division or Business Unit Competencies

Competencies contribute to individuals, teams and organisations becoming or having capability to compete, survive and thrive. Competencies are like dynamic building blocks that are most effective when strategy-matching and tightly focused on delivering measurable business results and value.

Inside organisations, from a structural system perspective, the types of strategies and approaches to identified issues and problems. They are more commonly employed within organisations. They can also be specialists in one area within a field and offer advice related to that specific area or they can be generalists.

As already raised, Business Analysts are agents of change and improvement. There are, however, different types of BAs. Another common type of analyst is a Systems Analyst. Business Analysts and System Analysts are technically different roles. Table 2-2 shows the similarities and differences in organisational capabilities to deliver strategies and plans. These are also clustered into categories. We call these division (business unit) or team competencies (as per Table 2-3).

For example, a Battery Electric Vehicle (BEV) Manufacturer such as TESLA is organized (structured) under technical / functional competency categories.

Division competencies include Finance; Accounting; Legal; Technology; Supply Chain; People; Environmental, Safety and Health; Heavy Trucking; Powertrain and Energy Engineering; Vehicle Engineering; Tesla Automation; and Sales.

Under each of these divisional categories of competency, are functional or technical subcategories of team then individual competencies. Knowledge, skills, attributes and experience are the building blocks of competencies.

Here it is useful to understand how capabilities interact across different subsystems.

Capabilities across Subsystems

To understand the focus of consultants and BAs in a digital world, let's return to the discussion of organisation subsystems in Table 2-1. For example, several teams may have identified Project Management as a core competency. The associated knowledge, skills and experience that make up this competency might include project planning; budget planning; risk management; competency in specific project management tools (JIRA,

Trello, Monday.com); and, SCRUM or Agile methods.

We have already indicated that IS consultants and BAs, especially Systems BAs, tend to focus more on the structural and technical subsystems.

Structural Subsystem Capabilities

Structural subsystem capabilities and associated competencies cover the way that tasks are divided and integrated, how workflows through the organisation's systems, the business rules and procedures that apply to these processes and workflows, as well as the authorities associated with these functions.

Here, approaches and tools such as business process mapping, process improvement, process mining and process automation (including robotic process automation) become essential. This is because there are efficiencies and cost savings in these approaches and they are key considerations during digital transformation.

Technical Subsystem Capabilities

Technical subsystem capabilities and associated competencies cover the use of equipment and facilities and the knowledge and techniques people employ to perform tasks. Each subsystem employs different strategies. Each requires specific capabilities and competencies that are technically oriented or more people oriented. The focus or combination of competences is unique to each project or activity.

Technical subsystems can be occupation specific such as finance, marketing, operations, IT. In a digital world, the specific technology and software that provides support to these organisation and associated role capabilities are important considerations for process, system, information, platform and ecosystem architecture.

Very large IS consulting organisations will employ non-IS consultants and BAs (e.g. Organisational Psychologists) and other analyst types to manage the effects of technology or process change in very specific circumstances. It all comes down to the capabilities and competencies required to get the work done well.

Consultant and Business Analyst Capabilities

In their roles in such assignments and in project teams, IS consultants and BAs must have a mixture of domain and technical skills. In addition, they must also possess (and professionally develop) generic business and professional skills. These include researching, writing, presenting, conducting engagement meetings, managing a professional services team and developing relationships with potential and existing clients.

These skills all contribute to what we describe as the ***Art of Influence***. Later in the book we describe techniques that enhance your influencing capabilities.

Comparison of Consultants' and BAs' Core Competencies

Generally, core skills depend on the consultant or BA's specific industry or functional expertise. In Table 2-4, we compare examples of the core skills of a consultant and a business analyst showing similarities and differences. Items added in bold italics align with examples from the SFIA 9 Business Analysts and Project Management bodies of knowledge (see 2.13 for more information).

As Table 2-4 illustrates, both roles can have generalists who have a wider range of competencies and skills. Some of the skills highlighted apply to senior more advanced BA and consultant roles and are provided to illustrate the notion of competencies and associated skills and knowledge.

More advanced levels tend to be evident in senior, more experienced people. While there are some common skills and knowledge requirements between consultants and business analysts, both roles also require a set of core skills involving eliciting information, conducting professional research, analysing, communicating, testing, and verifying requirements, plus the ability to identify opportunities to solve business problems and improve processes.

Although BAs and consultants can have overlapping duties, they differ primarily in one area. While analysts and consultants alike review business operations for their strengths and weaknesses, consultants are more likely to recommend than help management and project teams implement recommended changes across a division or an entire organisation.

There are also certain capabilities that only a proportion of IS consultants and BAs possess: the ability to innovate and the ability to inspire. Through training, increased self-awareness and constant testing of one's limits, you can develop these rare and valuable capabilities and reach the very top of your profession.

SFIA 9 - Competency Sets for Consultants and BAs

The Skills Framework for the Information Age (SFIA [9]) is a global competency and skills framework for the digital world. It is a model for describing and managing skills and competencies for professionals working in Information and Communications Technology (ICT), software engineering, and digital transformation.

To access deeper descriptions of the competencies required by consultants and BAs, both the Business Analysts Body of Knowledge (BABOK) and the

Project Management Body of Knowledge (PMBOK) competency sets have been mapped by the SFIA – currently version nine is available via the SFIA website in multiple languages. The framework provides levels of competency across a range of job roles from junior, (entry level 1) to advanced specialists, managers and leaders (level 7) with governance accountability.

Top Tip: Competencies contribute to individuals, teams, division and organisations developing or having the capability to compete, survive and thrive. Competencies are like building blocks that are most effective when strategy-matching and developed deliberately to build the capability to deliver measurable value. Consulting firms must take deliberate decisions when considering the development of new competencies to enter new market segments e.g. do we develop these competencies in-house through education and training or buy in new competencies through recruitment.

Table 2-4 Core competencies and skills of IS Consultants and BA's

Core Competencies	Business Analyst	IS Consultant
Communication	Effective communicator, able to facilitate work meetings, ask the right questions, actively listen and take in new information. Able to write and present reports. Has advanced skills in Stakeholder relationship management	Broad business communication skills. Can communicate with stakeholders, clients, and staff to ask questions and elicit information. Able to provide and present professional-quality proposals and reports, both verbally and in writing.
Business research	Able to conduct advanced professional business research and business situation analysis; business modelling	Able to conduct advanced professional business research and business situation analysis; business modelling.
Technical	Knowledge of software and systems, able to use software and systems to analyse data and information. Skills in acceptance testing	Technical expertise: able to use software and systems to analyse data and information. Knowledge of systems design and technical architecture.

Core Competencies	Business Analyst	IS Consultant
Elicitation and Analysis	Applies analytical and critical thinking skills to elicitation and analysis to identify problems, root causes and opportunities, and develop solutions: Advanced skills and knowledge of requirements definition and management; and feasibility assessment.	Applies analytical and critical thinking skills to elicitation and analysis to identify problems, root causes and opportunities, and develop solutions: Advanced skills and knowledge of requirements definition and management; and feasibility assessment.
Interpersonal and relational	Able to work with others, build relationships, and collaborate	Able to work with others at all levels, build relationships, influence, resolve conflicts and collaborate.
Business	Knowledge of business processes and operations. Has identified areas of specialisation such as finance, HR, IT, legal, marketing, operations. Has competencies in Benefits management	Knowledge of business processes and operations. Has expertise in areas of sector capability (See Figure 2-4) and specialist competencies such as finance, HR, IT, legal, marketing, operations. Has competencies in Benefits management
Project Management and Governance	Able to establish and manage projects, develop project plans, and manage project teams. Able to analyse project impacts, develop project approaches, plans, budgets, manage project risks and governance, and manage project teams	Able to establish and manage projects, develop project plans, and manage project teams. able to analyse project impacts, develop project approaches, plans, budgets, manage project risks and governance, and manage project teams. Has skills in program management.

Chapter Summary

The purpose of this book is not to discuss what technology to apply to different situations. The book is about the IS consulting / BA processes used by top professionals. So, we offer the following definition:

Information Systems Consultants and Business Analysts expertly combine information and technology with people and capability approaches (staff, customers, management and stakeholders) to achieve beneficial outcomes for the client organisation that adds value to the organisation's vision, goals and culture.

From project to project, and activity to activity, the extent of involvement by staff, customers, management and other stakeholders will vary. This is an important consideration in planning for, and executing, any change or transformation project.

Recently, a consulting manager from one of the large international IS consulting organisations stood up in a meeting and said, "the success of all systems implementations lay in managing the people well".

A very wise statement - but what this person was reflecting on was their greater responsibility in the project to their client and the client's personnel. In other words, as a consulting manager, he was dealing more with the effects of the change in technology on the stakeholders rather than just the change in the technical environment. This issue cannot be ignored - it must remain the top priority for the principal consultant on the project. The success of projects is experienced by people (not technology). This brings us back to the subsystem's framework in Table 1-1.While IS consultants and BAs tend to mainly work within the Structural and Technical areas, these subsystems are inextricably linked to the other subsystems: Psychosocial, Goals & Values and Management.

Experienced practitioners always seek out and consider the strategies, plans and goals of an organisation before they commence their work. Aligning specific business goals with technical, people and process work offers the most beneficial outcomes for both the client and the practitioner.

This brings us to the topic of consultants versus business analysts. Are they really any different? In many ways... no they are not. Most Information and Technology (IT) consultants (and independent contractors) are specialists who move from organisation to organisation, plying their technical trade, supplementing and complementing organisational capabilities and competencies.

To all intents and purposes, a BA is a type of consultant: they tend to be internal consultants moving from division to division and project to project.

What normally differentiates them is the breadth and depth of activities undertaken in each assignment and the range of organisations in which they operate. When the change requirement is larger and needs several different skills, a consulting organisation is sometimes better able to coordinate these skills more effectively because they are external, and likely more independent.

In the next chapter we focus on what it takes to become a top professional practitioner.

Endnotes

6. Maister, D. H. (1993). Managing the Professional Services Firm. Free Press, New York.

7. Schein, E.H. (1978) Career Dynamics Matching Individual and Organisational Needs. Addison-Wesley Publishing Company, Boston.

8. Teece, D. J., Pisano, G., & Shuen, A. (1997). Dynamic capabilities and strategic management. Strategic Management Journal, 18(7), 509-533. http://www.jstor.org/stable/3088148

9. https://sfia-online.org

Chapter 3 - Becoming a Professional Practitioner

Chapter guide

In this chapter we focus on what it takes to be more than just average. In other words, we double down on developing or improving the capabilities, competencies, skills, knowledge and attributes required of a top professional. We:

- Introduce the consulting and engagement life cycles
- Build the foundation of your practitioner toolbox to benefit you and your career development at any stage
- Identify clients, covering active and passive engagement
- Establish how to create a good impression for the right reasons
- Discuss selling yourself and your organisation or part of the business
- Establish credibility: understanding and using ethos, pathos and logos (see chapter 4).

Many of the concepts in this chapter are used throughout the rest of the book.

Introduction to becoming a Top Practitioner

For client in our increasingly digitized world, an "IT project" is a 20th century concept. By now you will have a strong sense that digital transformation, information transformation and technology transformation are simply about business and organisational transformation.

Today, Chief Information Officers (CIOs), Chief Digital Officers (CDOs) and other executives responsible for information systems are engaged in the general strategy-making and management of the overall organisation. Information systems have permeated every corner of the organisation (see Chapter 1 for more detail on the range of Information Systems). Without them, most organisations would quickly fail to compete, discontinue operations and fall into utter chaos. Today, transformation projects, more than ever, need to contribute to the overall success of the organisation.

In Chapters 1 and 2 we looked at the environment that practitioners work in and the role they play. We have discussed the capabilities and competencies these professionals have (or need to develop) and introduced why organisations use IS consultants and BAs.

Now it's time to build the foundation capabilities of your practitioner toolbox based around a lifecycle model relevant to both consultants and BAs. Understanding the consulting lifecycle and how to apply it is where top consultants and BAs can add real value.

An introduction to Lifecycle Models

The reasons that drive the market towards the use of external or internal practitioners is the basis of the lifecycle models and principles presented in this chapter. Lifecycles are one of the key concepts of processes models such as project management, content and software development, and systems engineering. A lifecycle model is a flexible approach that can be used in a variety of practitioner investigation tasks and to guide the completion of projects and assignments. Lifecycles for both processes and systems consist of a series of stages that generally move from analysis and creation to review and termination. The stages are usually defined by what the process does and what it needs to do next. Lifecycles play an essential role in project planning, monitoring, reporting and governance.

Each stage of a well conceptualized lifecycle is regulated by:

1. Agreed outcomes;
2. The project and communications approach; and
3. Specified measures for the completion of each stage.

Life cycles are an excellent way of establishing clarity and trust between project sponsors / owners and practitioners brought in to help analyse and solve problems.

Each stage of a lifecycle represents a set of management decision points. In a well-run project or program of work, each stage can be used to establish that the system is mature enough or completed to the agreed standard. This alignment between agreed outcomes, the process and agreement to leave one stage and move to the next, is sometimes called project or process governance.

Different Types of Lifecycles

There are different types of lifecycles depending on the context in which they are used. For example, software development has a well-known process lifecycle that includes stages such as planning, design, implementation, testing, and maintenance.

In some cases, the circularity of the model is inexplicable.

Figure 3-1 Generic Lifecycle Models

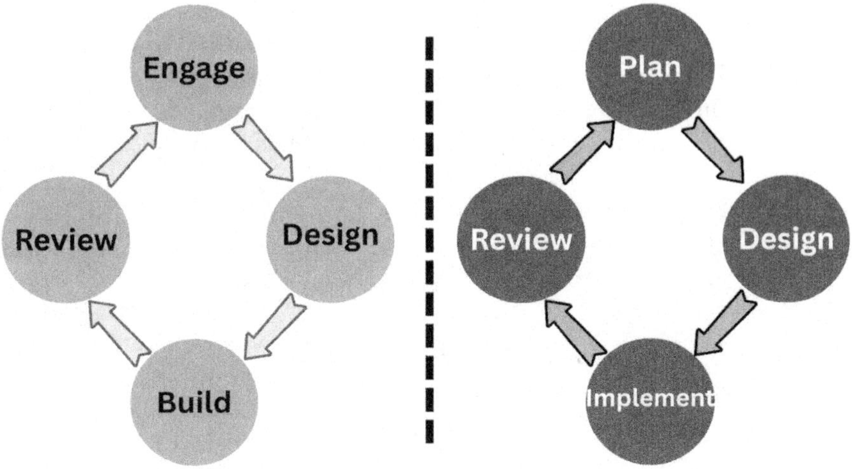

The IS Consulting and BA lifecycle model

In this section we introduce generic models and present a consulting and BA practitioner lifecycle model.

There are many different types of consulting projects— engineering-centric, strategy-focused, human resource related, and so forth. A typical consulting or BA project has two important characteristics that drive additional challenges from a lifecycle perspective.

The projects you will likely be involved in are usually:

1. Relatively short in duration (<6 months), and are
2. Highly variable in both scope and deliverables.

The high level of variability in your work as a practitioner is what makes approaching each engagement and situation in a systematic way. Developing the skills and approaches used by top practitioners helps you set up any assignment or project for success – for your client and for you.

A lifecycle relevant to the work you are doing helps keep your project organised and on track from establishment (or initiation) to closure. In Figure 3-1 there are two models shown side-by side. They are similar and used to illustrate other models you may have already come across.

Engaging, planning, and designing are about defining and agreeing the 'job'. These phases can also be referred to by external consultants as 'getting the job'.

Phases such as building, implementing, managing, or operating, are concerned with 'doing the job'. To align more closely with the role accountabilities and approaches top practitioners use, we have refined the

Consulting and BA practice model shown in Figure 3-2.

This model is made up of two parts. The central section is about 'getting the job', while the outlying circles are concerned with 'doing the job'. There is no circularity because each of the lifecycle phases can comprise a single engagement. In the rest of this chapter, we go into detail about each of the four phases of the consulting and BA practitioner lifecycle. We dedicate Chapter 4 to engagement because it's a core capability!

Engagement enables and facilitates all other elements or phases to our practitioner model and shown in Figure 3-2. This model shows four phases:

3. Dialogue / Diagnose
4. Plan / Design
5. Perform
6. Review.

Figure 3-2 The Consulting Lifecycle

To introduce you to the outcomes of each phase, in Table 3-1, we summarise each phase along with examples of the capabilities and competencies needed (see also Table 2-4).

Table 3-1 Phases of the Consulting Lifecycle Model

Phase	Definition and Outcomes	Sample capabilities
Dialogue / diagnose	The Diagnose / Dialogue phase comprises interaction and discussion with stakeholders to identify the extent, nature and impact of a known issue or opportunity. This phase requires both consultants and BAs to demonstrate advanced skills in elicitation and analysis	• Communication • Interpersonal • Business • Technical • Current state Analysis
Plan / design	The Plan / Design phase comprises activities that determine a solution that resolves an issue or creates a business opportunity. It sets out the path to its creation and implementation.	• Business • Technical • Project Planning and design • (Risk Analysis) • (Change Impacts) • (Financial Analysis)
Perform	The Perform phase describes the set of activities that moves a client from its current state to some future state of operations.	• Interpersonal • Business • Technical • Project monitoring and reporting • Communication • Interpersonal
Review	The Review phase consists of two types of work: the first is the set of activities that assure the client that the Perform phase has delivered the expected benefits; the second is a variant of the Diagnosis / Dialogue phase, where consultants determine the cause of some known phenomenon that is affecting the well-being of an organisation.	• Interpersonal • Project Review • Technical • Analysis • Business

During each of these phases, the practitioner draws on a range of competencies for each capability, always cognizant of their relationship with the client to bring the right expertise and experience to the job, and to ensure the continuation of the current engagement. Such mindful practice builds trust and helps to lay the foundation for future engagements. A good relationship with your client is critical to its success.

Engagement not only starts the process of practitioner/client interactions, but also continues throughout each phase and beyond and is central to high functioning, productive business relationships. Engagement establishes and supports logos, pathos and ethos approaches, which we will explain later in the Endnotes (and see Ch 4).

To assure quality in their activities, practitioners should use discernible methods and frameworks throughout that are relevant to each stage of the lifecycle. Apart from the quality aspect, using methods and frameworks is a way to foster the client's confidence (logos, ethos and pathos)[10] that you have a process and path to completion.

Why Good Practice Methods Matter

Methods or methodologies distinguish practitioners - IS Consultants and BAs alike - as experts in their trade who use professional tools, to promote efficiency and effectiveness of their activities. They become your practitioner's toolbox.

Your practitioner toolbox needs to contain a good selection of the processes used to elicit, analyse and synthesize knowledge, information and data from people within the client or from stakeholders in their sphere of activity.

We will cover the frameworks and other analytical models, in Chapter 6 and Chapter 7. These frameworks are the logical structures that better guide and increase understanding of the situations you face in your professional endeavours.

Frameworks are often based on past positive experiences or theoretical academic or industrial research. They form a scaffold to organise the data you gather into a logical and digestible form and guide your professional processes.

Frameworks and models assist with Situation Analysis, Impact Analysis, and Change control to name a few. For example: Some years ago, when involved in analysing knowledge management issues in a financial systems implementation organisation, the framework we planned to employ used the common interview method developed by a top international academic.

A student practitioner was assigned to conduct interviews with staff in the systems area, spending 25 hours doing so. The interviews went well with over 20 staff participating.

On reviewing the data collected, however, we realized that the analyst had employed the methodology well but failed to base the questioning on the framework.

While we did manage to garner some interesting information from the interviews, and report back a few interesting findings, overall, the exercise was inefficient. The data was unstructured and by not focusing on the framework we were unable to use it to gain the expert insights we should have. A disappointing outcome.

This example highlights the need for everyone to be clear about the method to be used, and for standards and protocols to be clear.

Top practitioners constantly evaluate their effectiveness across all four phases of the lifecycle. They monitor and reflect on where they can add new, complementary competencies, or where they can develop more advanced skills. Now let's take an in-depth look at each phase, noting that Chapter 5 is dedicated to engagement.

Dialogue / Diagnose

Dialogue and diagnose: these two words are strongly related. 'Dia'- is a Greek word meaning "between".

Dialogue is based on logos (logic) and here refers to oration or logical speech "between" two parties. Diagnose means to learn or discern, again "between" two parties.

The Purpose of the Diagnose / Dialogue Phase

The purpose of the Diagnose / Dialogue phase is to conduct a two-way investigation of technical and structural sub-systems within the client organisation. In this phase, it is imperative for the practitioner to involve the client in their deliberations, so that the two parties can discover and agree on the needs to be addressed in the project. In general, this phase is an opportunity to:

- Elicit the problem or opportunity in detail, using fact finding and questioning techniques to establish root causes and priorities;
- Analyse these discovered facts; re-engage where there are gaps in data or where root causes are not yet evident or agreed;
- Synthesize them into a useful, client-friendly format for feedback to the client.

The methodology and the framework used in the Diagnose / Dialogue phase need to be closely aligned; when they are not, time is wasted, and little is learnt from consultant activities.

Methodologies used for the Dialogue / Diagnose Phase

Apart from interviews to elicit issues and expectations, common techniques (heuristics) include:

- Business process mapping
- Business analysis techniques (of which there are many - a good reference is the Business Analysts Body of Knowledge)[11]
- Analysis of data structures
- Exploration of the technical infrastructure
- Requirements analysis for applications and database systems
- Walkthroughs of current systems and workflows and other information systems investigations.

In the Dialogue / Diagnose phase, practitioners also investigate psychosocial factors such as staff satisfaction, cultural issues, commitment to current systems, political and management issues, and perhaps the testing of resistance to information systems changes. The methods and frameworks are endless. Some are proprietary while others are public and common.

The Outcome of Dialogue / Diagnose

The output, normally an initial report with ideas and options to discuss with the client, may eventually contribute to a proposal to address identified issues. This critical phase clarifies the outcome and priorities of the client and provides practitioners with an opportunity to test their initial findings and thinking. These can be delivered in a variety of formats. Ultimately, this phase focuses on helping the client make an informed decision that will impact what you propose in future lifecycle phases, especially planning / designing and performing.

The Dialogue / Diagnose phase will succeed if the practitioner gains sufficient, high-quality insights into the issues, understands the context, gets to the heart of problems (identifies root causes), relates well to the client stakeholders they engage with, and can communicate the results of the diagnosis in a way that is understandable and useful to the client. We consider the process of conducting robust professional quality research a fundamental skill. We use a Research Canvas approach to discovering the data you need to gather as the basis for writing your report or proposal (see chapters 6 and 7) as well as the foundation for presenting your findings to the client (see chapters 8 and 9).

When writing a proposal, if the client is reticent about committing to engaging a consultant for the complete lifecycle, the consultant or BA can offer an exit point at the conclusion of this (or any) phase. This strategy lowers the risk in the eyes of the client. The Dialogue / Diagnose Phase, because of its focus on communication with the client, also presents an opportunity to build and strengthen the personal relationships between consulting and client personnel, as well as between BAs and senior leaders within their organisations. Once the current state of play is rendered during this stage, we move into the Plan / Design Phase.

Plan / Design

The Plan / Design phase may be a stand-alone client assignment. It is quite common for client organisations to hire consultants to conduct the first two phases with the engagement culminating in a report or proposal. The proposal and plan agreed in the Plan / Design phase allows you to communicate your ideas and suggested solutions for solving the identified problems to the client. Clients like to be kept informed. Always apply the no surprises' rule!

The Purpose of the Plan / Design Phase

The purpose of this phase is to provide quality facts and data, and either an initial research report or proposal to the client. Planning and designing business transformation projects are synergistic pursuits.

Consider the broad activities included in this phase:

- Designing solutions;
- Evaluating alternative solution designs;
- Planning for implementation of the selected solution; and,
- Reporting back to the client these solutions, plans and their effect on the business case for the project.

Each alternative design requires a different set of activities and consequently, a different plan. While one alternative solution may be ideal for the client, the risks involved in implementing the solution may void the business case. This is why we strongly advocate using current state analyses across the system, to accurately portray the immediate issues and challenges as well as the impact of possible solutions.

Presenting options to a client can be advantageous. However, if only one solution is presented, the decision to proceed may be a zero-sum game: you either continue the project or you don't. By presenting options, the client can decide between them. For you to lose the project completely, the client would need to reject all presented options.

When developing a business case for a client replacing an old system, the costs to the client will generally include the costs of the product and the costs of implementation. In the financial systems and enterprise systems world, the costs of implementation will often outweigh the costs of the software and hardware by a factor of two or more.

Methodologies used to Plan and Design

Many large consulting organisations and enterprise systems vendors have specific stepped processes for implementing large systems. If designing software for example, a client may choose between traditional waterfall methods or contemporary agile approaches.

When designing a system, database experts may employ specific rules in the derivation of data structures; business process designers may use different mapping and notation guidelines to create current and future state process maps; programmers and analysts may use a variety of tools and guides in the pursuit of their trade. It is not the purpose of this book to explain these design tools.

The design activity, along with all the activities in any medium to large project, will be planned in advance to promote efficiency and effective outputs and to help manage the implications of the change or transformation for the client. There are several information systems planning methods including Prince2®, PMP and Lean that practitioners employ on a regular basis.

The Outcome of Plan / Design

A quality execution of the Plan / Design phase is essential as the outcome will facilitate a decision point by your client. As a consultant, your proposal will determine whether your organisation gets the job. As a BA, your client will be able to make an informed decision about whether to go ahead with your proposed recommendations. Your clients must be able to determine the priorities in play, such as the financial investment, timing alongside other projects, and other resourcing decisions when considering progressing the proposed project.

The Plan / Design phase provides a promise of improvement and benefits to the client. While the Plan / Design phase is an active phase, i.e., usually easily identifiable activities that are therefore chargeable to the client if you are a consultant, it may be separate from the Perform phase described in the next section. A common outcome from this phase can be the signing a contract document for future work. It is important to remember that the plan and design you have created has not been realized yet; its success will be tested in the Perform stage. Effectively, you are developing a 'promise' of future benefit so there must be some sort of trust relationship established between client and consultant / BA. We explore how to establish trust through logic (logos) ethics (ethos) and relational skills (pathos) in Chapters 4 and 5.

Perform

The emphasis in the Perform phase is on the delivery of project outputs that provide beneficial outcomes to the client. This phase in the lifecycle can be the most difficult and troublesome. The risks are greater in this phase and should be managed carefully.

The Purpose of the Perform Phase

The purpose of the Perform phase is to deliver a designed solution in accordance with a set plan.

The plan is based on the beliefs of the consultant (and client) about the future activities of the project i.e. how the project will turn out. As mentioned previously, one of the objectives of the Plan/Design phase is to develop the client's confidence that the roadmap to completion is achievable.

The Outcome of the Perform Phase

The output of the Perform phase is a new process or system, delivered in accordance with the plan and design, which brings the promised benefits to the clients.

It would be foolish for any practitioner to believe that this phase is easy or that the estimates in the plan are perfect, or that the design will not change over the course of the project. It is important, therefore, to follow strict project management and project governance processes in this phase.

All the phases are inextricably linked. Poor quality in the activities of one phase will impact later phases. The next phase we will consider can occur at either the start or end of any consulting project. It is the review phase.

Review Phase

While these phases may occur in the order presented within a consulting lifecycle, it is much more useful to consider them as separate sets of activities or even types of IS consulting and BA practices, rather than ordered steps. Consider that you are always engaging and always reviewing, no matter what lifecycle phase you are substantially in at the time.

The Purpose of the Review Phase

The review stage is similar in purpose, nature and activity to the Dialogue / Diagnose phase.

A review activity at the beginning of a project considers an existing project or system and what steps need to be taken to meet the client's business objectives. Normally coming at the end of a project, the review should demonstrate to the client how your activities have delivered the required and agreed outputs and how these outputs are delivering / will deliver the beneficial outcomes for the client organisation. In many circumstances, a review is the only activity that the consultant is performing for the client.

A Review activity is different to a Dialogue / Diagnose activity. A review activity is done at varying levels of detail, appropriate to the situation, without a specific solution or design in mind. A Dialogue / Diagnose activity normally has a future state solution towards which the IS consultant is working, for example a specific financial systems package, website, system or process improvement. A Review activity is associated with the current state.

The Outcomes of the Review phase

So, reviews are conducted to achieve a wide range of outcomes. Depending on the size and scope of a project or assignment, one or a combination of the following outcomes might apply:

1. To assure the client is meeting any relevant regulatory or legislative requirements;
2. To better understand why an issue, which may be either detrimental or advantageous to the client, is occurring;
3. To gain an objective perspective on an issue concerning the organisation or environment in which it operates (industry, region, country);
4. To provide decision-makers with additional information so they can make a more informed decision;
5. To gain a third-party opinion on an issue or opportunity to support an internal view; and,
6. To consider the activities taken by the practitioner in a project to ensure they have met the common and understood objectives to the satisfaction of the client.

Sometimes, the engagement process does not allow the consultant to gain an appreciation, first-hand, of the issue(s) that need to be dealt with in a project.

For example, when a client puts out a tender for implementation work (e.g. a new accounting system or enterprise system) it may include the client's view of their requirements based on their understanding of the existing systems. However, changed system architectures or new systems may operate in completely different ways. A prudent practitioner, in this case, will build in a preliminary review stage (to evaluate the current state) to ensure they proceed along a path (based on analysing the impact of proposed options) that will optimize the new systems' architecture for the benefit of the client.

Furthermore, without the foresight of knowing how a different system will affect their organisation's processes, tenders for a new system may assume that future systems will work similarly to their current systems.

Good practitioners will always have some internal review processes to measure their effectiveness in an assignment or client engagement. These processes are generally carried out at an engagement, team, management and individual level. Such reviews are essential to promote continuous improvement at all levels within the organisation.

Personal internal reviews may be carried out by the engagement partner or principal consultant and range across a wide array of topics including issues concerning: the work, the client personnel, other consultants on the project, tools or techniques; as-a-service options; supply chain issues; possible future work arising from the project; and, activities, techniques, methods that may be generalized (formalized into a method) and used in other clients.

Chapter Summary

This chapter introduced the IS consulting and Business Analyst lifecycle consisting of the Engagement, Diagnose / Dialogue, Plan/Design, Perform and Review phases.

While these phases may occur in some order it is just as common to have them occur individually or in parallel. Flexibility is the key !!

There is no real circularity in the model in Figure 3-2 because each of the phases shown can represent a single engagement.

Movement around a practitioner's lifecycle can be backwards or forwards. The client-consultant or BA-management relationship can move seamlessly from engagement (project initiation or kick-off) to other parts of the lifecycle and back to the engagement phase as requirements change or new needs are identified.

So, it is essential we recognize that client and stakeholder engagement is a continuous activity throughout all lifecycle phases, which is why we dedicate the next chapter to this important skill.

The outputs of all the phases are a mixture of insight (logos), relational skills (pathos) and promises (ethos). We cover these three concepts throughout the rest of the book.

Engagement is the focus of the next chapter. It is the most important skill that an IS Consultant or Business Analyst can have. The continuity, growth and very survival of a consulting firm or BA practice within an organisation are based on the capability of those who engage and ultimately secure clients.

Endnotes

10. A full explanation of logos, pathos and ethos is contained in Ch 4. Briefly logos encompasses logic, pathos relates to emotions and ethos is about ethics and trustworthiness.

11. Business Analysts can use the BABOK (Business Analysts Body of Knowledge) book to check skills and techniques which are listed in the Appendix section. It is an excellent resource for ongoing professional development. BABOK aligned competencies can also be found in the SFIA framework

Chapter 4 - Engagement: Building your Influence Toolbox

Chapter Guide

In this chapter we focus on the critical role of engagement throughout the consulting and BA lifecycle. We:

- Introduce the importance of engagement as the Art of Influence
- Identify types of clients and where to find them
- Establish a foundation of credibility - conveying a professional approach through understanding using ethos, pathos and logos in action
- Plan to engage
- Identify preliminary needs
- Identify influencers and decision-makers
- Talk about how to get an appointment
- Plan to respond
- Consider engagement techniques, covering selling vs engaging
- Identify what to think about when your engagement meeting is confirmed
- Summarise our advice.

An Introduction to the Essential Role of Engagement

No matter what industry or organisation type a practitioner is working in, a planned approach to client engagement is helpful and recommended.

Engagement is a process that underpins a consultant or BA's success. Without clients, an IS consulting organisation will not last very long. It does not matter how proficient the IS consultants are at their technical field, no clients means no revenue. Engagement starts the process of getting the business (for consultants) and clarifying and agreeing project requirements (for all practitioners).

In a consulting firm, typically, it is the owners, partners, directors, or principal consultants who are responsible for bringing fees into the organisation. As consultants grow and advance in their career, so do their revenue responsibilities.

Similarly, it is commonly senior business analysts who are called on to lead the engagement for an assignment within an organisation. However, even the most junior (entry level or even intern) BAs must quickly develop advanced engagement skills to progress in their career. Engagement is an essential activity as well as a core capability of all consultants and BAs.

Consider again the IS Consulting and Business Analysis Lifecycle Model (in chapter 2) and the four activity phases. During each of these phases, the practitioner must be cognizant of their relationship with the client to progress the proposed or current engagement, and to lay the foundation for future engagements.

So, engagement not only starts the process of practitioner-client interaction, but engagement also continues throughout the life of that assignment or project and beyond.

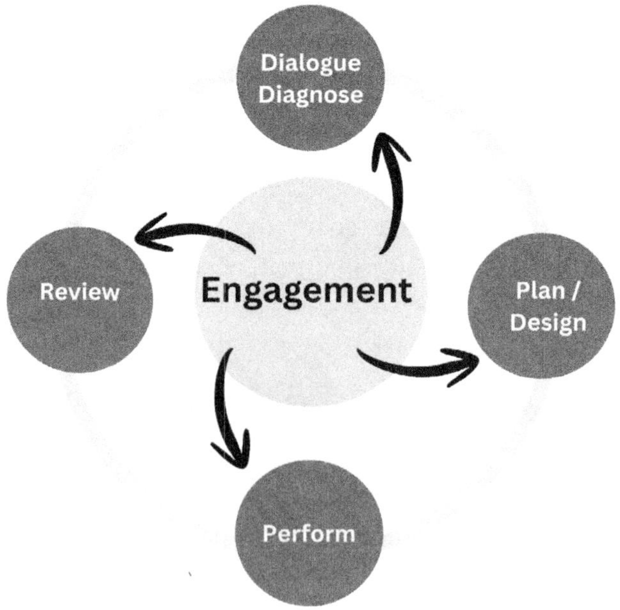

Figure 4-1 Engagement is central to all lifecycle phases

Engagement is a two-way process!

Client engagement is a core capability for business analysts and consultants alike. This is because your range of communication and related engagement competencies help build and maintain a positive relationship with clients and colleagues.Engagement is present in one form or another throughout the consulting and BA lifecycle as shown in Figure 4-1.

The main goals of engagement are to build trust with clients, establish clarity and agreement about the work to be done, and to establish yourself as an expert in your field. Engagement, done well, can also help resolve future conflicts and avoid misunderstandings in the process.

The Engagement Process

Figure 4-2 highlights the two-way nature of engagement as well as the steps in each engagement.

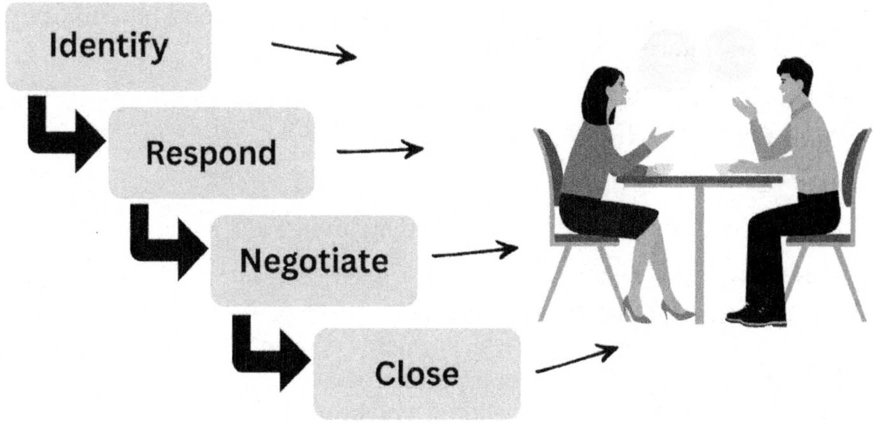

Figure 4-2 Steps in the Engagement Process - a two way street

Once the client and their needs are identified, determined, and agreed, the practitioner will respond with a course of action. The client may not immediately accept the full proposal from an IS consultant, in which case a period of negotiation will then ensue.

At the end of the negotiation process, the client and IS consultant will agree on a schedule of activity thus bringing the initial engagement process to a close. Closing is the process of getting final agreement to proceed to the next stage or to enact a consulting or BA assignment. Asking a client to commit to spending money on the proposed assignment is difficult for some people. Later in the chapter we will consider some techniques that experienced consultants use on a regular basis.

It is easy to see how the consulting and BA lifecycle works along-side each other and why each step of the lifecycle relies on engagement. Core engagement capabilities are the same or similar throughout each stage of the lifecycle.

Engagement Capability and associated Competencies

Effective communication competencies and skills sit at the heart of engagement with five of the eight competencies below representing various aspects and applications of communication. Some of the competencies (and a sample of skills) that make up the building blocks of the engagement capability are:

- Relationship management
- Communication (verbal, written, presentation skills)
- Interpersonal skills (listening, asking questions, reframing, checking understanding, summarizing skills, and personally building relationships)
- Negotiation
- Solution selling
- Business acumen
- Account management and engagement planning
- Time management.

When combined, these competencies comprise the Art of Influence. Alongside these competencies are business and personal organisational skills. Personal organisation competencies are equally important in client engagement because they help keep track of clients and their needs, and keep you, as professionals, organised and on track. Good organisational skills also help you to delegate tasks and manage time.

In the very competitive world of IS consulting, those with better engagement skills are given the opportunity to thrive, while those with poor engagement skills, irrespective of their technical skills, often do not even get the opportunity to move into the active phases of the IS consulting lifecycle. Here is a real life example (with the name changed).

Consider the story of Rob. Rob is an expert in several areas of technical programming. He has worked for a number of organisations as both an employee and a contractor. Rob is a kind man, a good father, and a reliable friend. He is very pedantic in his work, detail-oriented and provides a solid work output by his considerable skills and high-level of expertise. But Rob, like many others, is shy and not a natural conversationalist when meeting new people. He needs other people to make the connection and sell his skills, so he works for companies or has contracting organisations place him with clients. Cold calling would be a frightening and unnatural experience for him. Once placed within a client, however, Rob gets on well with others and produces good work. In the consulting world, getting the work is sometimes called 'rainmaking'. Rob is not a rainmaker; he is a doer. As a single IS consultant, responsible for generating his own work, Rob tried but did not do very well.

So now we turn our attention to the steps in the Engagement phase. The first of these steps is to identify the client and identify their potential assignment. In discussing this topic, we will touch on aspects of Marketing and Brand concepts.

Identify the Client

Clients can be identified using active and passive engagement approaches.

Passive Engagement

In this section we will talk about the 'how', the medium of communication and to a certain extent the 'who', i.e., clients (or project sponsors). Before we consider how consultants and BAs identify clients in a proactive manner, let us consider the ways that clients can identify practitioners in a passive manner.

The most common and logical way that clients can identify you is through advertising. Smaller IS Consulting organisations, however, do not have the financial means to aggressively advertise their services through traditional media outlets such as radio, television and the printed press. Luckily, consultants and BAs often have the tools and know-how to build their profile using social media.

Using Social Media and Websites

The objective of social media marketing is to build a professional persona that will attract the right type of clients and the right type of work. The profile that you create builds your brand.

When a potential client becomes aware of you personally, or the services you offer, they will often want to seek further information, i.e. your profile and experience.

The first port of call will be either your professional profile on a forum such as LinkedIn or your website. These forums will inform potential clients about you and what you have to offer. These forums should reflect your brand: your industry experience, capabilities, seniority and market position. Here is where clear, concise, and authentic communication starts. If it's your website, it must faithfully present the services that you offer.

While you may or may not name past clients, some case studies of past engagements, explanations of your offerings and written endorsements are all common LinkedIn and website features. Without such profiling you could be considered on a spectrum ranging from insubstantial to invisible.

LinkedIn is commonly used by clients to check your profile. Influential social networking sites in vogue now, include Facebook, X (Twitter) and LinkedIn. You must decide what sites you will use to showcase your capabilities. Clients who value your networking ability will check these social networks to determine whether they have common links or whether other clients have recommended you. They might also find you through a Google search, which will also show whether you have other mentions, e.g. from past presentations, published articles, news items and other public references. Potential clients could also check to see whether you 'blog' or 'tweet' on X or partake in other social media activities that showcase your expertise, influence, innovative nature, and ability to deliver. Newsletters work for some people, but they can become annoying spam unless very interesting. Short articles on LinkedIn can be effective.

Other ways to build your profile is to publish and present on topics related to your consulting practice or areas of BA specialization. A common way of doing this is to invite current and prospective clients to a breakfast or lunch event with a guest speaker providing a perspective on current issues. Topics should be chosen carefully to maximize discussion and promote networking between your consulting personnel and invitees. Publishing articles in appropriate business magazines, online portals and conferences also promote your profile. Books or book chapters also enhance your reputation. The key is to ensure that any online profile and activity is up to a professional standard and serves as a passive means for clients or employers to build a strong and helpful sense of the value you could add to a consulting or BA assignment.

Your website is an important part of passive engagement. Apart from showcasing your capabilities by demonstrating your achievements with past clients and partnerships with appropriate firms, you can demonstrate your expertise with thought-provoking content that connects with your target market. A Search Engine Optimization (SEO) strategy will assist potential clients to find you. Importantly, there must be an easy mechanism for potential clients to contact you. Many consulting firms rely solely on in-bound leads from their website to generate their business activity. To convert these in-bound leads into paying clients involves the skills described in the Active Engagement sections below.

Selling Individuals vs. Selling the Organisation

If your profile is built on the personal expertise of the organisation's consultants, then your general approach should be to promote the individuals in your organisation.

If, however, your profile is built on efficient and effective organisation processes, then your approach should be to promote the organisation as a whole.

A risk in promoting individuals is that they may leave the organisation and leverage their individual profile to steal clients from your client base. You can reduce this risk with individual contracts that limit such behaviour.

Active Engagement

The passive approaches above are designed to attract potential clients into your sphere of influence. Be aware that consulting, particularly in the engagement phase, is a contact sport! The first critical step of active engagement is the warm or cold call that leads to a formal engagement meeting. Some organisations cold call potential clients or hire telemarketing organisations to cold call on their behalf.

Cold, Warm and 'Hot' Calling

A cold call is when the two parties in the call do not know each other. The purpose of the cold call is to set up the engagement meeting.

A warm call is when the parties have been introduced either through the passive activities discussed above, e.g. in-bound leads, or by a trusted third party. Trusted third parties include friends, family members, business colleagues, suppliers, clients, fellow consultants, and organisation members. An introduction from a third party increases the likelihood of engagement success. Widening your network and encouraging them to refer you to business opportunities will increase the number of warm calls.

The best type of call is the hot call. A hot call is when a potential client contacts you to discuss potential opportunities. Hot calls should be prioritised in your meeting schedule.

Responding to tenders and Requests for Proposal

Another type of active engagement is a response to a public or limited tender for work. Favored by governments and large organisations, tenders promote fairness in procurement activities.

Both government and more commercial organisations can also ask for a response to a Request for Proposal (RFP) or for Expressions of Interest (EoI). All types of such requests are designed to take the subjectivity out of choosing the best candidate for the engagement. The document structure purposefully guides the tendering parties' responses towards a specific set of requirements.

Tendering and RFP processes, therefore, are based on logos (logic) and ethos (ethics) and are supposed to be devoid of pathos (emotion). Any emotional relationship between the parties is put to one side during the choice process. It is our contention, however, that creating a positive relationship with any potential client will inject some pathos (emotion) into the tender process and increase your chances of success. Tender and RFP evaluators can subconsciously favor people that they like.

The Professional Relationship – in person, by phone or online

To maximize your influence, it is preferable to talk to clients face-to-face or at a minimum, by telephone or video conference, if a face-to-face meeting is difficult or expensive. Video conferencing channels such as Teams, Zoom, Messenger and WhatsApp have become increasingly popular since the pandemic.

Ultimately, the best relationship with a potential client is an existing good relationship. In other words, your current and past client base can offer the best opportunities for further work. For this reason, you should prioritise your ongoing marketing efforts towards seeking further work from existing clients. Once you have identified the client, next we identify the need.

Identify the Need

The purpose of this phase is to identify the real need. As you will discover, clients and project sponsors will often engage with practitioners (internal or external) to solve a problem that they or another person in their organisation has identified. Top performing practitioners always do two things:

- Conduct background research (at this stage and in the process of drafting a proposal – see Chapter 8). They do this to 'pre-qualify' i.e., establish whether the problem, as presented, is the actual problem, or a symptom of the problem; and,
- Pre-prepare questions based on their initial background research.

What sets aside top professionals from the rest is thorough preparation for engaging, every time and at every stage of the lifecycle. Preparation is the one of the superpowers of top consultants.

Preparation – how to 'Pre-qualify' ahead of engaging

It is very common that the identification of the client and their perceived need will happen at the same time. This is where preparation is invaluable. Practitioners should take steps to 'pre-qualify' the potential client by performing an initial diagnosis of their need.

To pre-qualify means to gather background information to qualify or certify someone or something as a potential client or to test preliminary requirements for a potential opportunity. For example, pre-qualifying for a mortgage means that a lender has done a basic review of your credit and found that you might qualify for a loan.

Using this 'pre-qualifying' approach helps practitioners avoid the following embarrassing and unnecessary situation: this happens where they agree to resolve an issue, based on the assessment of the client, only to find the issue is more complex, will take more resources than initially estimated, or is quite different to the situation described by the client. The issue may also lie outside the practitioner's experience, expertise or job type. Furthermore, in this pre-qualification process, practitioners can assess the value that their services will deliver to the potential client organisation or business unit. As your consulting practice grows, you may no longer want to accept smaller assignments. All assignments generate overhead costs and if your client pipeline is generating a constant supply of larger assignments, this can reduce overheads.

> Not long ago we were brought in to assist with a project inside a government department that was clearly in trouble. The project was behind, and cost overruns were starting to appear. This was a very technical implementation of a major system. The BA assigned to the work came from a people and organisation change background. He had no prior experience of technical systems implementation yet had been assigned to manage the project because he was a senior BA.
>
> When we conducted our pre-qualifying preparation, we discovered that he had been on regular sick leave for stress-related illness and was talking about leaving the organisation. Clearly this was not a good situation for either the organisation or the BA.
>
> The organisation could have avoided this by having an in-depth knowledge of the specific skills each of their BAs had so that they could better match people with the work. And the BA might have asked pre-qualifying questions about the project to establish, and then discuss, whether they had the right capabilities and competencies to do the work.

While it may be tantalizing for consultants to accept an assignment that delivers little or no value for the client, particularly if your consulting organisation is a little desperate for work, the ramifications are potentially quite destructive for the consulting organisation's reputation. The same applies to BAs. Accepting work or allowing yourself to be assigned to a project where you do not have the right experience or expertise can lead to a bad situation for you and your organisation.A clear and agreed identification of the need combined with a joint understanding with the client or project sponsor of how the assignment activities will benefit the client, is a recipe for good outcomes for all parties involved. It is a source of positive references, further work and career progression. Practitioners carefully think through whether they are the right person or organisation for the assignment to increase the chances of successful outcomes. It would be foolish to not take this step!

Pre-qualification requires several considerations. You would be mad not to consider the following.

Table 4-1 U BE MAD

U BE MAD

Understand	The practitioner should be capable of understanding the need within the context of the domain of expertise required, the organisation's situation and the external environment (Sector and Industry and competitive or other forces) within which the organisation operates. Current state and PESTLE analysis are useful tools for this.
Benefit	There should be measurable benefits to the organisation (see Chapter 7 for more on this). There may also be a capability of competency development benefit to the practitioner, their firm or the client organisation.
Execute	Both consulting firms and their associates (inside and outside of the firm) as well as BAs must have the capability and mix of competencies, necessary approaches and activities to execute the assignment. Maturity, Capability and/or Training Needs Analyses can be very useful in establishing this.
Money	Budget to conduct the project through all phases of the lifecycle needs to be sufficient. Clients must also have the necessary funds to pay for external consulting services. Financial analysis such as cost / benefit; break-even analysis or Total Cost of Ownership can be useful.
Authority	The project sponsor must have the necessary delegated authority to engage the consultant or BA and approve expenditure. Consultants must take steps to seek proper authority within the organisation if this is not present.

U BE MAD

Desire	The client must also want to pursue the activities agreed with the practitioner and have the commitment (desire) to see the changes through. They must be able to cooperate and collaborate with the practitioner. This may sound counter intuitive. However, it is not uncommon for managers, even senior leaders, to be pressured into hiring consultants or leading change programs they are not fully on board with or are fearful of change impacts. Impact analysis and pre-qualifying questions are useful

U BE MAD

Even if the need is set out in a formal document, as a top practitioner you will take steps to satisfy yourself that:

- you can **Understand** the client's need;
- that the practitioner's actions will provide measurable **Benefit** to the client;
- you can **Execute** the required activities;
- that the necessary actions are within the budget of the client i.e., they have the Money;
- that the decision-maker or key contact has the **Authority** to engage the client and to approve the monies to be expended; and,
- the client really wants the work done - they have the **Desire** to do the work and see it through to completion.

A simple way to remember these steps is to believe that U would have to BE MAD not to carefully consider all these points prior to accepting the consulting assignment or embarking on a BA project.

Clients often have a long process of identifying their need and concluding that the engagement of an external consultant is their proper course of action to address that need. Alternatively, BAs can get caught up in a 'knee-jerk' reaction to a situation within their organisation. They still need to work through the appropriate lifecycle steps to ensure that a systems approach is taken, especially if there are significant people, process, data or technology implications across the problem and impacts (risks and opportunities) from any solution being sought.

Where do decision-makers get their advice?

During this time of identification and decision-making, clients take advice from a range of people. As shown in Figure 4-3, these include colleagues, management, staff, close advisers and their external network including friends, family and acquaintances. If you can become aware of the issues arising in a client organisation and get involved in the advice process at an early stage, then you may be able to influence the outcome or at least facilitate the call to action.

As shown, the decision-maker takes advice from a range of trusted advisers towards an outcome - the ability to make an informed decision and act.

Becoming a trusted source of expertise for friends, acquaintances and colleagues should be a lifelong pursuit for every IS consultant. But be aware that people will only ask you for advice informally if you are prepared to advise them informally; in other words, for free.

Charging friends and colleagues for every single piece of advice will inhibit their seeking your counsel. Remember, it is often not the preliminary advice that earns you fees or gets you noticed as a BA inside your organisation. It is the activities and actions over days or weeks of effort that generates the outcomes.

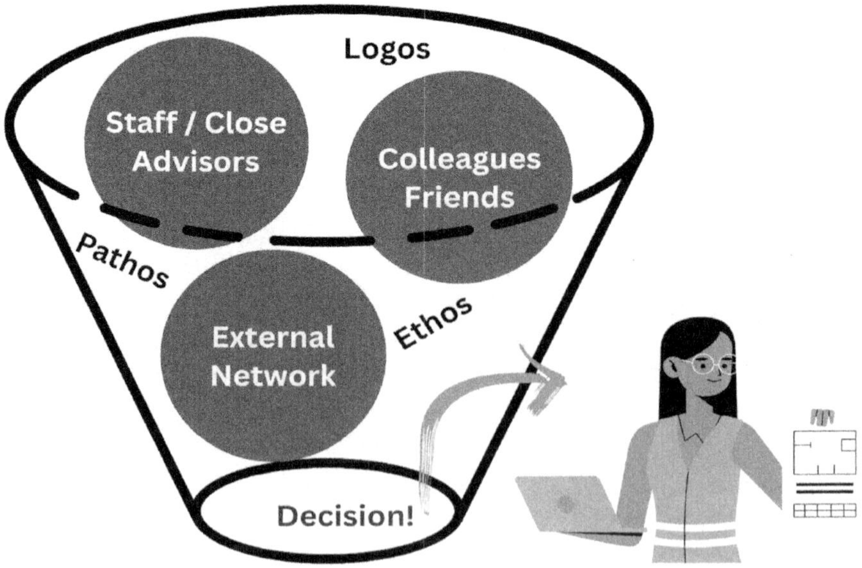

Figure 4-3 Where Decision Makers seek Advice

Many professionals offer free initial advice so they can pre-qualify the client and set out a course of action that will eventually produce revenue for the consultant or ensure you are part of premier projects as a BA. Once again, the breadth of your network is critical to your success.

Consider these questions:

- How well known are you?
- How influential are you?
- How wide is your network?
- How well can you apply your expertise to solve others' problems?

These questions are a measure of your revenue generation ability as well as an indication of your possible career progression. The more positively you can answer these questions, the better you will be at attracting clients and management attention and identifying their needs.

Having completed this identification phase, practitioners now respond to the client's needs.

Respond

A significant factor in your success as a practitioner is understanding the Art of Influence. To illustrate how to establish your credibility and therefore your ability to influence the client to act (hire your consulting firm or employ you as a BA), we draw on one of the oldest business models still in use today, the Rhetorical Triangle.

The Art of Influence using the Rhetorical Triangle

Rhetoric is the ancient art of using language to persuade. If you use it well, your colleagues, clients and audiences more easily understand what you're saying and will more likely be influenced.

The power of the model is that it helps you make all your professional (and personal) communications personalized, credible and engaging.

When you prepare a written document, a speech or presentation, consider the three elements of the triangle in Figure 4-4. If your communication is lacking in any of the three areas, you'll decrease the overall impact of your message.

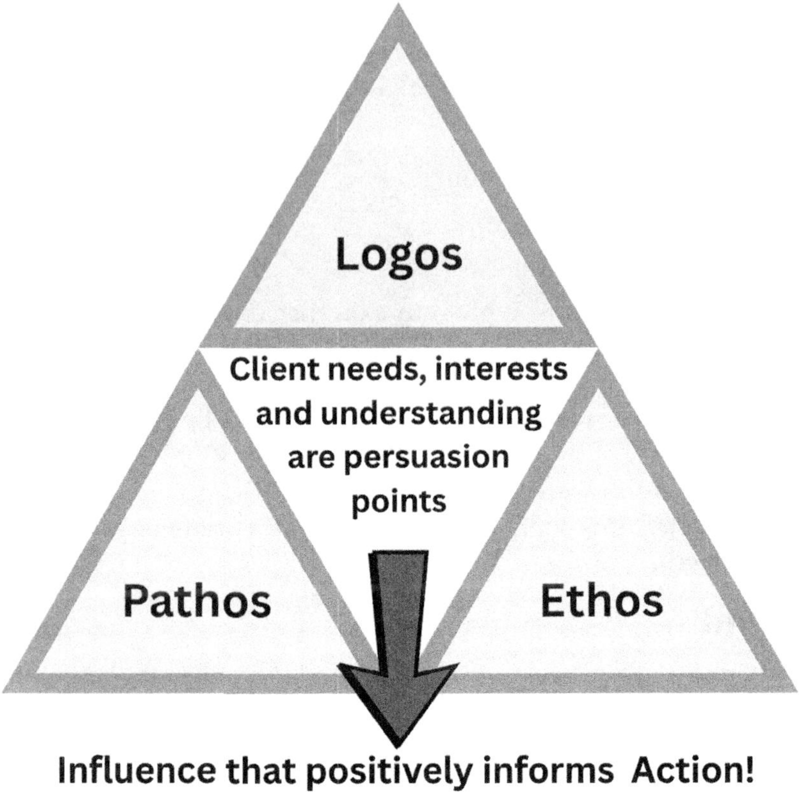

Figure 4-4 Modern use of the Rhetorical Triangle

Next, we apply ethos, pathos and logos to the art of persuasion.

Identify your Persuasion Points using Ethos, Pathos and Logos

The three points on the Rhetorical Triangle as shown in Figure 4-4 (ethos, pathos and logos) relate directly to the three classic enticements you should consider when communicating. Each helps establish and set the outcome or call to action you and your client need from the meeting.

Ethos Establish your credibility and your authority as a reliable and trustworthy source. Show you are trustworthy through your tone, style and behaviour.

Establish your ***personal credibility***. Provide information about your background and expertise, using examples relevant to the client. Use expert testimony, in other words, third-party references.

Consider the purpose and desired outcome of your communication or engagement: What is your audience's need for, or interest in communication or engagement with you? What is their likely ability to understand what you're going to talk about? Do not assume that people understand highly technical issues, even people who work in IT!

Is the outcome of the engagement step to: Elicit background information? To educate? To persuade or change a perspective? To present ideas?

Always be clear about the purpose and outcome for each engagement step and craft your meeting engagement accordingly. We will discuss this further in Chapter 5.

Pathos Understanding the person you're meeting with, or your audience if there is more than one, enables you to connect with them about identified needs and interests and enhances your message creating more impact.

Take any opportunity to appeal to the emotional side of your audience by relating to them through their values and interests, especially how they feel about resolving their business challenges. Build an emotional connection. Understand how your client, colleague or audience feels about the impact of the problem on the organisation, their division or team or their role, and also how they feel about the resolution of the problem. Identify the real value they need from an engagement and any possible resistance. Such an appeal must be appropriate and honest, otherwise people can feel manipulated.

When preparing your pathos approach, consider your audience. What are their expectations? (Knowing the type of problem, you are going to discuss) what are their likely stressors? What might be the emotional outcome of resolving the challenges they face? What do I want them to take away?

Consider how you can connect with them emotionally, from a position of truly understanding, their values, their concerns, status and the amount of risk or stress each situation is causing.

What emotions do I want to evoke? In what ways can I genuinely empathize? Where have I worked on similar problems and what was the outcome for the client? Do I use anecdotes or personal stories?

Logos Think about the context of your message and craft a solid appeal based on reason.

Appeal to your audience's intelligence with well-constructed, fact-based, and clearly argued ideas. Provide trend data, statistics, case studies, examples etc. to build a logical reason for acting (including hiring you or your firm).

Review your engagement preparation or communication and ask, "Is the message logical?"

Think about how talking with your client or manager (if you are a BA) and consider how you'll present the information.

What type of reasoning will I use? How will I support my position? With statistics? Evidence? Observations? What tone will I use? Formal or informal? What is the best way to communicate the message? Issues paper? Presentation? Email? Report?

Consider any events surrounding the engagement or communication: What background information do I need to supply? Are there important counter-arguments I should bring up and deal with? Does the method or location of my communication fit with its message?

We continue to build your Influence Toolbox throughout the rest of the book, based on the Rhetorical Triangle.

When considering the use of the rhetorical triangle in practicing your art of influence, you may note that certain clients (or their influencers) react more positively to ethos, pathos or logos approaches. Be sensitive to these reactions. Style flexibility is based on being prepared, being able to read a situation accurately, and remaining calm.

Documenting your response to the client

A response to the client and their needs must be documented in some way. This could take the form of a summary email if the engagement is initial or part of establishing needs. When more advanced, an engagement letter, a report, short document, or more formal Tender or Request For Proposal (RFP) response is appropriate. From here, we will refer to this response as a consulting proposal. (Proposals are covered in depth in Chapter 8.) You may also consider backing up your report or proposal by presenting key information through a presentation (see chapter 9).

While a consulting proposal is an important document in the consulting lifecycle, it predominantly conveys the logos (logic) component of the engagement process. However, the pathos (emotional) component is more powerful and influential, because it touches on how the client is feeling about the problem and the potential project (how stressed, worried or personally impacted for example).

Because IS consulting is predominantly the provision of personal services, the personalities involved are as important as the logical components set out in the consulting proposal. ***It is important to remember that COMPANIES DO NOT engage consultants, PEOPLE DO!*** Reaching out and forming a relationship with the people in the target client organisation (or division for BAs) will increase your chances of engagement success.

Three Main Communication Channels during Engagement

The foundation communication event of all practitioner engagements is the consultation meeting. This is the pre-agreement discussion where the potential client and the BA or IS consultant determine the objectives, scope of activities, and terms and conditions of the proposed consulting assignment.

To engage successfully both parties must be satisfied that the arrangements will be suitable in meeting their myriads of business objectives. The three principal communication channels in the engagement process are:

- The **Consulting Meeting**, where information is exchanged to better understand the client and their need and relationships are built between the principal players involved in the process;
- The **Consulting Proposal**, which sets out the needs of the client and how the IS consulting organisation will respond to those needs; and,
- The **Consulting Presentation**, during which the consultant interactively explains the key points presented in the proposal and clarifies any queries that the prospective client may have.

Each of these very important consulting competency areas are discussed in detail in chapters 5-9. Before a response to a client becomes an agreement, there is usually a need to negotiate the next phase in the engagement process. Creating an agreement that suits both parties is an exercise in seeking and exchanging information about the issues and satisfying each other that a fair and equitable deal has been achieved for all parties involved.

This process of give and take is negotiation, an important competency for all practitioners.

Negotiating

Negotiation is a process that calls into play logos, pathos and ethos (logic, emotion and ethics). Such is the importance of this skill to IS Consulting, we have devoted Chapter 11 to the techniques involved in the negotiation process. Once the negotiation phase is nearing completion, it is time to close the deal.

Closing

The word 'closing' is a gerund[12] to describe a transaction finalization type. Closing the deal can happen at any time in the life-cycle process. A client or project sponsor may call you to discuss an issue or assignment with the intention of engaging you or your IS consulting organisation to resolve the issue or complete the assigned work. This is called uncontested work. In other words, you are not competing with any other consultant for the assignment.

Naturally, if the assignment passes the U BE MAD test, this is the best type of work to get because there are virtually no engagement costs.

Some believe that closing the deal is its finalization and this is only partially true. Our belief is that Closing is the chain of events that occur while the consultant or BA is keeping the transaction active or 'in play' during its final stages. This happens where the client's decision-maker is actively considering whether or not your proposal is worthy of acceptance and the consultant is using their negotiation skills to overcome any objections or issues that are stopping the decision-maker from deciding in the consultant's favour. The more negotiation skills you possess, the greater opportunity you have to influence the outcome.

Close Types

There are several types of close, which are communicated in any number of ways: verbal, email, letter, phone call etc. Here are some of the different types.

Explicit Close

This type of close concludes the negotiation process and explicitly gives authority to the consultant to start work on the assignment. An explicit hard close is normally associated with formal documentation that clearly states the deal is done. Example: The signing of a contract or engagement letter between the consultant and client that sets out the objectives, activities, terms and conditions.

> **Consultant/BA**: Would you like us to start work on this?
> Client: Yes.
> **Consultant/BA**: We will prepare the contracts / paperwork for your signature.

Implicit or Presumptive Close

This type of close occurs when the consultant asks whether they should commence some aspect of the work, such as an initial review. The practitioner is presuming that the deal is concluded, and the client is happy to proceed at least with some preliminary work. Once a consultant starts a project with the client it is likely that they will continue. The implicit hard close may not succeed. Furthermore, the presumption of a successful deal may annoy the client if they are still not happy with the activities, terms or conditions. In other words, they still have objections that need to be overcome (through negotiation), which the practitioner has not adequately explored. Here's an example:

> **Consultant/BA:** Why don't we set aside some time on Monday to formally plan our approach to this project. This will only involve a couple of days' work and you can decide whether you want to continue.
> **Client**: Sounds good, I will create a meeting invitation.

With this type of closing strategy, it helps to involve the client in the activity so that they gain some process ownership.

This or That

The 'this or that' close can be either a hard or soft close. Offering the client, a choice of actions to go forward gives decision-makers an opportunity to decide, something they often like to do.

> **Consultant/BA**: "We can either approach this development using a traditional waterfall approach or given the novelty of the system perhaps you might consider using an agile methodology. Which do you prefer?"

It is both a hard and soft close because the client may want more information about the different approaches before making a final decision. Or, they may just decide on the spot!

The 'if' Close

Should a client still have concerns about any aspects of the deal, the consultant can use one of the shortest but most powerful words in negotiation: 'if'. The principle of the 'if' close is that the consultant can form the closing question in the following format.

> **Consultant/BA**: If we can [overcome / resolve / address] your [issues and concerns] then should we proceed with this engagement?

Hopefully the answer will be yes and the close is a hard close. If the answer is no, then more dialogue is required to identify the needs and requirements of the client.

Note that these extra needs and requirements may concern the engagement terms, the client and their situation, key personnel or methods of the consultant, or a personal requirement / preference of the decision¬ maker.

These are points worth exploring. Or you can use the soft close and simply ask what points need further consideration!

The Soft Close

The soft close is a technique to sound out the client about their readiness to make a final decision. Experienced practitioners will know that asking for a commitment from a client (hard close) too early will force them into a corner and possibly trigger a premature (or even aggressive) rejection of your proposal. A soft close allows the client to communicate their willingness to continue negotiating towards a beneficial outcome. Done well, a soft close will keep the client 'in play' and not threaten the good work done so far. A consultant or BA may employ a number of soft closes during the engagement process. A soft close indicates your progress towards a conclusion. Example:

> **Consultant/BA**: Are we on the right track?
> Are there any more issues that we need to sort out before wrapping up our discussion?

Note: changing your language to 'closing the deal' or 'starting the work' hardens this close technique. Remember, a premature hard close can be off-putting if the client is not ready.

Closing Techniques Practitioners should use with great caution

Here are some closing techniques to use with extreme care.

Price reduction

This can reduce the professional brand and image of the consulting organisation. However, it is not unusual for IS consultants to state that the quoted rates are reduced for some reason or another. It is not recommended that you reduce the price as a deal closer, because it gives the impression that it was too high in the first place. Savvy clients may also ask for price reductions based on unhappiness about certain aspects of work delivered. Sometimes this is reasonable, and other times it is just a technique to save them some money.

If successful on one occasion, look out for further attempts at reducing invoices in the future. At some point, if the requests are spurious, you need to be firm about payment. Ensure your contract terms and conditions give you sufficient flexibility.

Flexibility rather than discounting for consultants?

Consider presenting your rates for the work as a scale. We have used this approach effectively for large and small clients.

For example, indicative rates for a senior practitioner might be $250 per hour for up to 200 hours work, $175 for over 200 and up to 400 hours and so on. You're not discounting in the traditional sense, rather, you're incentivizing the client to commit to an amount of time at an agreed rate.

The success of this approach is dependent on your ability to competently estimate time and resources (as covered in chapter 8, 'The Back End'.)

Time restriction on making a decision

This can be used under certain circumstances. The availability of staff can create time restrictions. It is reasonable to put a time limit on the acceptance of a proposal, but the limit needs to reflect the professional nature of the industry.

Criticism of other organisations

If you know of other organisations competing for the business, resist the temptation to criticise them. The client can view this behaviour as unprofessional.

Reciprocity

If you have provided some favour, service or advice to the client in the past then mentioning it in the close can trigger a feeling of reciprocity in the client. Some clients feel the need to reciprocate your unsolicited past services by offering you the engagement. Be careful you don't explicitly ask for the return of favour, because this can back them into a corner and trigger an unexpected, possibly aggressive response.

Other Engagement Techniques

The Rule of Three

In public speaking, orators, politicians and other presenters constantly use the Rule of Three. The Rule of Three is a curiosity that has been around since the early Greek philosophers.

For some reason people react favorably to information or phrases presented in threes. When combined with other speaking techniques, such as repetition and Attribute, Purpose, Value (APV) construction, it can increase

> **Example** - using Rule of Three, repetition and APV construction:
> "For this project we will provide great people, great service and great outcomes".

your influence. [See chapter 7 for a fuller explanation of APV and its uses.]

Politicians and advertising companies use the Rule of Three all the time. One of their favourite techniques is start the three words with the same letter.

> **Example** - When commenting on military dispute between two countries, a politician might call for "De-escalation, Dialogue and Diplomacy". Or in advertising you often see "Big. Bold. Beautiful.", "Fun. Fast. Friendly." or "Smart. Simple. Secure".

The technical term for words starting with the same letter or words that rhyme is phonetic cohesion, a well-known influencing technique.

Some people combine the Rule of Three with This or That, offering three alternative ways forward for the client.

Adviser Close

The adviser close occurs when you direct your final overtures to the identified adviser, influencer or companion of the targeted decision-maker.

If a decision-maker brings along a companion to engagement meetings, there is often a reason, normally so the decision-maker can discuss or obtain a second opinion about your proposal.

Since the adviser will not be held as responsible for the final decision as the decision-maker, they are more likely to be influenced by logos, pathos or ethos engagement approaches. Furthermore, addressing the advisor and asking their opinion recognizes their power and influence and may elicit a positive emotional response from them.

If you can target your dialogue towards the adviser, build a relationship with them, and recognize their importance, you may bring them on side and perhaps join you in influencing the decision-maker towards a beneficial decision.

Bonus Close

The Bonus Close is a variation on the time restriction close. The Bonus Close is where you offer a free or cheap additional service should the client agree to the engagement.

> **Example** - If you go ahead, we have an expert in this area visiting from the UK next week. If you would like to spend a little time with him, we can arrange that – there would be no charge for this.

Negative Benefit Close

This close should be used with caution. The Negative Benefit Close, sometimes called the "Neg" is where you ask the client what would happen if you don't go ahead with this assignment. What impact will it have on their business? There are many, many types of close. These are just a few techniques that we hope will assist you in engaging more clients.

Selling vs. Engaging

We recommend that practitioners, especially consultants avoid terms such as selling, sales pitch, meeting budgets, account management, commission and other traditional sales terms when dealing with clients. This kind of selling language can detract from the professional image that an IS consultant needs to portray. Of course, we do suggest that consultants should draw from the tools of influence that our colleagues in traditional sales roles employ. IS consultants have a lot to learn from sales personnel. However, clients in the information and technology industries deal with sales personnel all the time and are very familiar with their techniques, including closes.

When the Deal is Done

While many deals are done verbally, or on a 'handshake' within a trust relationship between the two parties, it is useful to always remember the following 'wise words'.The first is a saying attributed to Samuel Goldwyn in the 19th Century and the second saying was from Chris, a lawyer colleague:

A verbal contract is not worth the paper it is written on.

In contracts, trust is not an issue.

What Chris meant by this second saying was that many times during a contract negotiation, the other party would say 'you just have to trust that we will do this'. Chris's response to this was that should a dispute end up in court, by which time the trust relationship has completely dissipated, the judge would usually give more weight to the contract's written terms. The parties involved should also include all promises in writing, especially ones that any party suggested should be based on trust alone! This can be in the form of an engagement letter, contract, Statement of Intent or even just a follow-up email. Just get it in writing!

Chapter Summary

In this chapter we considered the Engagement Phase of the IS Consulting and BA lifecycle. These steps are Identify, Respond, Negotiate and Close. Mastering the consulting techniques of the Engagement phase will prepare you for senior roles in consulting organisations.

End Notes

12. A gerund is a noun derived from a verb, such as when you describe the sport of 'sailing' or the hobby of 'knitting'.

Chapter 5 - Professional and Productive Client Engagement Meetings

Chapter guide

In this chapter we introduce how to plan and conduct professional, productive meetings based on a seven-step model. The approach helps make sure every aspect of your client engagement is planned and conducted to a high professional standard. Taking a disciplined approach to planning and communicating within the meeting ensures you and the client do not waste any time and that all parties agree on the issues and possible outcomes. Well-planned and conducted meetings set the foundation for successful relationships and quality outcomes. We cover:

- Seven steps to meeting success
- Meeting with the right person or people
- Preparation and pre-engagement
- Introductions
- Rapport Building
- Checking objectives and constraints
- Discussion and keeping on track
- Concluding: summarizing and agreeing next steps
- Following up – reporting back
- Summary

Throughout the chapter we provide examples of how to use logos, pathos and ethos to build your credibility as a practitioner, by learning how to target your client engagement.

Planning and conducting meetings that get results

There's nothing worse than a meeting where attendees leave thinking, 'That was a complete waste of time!'

During the consulting lifecycle, you may meet one or more people from the client organisation before presenting your written proposal to them. These meetings vary considerably in purpose,structure, and objectives. Without careful planning you increase the risk of wastingeveryone's time which in turn risks eroding trust (ethos and pathos) and confidence - in you or your firm or you as a BA - as the logical choice to select for the project (logos).

Planning, scheduling, running and following up engagement meetings are core competencies for consultants and BAs alike. Practitioners are always in engagement mode, using a broad set of competencies to successfully establish and work through an assignment, look for the next assignment, or seek to extend an existing engagement.

The most complex interaction is when a group from the consulting firm or BA team meets with a group from the potential client or business areas concerned. In the following discussion, we assume these scenarios. Naturally, the techniques and issues discussed equally apply to a one-on-one discussion and in your personal life.

Productive meetings require mastery of the Rhetorical Triangle

Meetings are a melting pot of logic, emotion and ethics (logos, pathos and ethos). Too often, people in business believe that participants in commercial discussions always act rationally. This is rarely the case. Humans are driven by their natural instincts and intuition, i.e. their personality, forged by individual life experiences and existence within a complex web of personal and organisational politics.

If you are meeting your potential clients for the first time, then your key word is exploration.

As Greg's dad, a senior sales executive, often said:

"God gave you two ears and only one mouth for a reason son."

The message he was conveying was that we should listen twice as much as we talk!

If you want to plan and host a successful meeting, you'll need a proper framework and time management strategy to lead the discussion in the right direction.

To achieve this, we explore how people operate in an engagement meeting context. First, we will look at a general structure for engagement meetings (from here on in we just call them meetings) and then we will explore the dynamics of these encounters.

So, our objective in this chapter is to assure you that effective (well-planned and conducted) meetings leave everyone feeling organised, motivated, and clear on what they need to get done before-hand, during and in the following days or weeks.

We explore how people operate in a meeting context. First, we will look at a general structure for engagement meetings. We expand on your 'killer questions' toolbox and consider the dynamics of meetings to ensure you and your client obtain value from them.

Seven Steps to Meeting Success

Over the years, we have developed a seven-step process for engagement meetings (as seen in Figure 5-1) to assist practitioners in achieving a targeted, focused meeting that achieves results.

The seven steps we suggest are not supposed to be a prescriptive approach, but rather a framework for practitioners to plan and conduct highly focused, productive and successful meetings in their own unique way. As show in Figure 5-1, The planning happens before – naturally it covers planning for all the other six steps. Steps two to seven usually happen during or after the meeting. You may have extra steps and techniques - that is fine. But make sure that you cover all the basics contained in the steps introduced.

Step 1: Purpose, Pre-Meeting Preparation and Pre-Engagement

Here, Benjamin Franklin's immortal words hold true for all practitioners:

"By failing to prepare, you are preparing to fail."

Top professionals know that the time taken to prepare for a meeting is time well spent. And we don't mean having a short discussion in the Uber / taxi going to the client premises!

Professionals prepare for a formal exercise with key personnel involved, e.g. partner or senior BA, so that the communications which underpin the engagement of a new client, are conducted with clear objectives and intent.

Plan every Engagement, especially Meetings

Even if the client has initiated the meeting, you still have important preparations to make. The outcome of this set of activities will be a meeting date, time and attendees and a draft agenda, which has been sent to the client for input. If you or your team has initiated the meeting, then every step of this stage matters.

Figure 5-1 Seven Steps of Planning and Conducing an Engagement Meeting

Prepare for Dialogue

In any meeting, practitioners should purposefully prepare for a dialogue with a view to achieving objectives and outcomes that benefits the client. Overall objectives should help you and the client clarify what outcomes and outputs (the tangible outcomes of the project such as a new system or process) they are after, what work needs to be done and how the work might be done. These are serious matters, often with high risk and high cost for the potential or existing client.

Your ability to influence clients to consider or accept your advice will depend on your mastery of the logical (logos), relational (pathos) and ethical (ethos) dynamics.

Identify the Purpose, Objectives and Outcomes of every Meeting

This is a step that way too many practitioners leave out but is one you should always include. A meeting's purpose and outcomes can vary widely. Understanding and clarifying the purpose and outcomes of every meeting helps to establish a very focused, on-point agenda.

Outcomes are established by answering the following question: 'By the end of the meeting, we will have...' e.g.,

- Established whether we are the right type of consultancy to solve the client's problems;
- Identified the root cause/s of the articulated problem;
- Agreed areas of risk and opportunity;
- Identified key stakeholders;
- Identified relevant background documents.

There are of course an infinite number of possibilities depending on where in the lifecycle you are at, and the situation you're meeting about. Outcomes always start with a verb, an action word. You have a choice as to whether you share the outcomes that are important to you as a practitioner with the client depending on the purpose, objectives and outcomes.

If you want to make productive use of your and your client's time, our advice is to plan every type of professional (and important personal) communication based on a clear purpose, objective/s and outcome. This principle includes phone call, emails and presentations!

Establishing the meeting purpose involves defining the primary reason for the meeting, such as discussing project updates or making strategic decisions. This sets the overall agenda and ensures all participants understand the focus. Meeting objectives are specific goals that need to be achieved during the meeting, like reviewing a project timeline or discussing solution options. Meeting outcomes, on the other hand, are the tangible results or actions that come from the meeting, such as decisions made, tasks assigned, or next steps outlined.

While the purpose provides direction, objectives guide the discussion, and outcomes measure the meeting's success. The first thing you need to clarify is the purpose of the meeting. This will depend entirely on what stage of the lifecycle you're at.

Establishing the meeting purpose based on the lifecycle

Clarifying your meeting purpose is about establishing the foundation and initial understanding of the challenges or opportunities that the client is focusing on. Starting with a clarification of the meeting purpose makes it much easier to establish draft objectives for the meeting. The purpose generally depends on where you are up to in the consulting / BA lifecycle.

If this is a first meeting, the purpose is to meet the client or project leader, to establish the relationship and identify the problem or opportunity and other key information (Dialogue / Diagnose).

If this is a project kick off meeting, the purpose will be to get the project off the ground and officially get started on the project work. It's a jumping off point for the project team and client team (Plan / Design).

If this is a progress update meeting, the purpose will be to elicit feedback on findings and actions to date, establish any variances to the project or contract and generally gauge client satisfaction with the process, approach and results to date (Perform).

If this is a project review meeting, the purpose is to evaluate the project's performance from the client's perspective, focusing on three key areas: what was promised (measurable organisational value), what was delivered (tangible outcomes and outputs), and how the project was experienced (perceived value from the client or user perspective). We discuss these measures in Chapter 7.

Once the meeting purposes are established, associated objectives and outcomes can be determined.

Establishing Meeting Objectives

Establishing meeting objectives that align with the meeting purpose is crucial for business analysts to ensure productive and focused discussions. The meeting purpose sets the overarching reason for the gathering, such as discussing project updates or making strategic decisions. Meeting objectives, however, break down this purpose into specific, actionable goals that need to be achieved during the meeting. For instance, if the purpose is to discuss project updates, the objectives might include reviewing the project timeline, identifying completed and pending tasks, and addressing any issues or roadblocks.

By clearly defining these objectives, business analysts can guide the conversation effectively, keep participants on track, and ensure that the meeting yields tangible outcomes that support the overall purpose.

Establishing Meeting Outcomes

Establishing outcomes that relate to meeting objectives is essential for ensuring that the meeting achieves its intended goals. Meeting objectives are specific, actionable goals set to fulfil the meeting's purpose, such as reviewing a project timeline or brainstorming solutions. Outcomes, on the other hand, are the tangible results or actions that stem from these objectives. For example, if an objective is to identify project roadblocks, the corresponding outcome might be a list of agreed issues and assigned tasks to resolve them. By clearly defining these outcomes, business analysts can measure the success of the meeting and ensure that the objectives lead to meaningful and actionable results.

Clients and consultants will have different Objectives

Depending on when the meeting occurs in the lifecycle, clients and consultants will have their own objectives for any meeting. They will overlap e.g. a successful project outcome, but each party may also be seeking different outcomes depending on the situation.

The ***practitioner's objective*** will be to influence the client (especially at an initial engagement meeting) to take whatever action is required to engage them for an assignment (so long as the assignment is consistent with the capabilities and values of the consulting firm or BA team).

At an initial meeting, the ***client's primary objective*** is deciding whether to engage the consultant / BA or not. It is possible that the client has not really decided to engage anyone!

What happens if there are no Meeting Objectives?

Without objectives, meetings tend to wander aimlessly as the participants 'wing it'. This is an ineffective way to conduct a business meeting and doubly so for IS consultants and BAs. Your and your client's time is precious. Be prepared to present and conduct yourself professionally before, during and after each meeting. If one party has clear objectives and the other party does not, it provides more opportunity for the party with objectives to focus the discussion on achieving their outcomes. They will have an advantage.

Sometimes an initial and very general discussion with a potential client will not follow the steps. It can move into an engagement meeting without any agreement to a potential project in the offing.

A couple of years ago, a Chief Technical Officer (CTO) invited Greg to his office to discuss his firm's plans to change the business model of their company (a product comparison website firm). The competition was introducing click-through functionality so people using their websites could find the best deal and buy it immediately.

About 60 minutes in, Greg started providing information and examples to educate him about 'platform strategy' and how it applied to his situation. As far as he were concerned, we had passed the point of 'initial discussions' and were moving into a 'Dialogue/ Diagnose' phase. When he later reflected this in an email to arrange a follow-up meeting, the CTO replied saying they had not decided whether they were going to engage anyone to advise on their plans. Did Greg waste 90 minutes? No. He gained some valuable insights into an unfamiliar specialist industry and established the basis of a possible project!

Examples of how Purpose, Objectives and Outcomes work

Meeting purpose, objectives and outcomes can be varied and must relate to each other. A foundation that considers the logos, pathos and ethos of each outcome establishes a strong foundation for the entire engagement. This approach sets the practitioner up to target the right decision makers, add measurable value through well-established needs, strategic priorities and project governance. Consider the following examples in Table 5-1.

As you can see in table 5-1, there will likely be more than one meeting purpose, objective and outcome. This largely depends on whether you're meeting for the first time, or if you are already engaged in an assignment with the client.

Prepare meeting logistics – pay attention to the detail!

Having identified the meeting purpose, objectives and outcomes we now suggest targeting who should attend, establish the date, time, duration and venue (online, in-person or a blend) identifying presentation equipment needs (if required) and craft and send a draft agenda.

Table 5-1 Examples of meeting objectives

Purpose or situation	Practitioner's objectives	Practitioner's outcome
Rapport and relationship building.	Establishing the relationship (pathos) and your credibility (ethos)	Building pathos and ethos basis of the relationship
Identifying how decisions are made within the client organisation.	Clarifying roles and responsibilities. Identifying the decision-makers. (As a consultant) discovering who your firm might be competing with.	Establishing ethos and pathos based on knowing how to target engagement, decision-making and governance
Exploring company goals and strategy associated with the project.	Establishing alignment between the project and the client's strategy and business plan.	Establishing the foundation of logos and pathos based on strategic alignment, measurable value and governance reporting requirements.
Exploring the needs of the client organisation	Understanding problems, issues and possible causes. Looking for 'hot-buttons' and quick wins around company objectives or the decision-maker's personal objectives.	Establishing logos and pathos based on aligning with identified needs, exploring root causes and aligning goals and values
Exploring the personal needs of the decision-maker (may not be the same).	Identifying what type or style of leadership and culture the key players have and their personal values.	Establishing ethos and pathos based on aligning culture, goals and values
Exploring issues of importance, impact and urgency: getting to root causes and identifying 'show-stoppers'.	Establishing where aspects of the problems have the highest consequences or impacts if not resolved. Adding value by getting to the heart of problems. Updating the client on information they may have been seeking or of which they were unaware.	Establishing strong logos and pathos and identifying areas of greatest impact and priority for further exploration and research

Purpose or situation	Practitioner's objectives	Practitioner's outcome
Identifying sources of information	Gaining access to key documents such as strategies, business plans, previous research and analysis (from within the organisation and from other sources such as industry peak bodies.	Establishing strong logos by obtaining the right information to inform analysis and planning.
Discovering barriers and points of resistance.	Identifying levels of technical and change maturity. Identifying change impacts and risks. Determining whether there have been any positive or negative experiences with consultants or BAs to repeat or avoid.	Establishing strong logos and pathos and identifying areas of change and leadership maturity and capability that could prevent the client achieving the desired ROI
Exploring approach, measurement and governance expectations.	Checking preferences and approaches to design, planning, project methods, measures of success and communication preferences.	Establishing strong logos, pathos and ethos based on Measurable Organisation Value and Client Calculated Value and client governance preferences.

Plan meeting details

A quick preliminary phone call with the client is an ideal way to get the basic logistics of any meeting sorted. You need to establish their preferences for, and consider:

- Who should attend;
- Date and time;
- Length of time available i.e. meeting duration;
- Time zones, working hours, and holidays;
- Place, including whether the meeting will be fully in person, a mix of in person and online, or fully online; and,
- Whether the client has any preferences for technology such as Teams or Zoom if partly or fully online.

We suggest using a simple checklist to make sure you have all the basics covered. You will find one in Appendix 1 at the end of this chapter.

Meetings are all about having the right people in the room. Leave a key person out, and you may not be able to progress matters, obtain crucial information or make an informed decision. If you have too many people in the room, things can get out of hand much more easily, become unfocused and a waste of time.

"For every additional meeting participant over seven, the likelihood of making a sound decision goes down by 10 percent, ...by the time you get 17 people, the chances of actually making a decision are zero"[13] .

The trick is to invite enough people to bring needed expertise or decision authority, without including so many that the discussion flies off course.

Each participant should have a role to play. That holds true for clients and practitioners as well. Again, it comes back to the purpose and objectives of your meeting. Bringing an inexperienced consultant or BA to a meeting can inform their skills training but you need to give them a role e.g. note-taking.

Let's say the purpose is to brainstorm an issue. Our experience suggests that around 10, maximum 15 people is plenty. Any more than that, practitioners really need skills and experience in creating and facilitating a co-design process. If your meeting purpose is to make decisions, four participants up to a maximum of seven is optimal. It comes down to who the key stakeholders are, who holds the budget and who is responsible and accountable for the outcome.

> **Top Tip:** Remember U BE MAD – for a decision to be made someone from the client side must have the Means, Authority and Desire to make a go-ahead decision.

Identify who needs to attend

We suggest you work with the client to have the optimal number in the room depending on your purpose, objectives, and outcome. If you can have a quick discussion with the client prior to the meeting, you can also clarify the other standard logistical matters.

Once you have established the parameters and logistics, it's time to craft and send the agenda.

Draft an Agenda

An agenda tells attendees what to expect during a meeting and how they can prepare for it. Ideally, you'll use your agenda to connect everyone with the meeting's purpose, objectives, and outcomes. You may even assign tasks or items to team members or other attendees. Taking this approach also provides the opportunity to manage the time taken for each agenda item and therefore to manage the time during the meeting.

A well-crafted meeting agenda maximizes the meeting's effectiveness and keeps everyone on track, as long as it is followed once in the meeting!

A productive, effective meeting needs a clear structure designed to achieve the purpose, objectives and outcomes.

Here are some tips:

- Create and share your meeting agenda as early as possible. Send as soon as practicable to allow as much time as possible for attendees to prepare for what's going to happen. If you send the agenda early, make it a draft, and encourage attendees to make suggested changes and additions. This gives everyone an opportunity to contribute and prepare.
- Provide any relevant pre-reading materials in advance. This can be the presentation slide deck, previous minutes or meeting notes, or a previous decision. This helps ensure everyone arriving at the meeting will be on the same page and ready to move the discussion forward rather than asking a ton of questions that wastes precious time.
- Assign or agree facilitators or a chairperson for the meeting as well as subject matter experts for each applicable agenda item. Make sure you let people know if they are expected to participate in this way and of any time constraints for their session. With preliminary client-consultant meetings no facilitator or chairperson would normally be appointed or required; rather, the discussion would be led by the senior principals.
- If using a facilitator or chairperson, have a quick preliminary discussion to agree areas of emphasis.
- Define and distinguish between different types of agenda items: informational, discussion topics, and action items.
- Clarify the purpose of each agenda item to help attendees understand what's most important and what to focus on.
- Prioritise each agenda item for urgency and importance. This helps identify those items that absolutely must be discussed during the meeting and any that can be addressed later if you run out of time – such decisions about priority should be made based on your objectives and outcomes.

- Create flow throughout the agenda to maximize efficiency. Cluster similar items together and ensure that items build from one to the next in a logical sequence.
- Plan and allocate enough time for each item on your agenda. Nobody will complain about a meeting that runs short, but running over time is not good practice.
- Use your meeting agenda during the meeting to track notes and action items and to stay focused.

Finally, we strongly recommend finding and using an agenda template to draft your agenda. There is a simple outline in Figure 5-2. If you are part of a consulting firm, or part of a BA team, your organisation may have templates that you're expected to use. However, templates are also easy to find online. Make sure that the items in the Figure 5-2 are at the top of your agenda to support a good flow and outcome.

> **Top Tip:** Include Action Items arising from your last meeting listed at the end of the agenda. Include the status (pending, completed) and who was responsible for completing them.

Figure 5-2 Sample meeting agenda

Agenda

Meeting purpose:
Meeting objectives:
Meeting outcomes: (if appropriate)

Date: **Time:**
Place: **Weblink:**

Attendees: (names and roles)

1. Welcome and Introductions (Chair)
2. Confirmation of agenda and time availability (Chair)
3. Business item (person leading discussion)
4. Business item (person leading discussion)
5. Other business (Chair)
6. Date for next meeting (Chair)

Prepare and send pre-meeting communications

Once you have crafted your draft agenda, it's time to send a meeting calendar invitation with a link to the draft agenda embedded, and attach other reading materials required to inform the meeting.

Make sure you put the most senior client first in the invitees' list and use the 'CC' function to invite your own team members. Keep your message short, perhaps stating the purpose of the meeting and inviting your attendees to make any suggested changes or additions to the agenda.

Even with consultation on the agenda items and the potential selection of a meeting chairperson from the client, the fact that you as a consultant or BA are shaping the agenda means that you have at least some, if not total control of how the meeting will proceed.

Yes, there is a lot of detailed work in establishing the basis of a professional, productive meeting. But remember, your credibility as a consultant, BA team or individual is at stake. We think it's worth it!

Step 2: Introductions

This is a simple step in the process and one that should be familiar to everyone. Of course, there will be introductions! So why list it as a formal step? Well, sometimes it just doesn't always happen in a group situation - someone starts the conversation before the introductions and the opportunity is lost.

So one must take the opportunity to discover the roles of everyone in a group meeting. Whomever is leading the consulting or BA team should ensure that everyone in the room is identified by name and role. Identifying participants' roles, especially client attendees, allows the consultants to address pertinent points to the appropriate people (logos). Discovering their names provides the consultants an opportunity to relate to them more personally (pathos) by using their names in conversation. Client personnel are usually in attendance for a reason. Introductions assist the consultants discover these reasons.

At other times, it will seem inappropriate and premature to determine everyone's role, because the group is large, or perhaps because the style of the principal client is a 'time-poor-get-down-to-business' type.

It is in the practitioner's interest to identify the roles of participants at the right time - before, during or after the meeting. Sometimes this is easily

> **Top Tip:** Always offer to exchange business cards at the beginning of a meeting to allow to use accurate names in your discussion and to identify the roles of participants.

achieved by the simple exchange of business cards.

If the meeting is not a first meeting, the leader of the meeting should have a list of names and roles of all client personnel who have attended prior meetings.

Prepare to introduce yourself and the team

To get an engagement meeting started, make sure that all participants have been formally introduced. Part of the introduction process should include each of the client attendee's roles in the company as well as the names and roles of the consulting or BA team. This better informs you of who the decision-makers may be and from whom they are taking advice. It is an opportunity to show-case the roles and skills within your practitioner firm or team.

Identify your value as a practitioner

It is important to be prepared to speak about yourself and the potential value you will bring to the assignment. Seriously! Do not head into or be in the meeting without preparing and practicing what you are going to say about who you are, what you do and the value you add. Because people often make judgments about practitioners quickly, the way you introduce yourself and what you say about yourself is critical. It's all about your personal value proposition: your personal 'brand'.

The best way to define your value is to look at it from a client's perspective. If you have done your background research, it should be relatively easy to answer these questions.

- Why have you been invited to attend this meeting?
- What are the client's goals and aspirations?
- What problems does the client need solved and what are the opportunities?
- What threats do they need addressed?
- What are their actual or potential pain points?
- How might your skills and experience build confidence that you're the right person for the role?

In other words, you need to define your personal value proposition to justify your presence.

Most clients aren't interested in hearing anyone rehash their resume or go on and on about what they've done in the past. They want to hear about who you are in a way that is relevant to them, the issues you're there to talk about, their business and what they are trying to achieve.

Your value proposition is one sentence, maybe two. It's clear, substantive, and compelling. Wherever possible and truthful to do so, we recommend this personal introductory statement be relevant to the client's meeting objectives and outcomes.

Your statement of value should include a brief description of what you offer that aligns with and will achieve the client's desired outcomes. It makes it clear why and how you are uniquely qualified to help them achieve those outcomes.

Instead of preparing to summarize your resume or cover everything you have done in the past, give one or two brief sentences about who you are and then one or two relevant (very short) statements about your value.

Introductions - who goes first?

If your lead BA or consultant is chairing the meeting, make sure that the client is invited to introduce themselves first. If necessary, ask any first-time client attendees to provide their name, role and a little bit about what they would like to achieve in the meeting. This allows a competent meeting chairperson to note any issues and adjust the agenda if necessary.

Conduct initial background research

How much effort you put into this stage depends on the amount of lead time there is before the meeting. Here we suggest the absolute minimum with the objective of ensuring you have at least basic knowledge of the client and their organisation. We explore this in greater detail on professional research in Chapter 6.

Check out the client's website to find key information such as industry research, annual reports and key staff profiles. Use publicly available information such as LinkedIn to find out about the client attendees. Understanding their backgrounds, experiences, career stage and possible motivations can provide a useful, targeted way to build initial rapport based on something that is of interest and meaningful to them.

This preparation is the foundation of the next step, rapport building once the meeting has started.

Step 3: Rapport building

It's possible that you may skip this step. However, it is still a valuable exercise to conduct background research on the organisation and people you are meeting with. There's no hard and fast rule – be sensitive to the client, based on what you know about them.

Rapport building with clients involves informal or semi-formal dialogue at the start of the meeting while people are settling in and the meeting is getting started. It can be a very important aspect of the engagement process. The objective of this step is to find some common ground with the client on a professional and/or personal level. Here's a brief example of rapport building at the beginning of a consulting meeting:

> **Practitioner**: "Good morning, Maisy! How was your weekend? Were you able to enjoy the beautiful weather?"
> **Client**: "Good morning Dan! Yes, I did. I went hiking with my family. We got to revisit an area of regenerating native bush that the family helped to plant. How about you?"
> **Practitioner**: "That sounds wonderful! It seems we have a shared interest in conservation and I'd love to talk more about it sometime. I'm excited to dive into our discussion today. Before we start, is there anything specific you'd like to address first or add to the agenda?"

Importance of rapport-building

If there's an opportunity, and rapport building suits the client's preferred engagement style, there are opportunities:

1. **Establishes Trust** (*logos and pathos*): Building rapport creates a foundation of trust, making clients feel comfortable and more likely to share important information.
2. **Enhances Communication:** (*logos*) When clients feel at ease, communication becomes more open and effective, leading to better understanding and collaboration.
3. **Fosters Connection** (*pathos and ethos*): Rapport helps in creating a positive and respectful relationship, which can lead to long-term partnerships.
4. **Increases Empathy** (*pathos*): Understanding the client's perspective and showing genuine interest in their well-being fosters empathy and strengthens the relationship.
5. **Improves Conflict Resolution** (ethos and pathos): A strong rapport allows for more constructive dialogue and effective resolution of any disagreements or conflicts.

Building rapport is essential for creating a productive and positive project environment. It sets the tone for the meeting and helps in achieving better outcomes for both the consultant and the client. Rapport builds the relationship between the two parties. This relationship widens the communication bandwidth, enabling greater information flow, more honest and open dialogue, and quicker conflict resolution. Under these conditions, trust will build between the two parties more quickly. Also, clients are more likely to award consulting work to people they like. However, quality rapport is only possible if you do your homework!

With practice, rapport building becomes easier. Client decisions are made based on the three themes repeated throughout this book: logos, pathos and ethos.

The Role of Logos, Pathos and Ethos in Decision-Making

How people with different personalities and decision styles make decisions are discussed in lots of books on management and leadership. We believe that decision-makers, based on their personality and experience, will consider their decisions based on a combination of logos, pathos and ethos. The logic (logos) of your proposed method and approach must be competitive with other similar proposals to be successful. So how do you get an edge over your competition?

Promoting your ETHOS is one way. By gaining trust through examples of similar past work and familiarity with their issues, you can strengthen your proposal employing Maister's Experience Firm approach. There ie a well-known phrase 'past performance is a good indicator of future performance'. Because the performance of your project is yet to be executed, your proposal is merely a promise of your future work quality. Third-party endorsements also assist to instil trust in your future performance. We discuss this further when we talk about writing a formal proposal.

Using PATHOS can assist in your pitch. Through killer questions you try and determine the underlying values of the decision-maker. Appealing to these values makes a powerful emotional connection.

Sharing the same values is a principal basis for camaraderie and eventually friendship. You are sending the message that you can do business together on an amicable basis. The values of the two organisations are shared. Issues will arise but can be managed based on these shared values.

Promoting your LOGOS even further is another way. Demonstrating your expertise is not just through talking about your past experience or talking up your knowledge. A top practitioner will ask pointed questions that show they understand the issues at hand. We will repeat this advice in the future - you are less likely to make an strategic engagement error with a question than you are by making a statement with which your client disagrees . By probing with killer questions, you demonstrate your expertise and its application to the issue.

Build logos, ethos and pathos – and behave well!

In a group meeting, each consultant should be responsible for creating a relationship with their client counterparts. Younger consultants should always remember that the younger clients will develop in their careers and become future key contacts in industry or government. Being dismissive, rude, or snobbish when you are twenty-two may lose you a potential client when you are forty-two. People remember.

It is always very heartening to watch a client's face light up with interest as you alight on exactly the topic that evokes their passion. However, pretending to be interested in something is tantamount to lying and when (not if) you are found out, that could end of your client relationship.

When do we just get down to business?

The rapport step may pass very quickly if the style of the principal client is to 'get down to business' because they are not interested in 'wasteful chit chat'. Be sensitive to this to avoid wasting the client's valuable time and at the same time, use any information gathered to help inform how you craft the purpose, objectives and outcomes of the meeting.

Step 4: Confirming the objectives and agenda, and time checking

Both the client and the BAs or consultants should come away from first meetings at any stage of the lifecycle with clear next steps and an idea of where things are heading. That's why it is essential to run a small confirmatory process at the start of every meeting.

If one of the attendees goes straight into talking or working through the main agenda, it is both appropriate and desirable to respectfully ask if the meeting could be paused to check these important parameters.Even if the client has initiated the meeting, it is appropriate and highly professional to ensure that the meeting gets off to the best possible start. Confirming objectives will focus the discussion and maximize the use of time for both parties.

This is the beginning of the journey for many consulting dialogues. The consulting or BA team should be well prepared for this discussion, having decided what objectives they want to achieve. Experienced consultants, who have executed similar assignments in the past, have an opportunity to demonstrate their knowledge (logos), but more importantly, demonstrate their insight into the real client issues.

Confirm who will lead the meeting

If this has not already been determined ahead of the meeting, now is the time.

In a consulting firm, this is usually the partner or most senior person attending the meeting: same with BAs. However, if there is an existing relationship between two people in the meeting, they should lead the introductions, to bring their principals together to conduct a discussion.

> **Example**: An up-and-coming consultant, Angus, has a friend from university, Charlie, whose firm needs IS services. They arrange a meeting between the management of the potential client (Charlie's boss) and representatives from the consulting firm e.g. Angus's boss.
> In this situation, Angus and Charlie would initiate the introductions, but the control of the meeting would then pass to their respective principals.

Moving through this stage can vary in the time taken

Often the confirmation of purpose, objectives and outcomes is a quick step that leads naturally into the general discussion step. Sometimes, however, the setting of objectives for the dialogue between client and consultant can take up the entire time of the initial meeting. This means that a subsequent meeting is required to continue the conversation and gain agreement on the important matters which require discourse and resolution between the parties. This may seem to be a drawn-out way to conduct an engagement.

When you are executing the assignment, you will be glad that you took the time to establish objectives, so that you can refer to them in your engagement outcomes.

When reflecting on this meeting, consultants may decide not to continue pursuing the engagement. These initial meetings consume time, the main scarce resource of a consulting firm. Consulting principals must decide whether they can recoup the time lost in engagement through the assignment fee structure. Similarly, consulting principals should consider the risk of pursuing an assignment that is outside their firm's capabilities.

One piece of advice from a colleague Andy (a consultant with many, many years of experience) on running the first meeting with a client:

- Don't talk solutions first in the meeting. Let people know that there will be a time to talk about their proposed solution, but it's just not now!

- Direct the discussion towards the situation AS-IS. The best way to talk about the AS-IS is to do it in a Delphi manner (all participants are experts contributing to an issue) so they cannot say 'you didn't tell us'.
- Ideally, have the same people at every meeting and no new people along the way (if it can be avoided) unless they add value in specialist technical areas.
- Show meeting attendees the AS-IS model you may have developed but you don't critique it: let them critique it. Let them fire the bullets that you wanted to fire! You see, the client personnel you are talking to in the meeting may be responsible for creating the AS-IS situation – this is why you don't critique it directly.

In summary, preparation for all stages is essential to ensure you are prepared to move into subsequent stages of the meeting process such as the general discussion.

Step 5: General discussion

You have set and agreed the objectives for your client-consultant dialogue, so now you can plan to systematically address these in the general discussion step. It is during this step that you apply the techniques that will help you influence the client to engage your services.

In this section we describe some advanced techniques that will assist you to influence the client towards your objectives, and as with all steps, we consider preparation.

Preparing for general discussion

Preparation for general discussion provides the practitioner with two advantages. If you prepare certain questions to ensure a comprehensive coverage of the client's needs, it will encourage you to inquire (in advance of the meeting) into their company, industry, environment and processes. During the conversation, you will have opportunities to use this preparation to demonstrate your expertise and insight into their situation. If you are a senior person, ask your juniors to conduct this research.

Consider the reasons why clients engage a practitioner.

One reason is that they do not have the systems or transitional knowledge to affect the desired change in their organisation. Clients are sometimes less able to determine whether your consulting firm has these skills and can effectively employ them. If they lack the capability for direct assessment of these core skills, they will rely on third party recommendations. However, every client can directly assess whether you understand the business. Therefore, apart from discussing the IS components and needs, and demonstrating your competence in the technical field, you must address the business considerations of the expected change in their firm.

Talk in terms of the value expected from your activities, and the business benefits they will accrue from your activities. We explore these techniques later in this chapter and discuss types of value further in Chapter 7 - Proposals.

Next, we move to our first very simple technique - keeping control of the conversation without being domineering.

Keep control of the meeting by asking questions

In any engagement meeting, a practitioner should aim to maintain control of the conversation's direction. This focuses the dialogue on the topics of interest to the consultant.

The way to guide the flow of conversation is to ask questions.

This is not meant to be an interrogation! It is an intelligent inquiry, mixed with reflections and observations on their answers. Polite behaviour dictates that people will answer your questions.

It is important to understand, as fully as possible, the client firm, its values, politics, ideal outcomes from the engagement, what they think are the issues and whether they have any preferences in the path towards a solution. The questions you have prepared when conducting background 'homework' ahead of the meeting will be invaluable at this stage.

Quite often, a client will ask a practitioner to meet with them to discuss a solution they would like consulting or BA help to implement. This should be approached cautiously (unless the organisation has invested considerable resources in conducting a current state analysis to determine the problem). More commonly this situation is ripe for the practitioner to politely ask whether they might ask some additional questions.

This is important for clients and practitioners alike. It is important for both parties to establish whether the problem as understood by the client is the problem or whether it is a symptom of the problem. It is good practice to ask questions to ensure that the root cause of the problems have been clearly identified.

If you determine that the problem the client has identified is merely a symptom and that alleviating this symptom will not result in reasonable benefits to the client, you may need to consider an initial Review Phase into your action plan.

However, it is just as important to ensure you are asking the right type of question rather than making a statement.

Questions vs statements

As in negotiation, statements create a position. So, if a consultant suggests a path towards the resolution in the form of a statement, the client may disagree with this strategy. This means that the consultant must now change their strategy (their position) or possibly lose the assignment or at least reduce the client's perception of your competence.

But what if the client keeps this poor view of your suggestion to themselves? Remember that polite behaviour does not dictate that one must respond to or comment on a statement. You may never know that the client is unimpressed with your suggestion. Frame your suggestions in question form to elicits a response from the client and does not tie you to a position.

Types of Questions

There are several types of questions that a practitioner can ask. In this section we cover probing questions, general questions as well as questions to establish outcomes and test proposed solutions and ideas. Some useful examples are in Tables 5-2 to 5-4.

Table 5-2 Probing Questions

Questions	Explanation
Are you certain about that?	This is asking the client to present confirmation, facts or other data to substantiate their claim.
What do you think about that?	Asking the client for a logos response.
How do you feel about that?	Asking the client for a pathos response.
What would you do about that?	Asking about what actions that a client would consider taking in response to an issue or opportunity.
What are the most important considerations to take into account when doing this project?	This will assist in identifying key values held by the client.

Questions	Explanation
Could you please explain it futher?	You are searching for the underlying rationale or value held that explains their statement or position.
Please tell me more.	Asking the client to continue to provide details about the topic under discussion.
What about you [name of another participant]? What are your thoughts?	In a group meeting, deflecting the questions to another participant to get their view or perhaps get them talking to better understand why they are present.

Table 5-3 Questions to establish Outcomes

Questions	Explanation
What does your organisation want to achieve from this project?	The response could be a vision, outputs, outcomes or benefits. Follow up with exploratory / probing questions.
What do you (as the senior leader / manager / project owner) want to achieve from this project?	Personal outcomes can differ from organisational outcomes. Sensitivity to each will held you target and pitch your strategy and approach.
What does the future look like with your identified problem solved? How will you measure success?	This is similar to the first question above but helps establish measureable value and governance processes

Top Tip: Skillful questioning enables the practitioner to find out what is driving the client's need, test possible strategies, determine any client concerns (or objections) and drive the conversation towards agreement on a mutual outcome.

Table 5-4 Questions to test Proposed Solutions or Ideas

Questions	Explanation
What might constrain you from taking that course of action?	Can elicit barriers and roadblocks that may be useful inputs into a SWOT or risk analysis.
What will enable you to take a course of action?	Can elicit other barriers and roadblocks and conditions that need to be in place to reach the intended outcomes.
Who are the main beneficiaries from this project or course of action?	Helps establish stakeholders, their needs, interests, and abilities to engage or participate.
What are the risks or unintended consequences of taking or not taking this action?	Can elicit initial risks and impacts of taking a course of action. Can also help to establish priorities and sequences for project planning.
Are we on the right track?	This is a 'soft' close, ensuring the client at least partially agrees with the direction the practitioner is taking the engagement discussion.
Should we proceed to preliminary work?	This is the 'hard' close. It should come after one or more 'soft' closes to ensure there are no further objections to overcome. You can use an 'if' close when futher objections reduce to one or two.

Establishing outcomes and testing ideas are crucial steps when planning a client meeting for several reasons:

- **Clarity and Focus:** Defining clear outcomes ensures that everyone involved understands the meeting's purpose and goals. This helps keep the discussion on track and productive.
- **Efficiency**: Knowing what you want to achieve allows you to structure the meeting efficiently, making the best use of everyone's time.
- **Preparation**: Testing ideas beforehand helps identify potential issues and refine your approach. This preparation can lead to more effective and persuasive presentations.

- **Client Satisfaction**: Clear outcomes and well-tested ideas demonstrate professionalism and thoroughness, which can build trust and satisfaction with your clients.
- **Measurable Success:** Establishing outcomes provides a way to measure the success of the meeting, helping you evaluate whether the objectives were met and what can be improved for future interactions.

By focusing on these aspects, you can ensure that your client meetings are purposeful, efficient, and successful.

The set of question examples in table 5-2 and 5-4 cover general questions, probing questions, establishing outcomes and testing ideas and actions. There are explanations of why and when you use these questions. People we I have trained in these techniques use these questions constantly in their practice. Two other technique they constantly use are the LAER and APV techniques.

The Listen, Acknowledge, Explore, Respond (LAER) Technique

When a client does not give a full answer or if you believe there is some underlying issue or unexplained rationale to their answer, then you can apply the LAER technique. See Table 5-5.

This technique needs to start with a high-quality probing or exploratory questions as highlighted in the two previous tables. And for LAER to work most effectively, the competency of active listening is essential! If you respond without exploring you risk responding without fully understanding the issue at hand. A poor response risks damaging your credibility as an expert. And remember to respond with a question rather than a statement. A question is how you Explore.

Once you fully understand the issue, you can then Respond. If you are still unsure of the underlying issue, you should continue to Explore until you feel confident with your proposed response. Responding too early risks make a statement that the client will reject outright - it's harder to regain your influence if that happens.

Table 5-5 Listen-Acknowledge-Explore-Respond (LAER) Technique

Action	How
LISTEN	Actively listen to the other person with the intent of understanding and when appropriate, reframing back to them your understanding of what they said in the Acknowledge step.
ACKNOWLEDGE	Respond in a way that demonstrates you have listened and understood. This could be an appreciation of how the situation might impact on or feel to the client, or by stating your understanding of the situation or problem the other has expressed using your own words.
EXPLORE	This could be in the form of a clarifying question, or questions to determine root causes, or to determine what the client has tried to do to remedy the problem so far, whether they have conducted any analysis of the problem, whether you could have access to any information relating to their challenges, and so on.
RESPOND	Only when you fully understand the rationale, underlying causes and surrounding issues should you respond. At the early stages this should always be pitched as 'early thinking'. Alternatively, it might be better to reflect on your exploration and get back to the client within an agreed period. If you're out of your depth, defer and discuss with a more knowledgeable colleague!

Here is an example of how that could work:

Client: "One of our issues is cash flow. We want to improve it."
Practitioner: Listens carefully and then Acknowledges: "I see, so your cash flow is weaker than what you would like." The Practitioner then Explores some more: "What are the main contributors to your cash flow issues? "
Client: "We are having problems collecting debts from our customers."
Practitioner may Explore some more: "Are your debt recovery processes satisfactory?"
Client: "No, our debtors are out of control. They are taking too long to pay."
Practitioner is ready to Respond now: "We should have a look at your debtors' system and the way you are going about collecting from slow paying customers. I believe we can help you there by firstly mapping your aged debtors' process."

The LAER technique is used in association with the Attribute – Purpose – Value (APV) technique.

Table 5-6 Attribute-Purpose-Value (APV) Technique

What	How
ATTRIBUTE	The attribute is the main characteristic of the item, solution, approach or strategy you are describing.
PURPOSE	The purpose describes what the attribute does, what role it performs
VALUE	The value statement describes how the attribute could assist the client to solve a problem or meet and objective.

The Attribute, Purpose, Value technique

This simple technique is another important language tool, providing practitioners with a structure for describing an approach or recommendations that aligns with the outcomes and benefits the client is seeking. Table 5-6 illustrates.

The technique divides a sentence into three parts: the first part describes the attribute - physical or virtual description of whatever it is you are wanting to talk about. The second part describes the function of the attribute - what it does. The third part describes the value proposition of the attribute - how it adds value to the client.

The following example shows how practitioners might use the APV and LAER techniques in conjunction. The client might be asked how the financial system will help them manage their business.

Consider the following example and explanation...

In this example, the practitioner uses APV, to establish the ability to advise and get agreement on how the client would like to proceed. Showing a process map of the client's aged debtor process, where the practitioner analysis identified gaps and what the future system would look like uses both logos and ethos to create an accurate basis for future discussions.

Practitioner: 'Let's pause for a moment to reflect on how you, as managers, feel about [pathos] your aged debtor's process. Can we consider what the impact of the current system is on you achieving your performance targets when you appear to have little control over customers not paying on time, or an easy ability to control the size of the aged debtors list?' [logos / pathos / ethos]
[This 'killer question' sets a foundation to determine what management feels about there being too many customers that owe them money, and their lack of control of that process.] ...
Practitioner: 'As you can see on this map of your aged debtor process [ATTRIBUTE], there are gaps in your organisation's support system and its capability to stratify the customers who owe money sorted by the length of time it has been owing and the amount owed (PURPOSE). Our recommended system has a function that allows the debtors clerk to target customers with large amounts outstanding or have owed money for a long period of time (VALUE).'

Akin to APV, another useful way to influence an outcome is to discuss options and solutions (if you are at that stage of the life-cycle) by using the language of benefits and stretch benefits. This approach also helps to build logos and pathos.

Using the Language of Benefits (APV) during Plan / Design

Understanding and effectively communicating the benefits (i.e. Value in the APV technique) of options and solutions is crucial in influencing client outcomes, especially at the Plan/Design phase of the life-cycle.

Benefits highlight the value and impact of a proposed solution, making it easier for clients to see the tangible and strategic advantages. Here's how you can use benefits language to influence client outcomes:

- ***Identify Immediate Benefits***: Start by identifying the immediate, tangible benefits that the client will experience upon implementing the solution. These could include cost savings, increased efficiency, reduced errors, or improved customer satisfaction. Clearly articulate these benefits to show the direct impact on the client's operations.

Example: "By implementing this new CRM system, you can expect a 20% reduction in customer response time, leading to higher customer satisfaction and retention."

- ***Highlight Stretch Benefits:*** Beyond the immediate benefits, emphasize the long-term, strategic advantages that the solution can bring. These stretch benefits often include market positioning, competitive advantage, innovation, and future growth opportunities.

Example: "With the new CRM system, you'll have access to advanced analytics that can help you identify market trends and tailor your marketing strategies, positioning your company as a market leader."

- ***Align Benefits with Client Goals:*** Ensure that the benefits you highlight are aligned with the client's overall business goals and objectives. This alignment helps in gaining buy-in from stakeholders and demonstrates that you understand their priorities.

Example: "This solution aligns with your goal of expanding into new markets by providing the scalability and flexibility needed to support your growth strategy."

- ***Use Data and Evidence:*** Support your claims with data, case studies, and evidence from similar projects. This adds credibility to your proposal and helps clients visualise the potential impact.

Example: "In a similar project, our client saw a 30% increase in sales within six months of implementing the new system. We believe you can achieve similar results."

- ***Communicate Clearly and Concisely:*** Use clear and concise language to communicate the benefits. Avoid jargon and focus on the value that the client will gain. Make sure your message is easy to understand and resonates with the client's needs.

Example: "This solution will streamline your processes, save time, and reduce costs, allowing you to focus on strategic initiatives.""

Using benefits to influence client outcomes involves identifying and clearly communicating both immediate and stretch benefits, aligning them with client goals, supporting your claims with evidence, and ensuring clear communication. By doing so, you can effectively demonstrate the value of your solution and influence positive client outcomes. Let's examine the following example.

Example: **Client Problem**: A client is struggling with outdated software systems that are causing inefficiencies and errors in their business processes. Communication objective: describe the client benefits of Implementing a New Software System: outcome increase logos and pathos.
Use logos benefit language first: 'By implementing a new, modern software system, the client can streamline their operations, reduce errors, and improve overall efficiency. For example, introducing an integrated ERP (Enterprise Resource Planning) system reduces manual data entry errors by around 30% and improves process efficiency by 25%, leading to significant time and cost savings.'
Use logos and pathos language to provide 'Stretch' (additional) benefits: 'This could mean that beyond the immediate improvements, the new software system will enable your firm to leverage advanced analytics and automation, positioning you for future growth and innovation. For example, with the new ERP system, your firm can now utilize real-time data analytics to make informed business decisions, leading to an estimated 15% increase in revenue through optimized inventory management and targeted marketing strategies.'

Importance of using value and benefits language

We highly recommend learning how to use Attribute, Purpose, Value (APV) and benefit and stretch benefit language to describe how options or an approach will potentially benefit the client. Such professional language is an important part of the art of influence. Value and benefit language:

- ***Motivates Stakeholders:*** Highlighting both immediate and long-term attributes, purpose value and benefits. This helps in gaining buy-in from stakeholders.
- ***Aligns Goals:*** Clearly defining benefits ensures that everyone is aligned towards common objectives.

- ***Demonstrates Value:*** Showing the stretch benefits emphasizes the strategic value of the solution, beyond an immediate fix.
- ***Encourages Innovation:*** Thinking about stretch benefits encourages creative problem-solving and innovation.

As with all other aspects of conducting a professional meeting, preparation is key, including preparing a range of contingency ('what if') questions ahead. But there are also other techniques that you can use to evaluate where the meeting has got to and how to respond during the meeting.

Technique - Stepping Outside

An advanced technique applied to engagement meetings and any other negotiation is 'stepping outside'. The discussion is happening on more than one level.

At its core, engagement is the exchange of words, the dialogue that the consultant is hoping to lead towards meeting their objective (i.e. a successful engagement outcome). This is the logos level.

At another level, it is the reaction to the dialogue by the client personnel. With some sensitivity and experience, a consultant should be able to observe the emotional reactions to points and approaches advanced by the team. This is the pathos level.

It is difficult for a single person to concentrate on the logos level and be aware of the pathos reactions. In past discussions where we have led a complex meeting, we have employed a person to intuit the emotional interplay and subtly inform us of their observations. This may involve the passing of notes, code words, signs or the suggestion of a break in proceedings so that the teams can confer.

With some experience and awareness, practitioners can become aware of subtle changes in the visage or body language of the clients, necessitating a change in game plan. Like a professional tennis player (with no on-court coach or adviser), whose planned pre-game strategy is failing, one has to become aware of this failure and change strategy accordingly. In other words, you have to step outside the logical flow and examine the emotional state(s) of your potential clients.

If possible, take a break (if alone perhaps a visit to the rest room) to review the situation and develop a different approach. You may wish to reschedule the meeting and prepare a different approach. Once you are aware that the path you are taking is wrong or not working as well as expected, you might revisit some probing questions to determine what or who is creating the blockage.

Gapping

The role of the IS consultant or BA is to facilitate a required change in the systems or processes of a client organisation.

Clients do not always know what they want, or what they think they want will not provide their expected beneficial outcome. It is unethical for practitioners to simply agree to undertake activities if they know it will not provide benefits to the client and / or have not advised them that the result may not be beneficial to their business. It is better for both the client's business and the consultant's reputation to withdraw from such an undertaking.

Sometimes during an engagement discussion, the practitioner must advise the client that they have an issue or opportunity, which the client has yet to identify.

There is a gap between their current situation and a future state that will improve their business condition. In other words, the practitioner is advising there is an issue to be rectified or an unidentified opportunity to be grasped. This process is called 'gapping'. Clients will not always immediately see the value from closing the gap.

The identification of these gaps, whether by the client or the consultant, is the necessary condition for an engagement to proceed. The goal of the engagement process is to recognize and understand these gaps, their implication for the client business and the steps to address them.

In summary, preparation for the general discussion is closely aligned with preparation for setting and agreeing objectives. Knowing key information about the company, its processes, objectives, strategy, competitive environment, and management will assist in driving the dialogue to a mutually beneficial outcome.

Step 6: Getting Agreement and Next Steps

The general discussion can be stimulating for the practitioner, satisfying the natural tendency to address new problems and win new work or undertake further work. But before any actions can be taken, the two parties must come to some agreement. The agreement does not necessarily have to be about executing the project, although this is the most preferable outcome for consultants. Use the negotiation techniques outlined in Chapter 11 to assist you in getting to the agreement outcome you seek.

If agreement can't be reached about execution, then it is advisable to gain agreement on some of the points discussed. Any accord between the parties lays a foundation for potential future contractual negotiations and the eventual execution of the project.

The principles towards reaching agreement on any outcome are the same. Even agreeing that more discussion is required is sufficient – you can set up a subsequent meeting to continue the engagement.

Generating a 'soft' or 'hard' Close

Essentially, the practitioner must ask the questions that will generate either a 'soft' close or a 'hard' close.

Soft close questions ask the client whether you are heading towards a final agreement resulting in the provision of services. You are not yet explicitly asking for the assignment. Another purpose of soft close questions is to identify any further objections or issues the client may need to be overcome before proceeding. Examples are:

- Are we on the right track?
- Are there any issues that you see arising from this course of action?
- How do you feel about the way we are progressing?
- Is this approach okay with you?

Once you feel confident that the issues have been cleared, you can proceed with a hard close question. Some examples are:

- Shall we proceed? I can start work on Monday.
- Let's get a contract drawn up.
- I will begin some preliminary work immediately and my office will send you the billing details.

Sometimes the agreement is not in place until the contract for services has been signed. For many smaller jobs, a detailed contract is not always put in place, however, some form of written correspondence is always warranted. The common instrument is an engagement letter or statement of intent, which sets out the scope of the engagement and includes all the relevant details.

An engagement letter is different to a proposal. A proposal sets out a detailed course of action. If you have already sent a proposal to the client, client, and the client agrees with the actions set out therein, the engagement letter will often reference the proposal rather than reiterating it. It is prudent for a consultant to seek legal advice to satisfy themselves that their contractual arrangements with clients are sound.

If agreement to proceed is not reached during any discussion, then move to establishing Next Steps with the client.

Establishing next steps

Next steps will vary according to the situation, but the minimal objective should be to keep discussing the engagement. In effect, the engagement process continues while the client is 'still in play' and finishes when the agreement to execute the project has been made.

While there may be several next steps including the preparation of a proposal or the furnishing of further information, the practitioner should always aim to meet and discuss these face-to-face. This enables the practitioner to see and sense the logical and emotional reactions to whatever materials or suggestions have been provided. When an in-person meeting is not convenient or possible, video chat is preferable to audio chat.

It is in the interests of the practitioner to keep control of the communication processes. This is not always possible, particularly during a formal competitive tender. But it is a goal, and the basis of project governance. The value of this should not be underestimated, especially if there are any disagreements down the track.

Step 7: Follow-up and communicating the outcomes

One way to keep control of the dialogue is to take responsibility for communicating the outcomes of the meeting. Once the meeting is concluded, advise the client that you will send some notes from the meeting. Not only does this record the understanding of the client's needs, it also provides material to base the agenda for the next encounter. It also communicates the client's needs from the practitioner's perspective.

An especially important thing to record is any agreements with the client about the outcomes or intention to execute the project. This means you have the basis for a subsequent meeting. In any follow up calls to arrange the next meeting, you can refer to the agreement to do so in the 'minutes'.

However, No amount of rapport-building or the use of 'benefits' language will overcome bad manners or inappropriate behaviour. All your hard work and preparation can come to nothing if you or one of your practitioner team unconsciously demonstrates a bad attitude or behaves inappropriately.

Your attitudes and behaviour can make or break an engagement

Finally, let's consider some behaviours and attitudes that consultants must keep in mind or avoid when engaging with clients. It can be so easy to unintentionally cause offence. You or your practitioner team may not have analysed who is going to be in the room. The very basics are understanding the age and stage, the gender or cultural characteristics of your client attendees (your communication recipients). Failing to analyse your clients' characteristics can be a real trap for any practitioner team.

So, let's start with the basics of what is it that people want and don't want to experience in engagement meetings, or in any aspect of their work life. Table 5-7 has some examples of poor but avoidable behaviour we have observed in client meetings, presentations and other business communications. In many ways, preparing to avoid unintentional problems such as poor attitudes and behaviour represents a checklist of why you need to prepare for every meeting carefully! It's all about personal effectiveness and style flexibility, both the topics of other very useful books and courses.

Importance of planning to avoid poor attitudes and behaviours

Let's face it, if you do not thoroughly understand who you are meeting with and prepare for all communication types, you could unintentionally behave inappropriately or send the wrong message in a wide range of ways.

Not adhering to good professional conduct has undone many a practitioner in the past, often without the practitioner even realising it. Let's flip some of our examples into the benefits of planning:

1. ***Builds Trust:*** Addressing and avoiding poor attitudes and behaviours helps in building and maintaining trust with the client.
2. ***Enhances Communication:*** Effective communication is key to understanding and solving client problems. Poor behaviours can hinder this process.
3. ***Fosters Collaboration:*** A positive attitude encourages collaboration and teamwork, leading to better outcomes.
4. ***Maintains Professionalism:*** Professional behaviour reflects well on both the consultant and the consulting firm, enhancing their reputation.

By being aware of poor attitudes and behaviours, practitioners can ensure more successful and productive client engagement meetings.

Table 5-7 shows how easy it is to unconsciously cause offence! Preparation and sensitivity to your audience are the key.

Table 5-7 Attitudes and Behaviours to avoid in client meetings

Poor Attitude/ Behaviour	Description	Impact on Client Engagement
Lack of Preparation	Consultant arrives unprepared, without understanding the client's business or the meeting agenda.	Undermines credibility and trust, leading to a lack of confidence in the consultant's abilities.
Unprofessional Behaviour	Consultant exhibits unprofessional behaviour, such as being late, using inappropriate language, or dressing inappropriately.	Diminishes the consultant's credibility and the client's perception of their professionalism.
Arrogance	Consultant displays a know-it-all attitude, dismissing the client's input and concerns.	Creates a hostile environment, discourages open communication, and damages the client-consultant relationship.
Poor Listening Skills	Consultant interrupts or fails to actively listen to the client's needs and feedback.	Leads to misunderstandings, missed opportunities, and solutions that do not address the client's actual problems.
Lack of Empathy	Consultant shows little understanding or concern for the client's challenges and emotions.	Erodes trust and rapport, making it difficult to build a strong working relationship.
Inflexibility	Consultant is rigid and unwilling to adapt to the client's changing needs or feedback.	Limits the effectiveness of the engagement, as the consultant may not provide the most relevant or effective solutions.
Interrupting	Not letting the client finish their point	The client can feel over-ridden or considers they have not been heard.
Criticizing	Suggesting the client has exercised poor judgement in the past	Causes distrust and concern that they have been made to look foolish in front of their boss or peers.
Judging	Suggesting the client is violating or out of alignment with their ethics.	Causes distrust and concern that they have been made to look foolish in front of their boss or peers.

Poor Attitude/ Behaviour	Description	Impact on Client Engagement
Catching the client unawares	Violating the 'no surprises' rule	Can catch the client unawares and make them feel foolish in front of their boss or peers
Embarrassing	Causing the client to feel embarrassed or insecure	Causes distrust and concern that they have been made to look foolish in front of their boss or peers
Accusing	Suggesting the client's personal needs are being put ahead of the organisation's needs.	Can result in termination of the engagement
Overpromising	Consultant makes unrealistic promises or commitments that cannot be delivered.	Leads to disappointment, frustration, and a loss of trust when expectations are not met.
Lack of Follow-Up	Consultant fails to follow up on action items or communication after the meeting.	Causes delays, confusion, and a perception of disinterest or lack of commitment to the client's success.

Chapter Summary

Our experience tells us that clients always value a practitioner being well prepared – we can always tell if a colleague is 'winging' it, unprepared. In many ways it is a mark of respect to the client and a measure of your professionalism to prepare before going to any meeting or sending a business communication of any sort.

The Seven Steps are not meant to be prescriptive, but rather to present guidance to practitioners in planning for and running more effective engagement meetings. As we have demonstrated, the competencies and skills we have highlighted can be applied widely to enhancing business (and personal) communication effectiveness.

Over time, and with practice, these seven steps become a way of thinking, a structured way of working as a professional. Everyone benefits from good process and efficient meeting practices. Practitioners benefit from developing an understanding of how our attitudes and behaviour i.e., how we engage with others and how we can unintentionally cause problems or offence. In many ways understanding how our attitudes and behaviours impact others is an ongoing journey as we grow and mature as professionals. The journey starts with a willingness to explore and expand our personal effectiveness. In other parts of this book, we present more advice and suggestions that are relevant to the meeting process.

The process so far has helped you clarify the client problem, perhaps identify and agree root causes and establish some initial thinking about solutions. But what do you do with all this information?

So far, you've planned to conduct at least your first formal engagement meeting with the client to start the process of planning to craft and present your ideas and solutions in the form of a proposal. You will also need to plan to present this in a client presentation.

In the next Chapters (6 and 7) we introduce the Proposal Planning Canvas to help you take the systems thinking, (see Chapter 2) approach that top practitioners apply.

Endnotes

13. Shellenbarger, S. (2016) A Manifesto to End Boring Meetings. Wall Street Journal.

Appendix 1 Sample Meeting Checklist

Before the meeting

- Get clear on the meeting purpose, objectives, and outcomes—check that a meeting is needed
- Determine who should attend
- Draft and include the meeting agenda and any required pre-reading material in the meeting invitation
- Advise attendees if you would like them to participate in any particular way during the meeting – e.g. present data or provide expert advice on a particular matter
- Include the meeting agenda and any required pre-reading material in the meeting invitation
- Determine the meeting length and occurrence
- Find a facilitator or chairperson (if needed) and share meeting materials in advance
- Consider whether any technology such as Teams or Zoom will be used, whether everyone has the right equipment and knows how to use it.

During the meeting

- Introduce yourself (with the camera turned on, if applicable)
- Reiterate your expectations and goals
- Share the rules of engagement
- Record the meeting (remember to ask permission) if needed
- Share your screen (if applicable)
- Monitor the meeting chat for questions or comments if applicable
- Assign tasks and provide a meeting summary especially capturing agreements if applicable.

After the meeting

- Document meeting notes and next steps
- Address follow-up items
- Ask for feedback about the meeting's effectiveness, if applicable.

Chapter 6- Common Analysis Frameworks and Tools

Chapter guide

In this chapter, we introduce the analysis of your clients' internal and external environments. While the chapter is by no means exhaustive, it informs the activities you will undertake in completing a BA research planning canvas (see Chapter 7). We also suggest that growing your confidence and competence in using common analytical frameworks and tools is essential to establishing the logos – the logic - of your work as a practitioner and establishing the basis for writing compelling proposals and reports.

You'll deepen your understanding of some of the concepts and processes already introduced and better understand the benefits of conducting high-quality background research for:

1. **Improved communication:** Well-documented research using common frameworks makes it easier to communicate findings to stakeholders. Clear and structured reports help in conveying complex information in an understandable manner.
2. **Strategic alignment:** High-quality research ensures that the project aligns with the overall business strategy. This alignment helps in achieving long-term business goals and enhances the project's value to the organisation.
3. **Informed decision-making:** High-quality research provides accurate and comprehensive data, enabling BAs to make well-informed decisions. This reduces the risk of errors and increases the likelihood of project success. It also helps increase the likelihood of your client achieving the anticipated return on the project investment.
4. **Enhanced efficiency:** Utilizing common tools and frameworks streamlines the research process, making it more efficient. This allows BAs to gather and analyse data more quickly, saving time and resources.

5. **Consistency and standardization:** Using established tools and frameworks ensures consistency in the research process. This standardization helps in comparing data across different projects and time periods, leading to deeper, more reliable insights, and increased client assurance.
6. **Risk mitigation:** Thorough background research helps identify potential risks early in the project. By understanding the market, competitors, and regulatory environment, and interdependencies practitioners can develop strategies to mitigate these risks.
7. **Competitive advantage:** Detailed research provides insights into market trends and competitor strategies. This information can be used to develop innovative solutions and gain a competitive edge.
8. **Enhanced collaboration:** Common tools and frameworks facilitate better collaboration among team members. Shared understanding and standardized processes improve teamwork and project outcomes.

By doing background research and leveraging these benefits, practitioners can deliver more effective and impactful solutions, ultimately adding significant value to the success of their projects and the organisation.

Introduction to Analysis Methods

We introduce the chapter by exploring exactly what external and internal heuristics (methods or approaches) can do for you, starting with how they are related.

Are Internal Analysis and External Analysis connected?

External analysis and internal analysis are interdependent. Completing one without the other can provide an incomplete picture that can detract from your ability to recommend a strategy, outcome or approach to the client.

Evaluating the external environment, the client's market and industry conditions, highlights where and how disruption or competition is occurring in an industry and brings focus onto potential opportunities and threats. Think creatively about where you might find relevant industry research, good practice and innovation examples.

Evaluating the internal environment – the organisation's assets, systems, processes and capabilities – can highlight potential weaknesses and strengths.

Combining analyses from both external and internal reviews gives you and the client a more integrated, holistic view of the overall situation when trying to change or improve something.

Additionally, quality analysis provides the opportunity to combine logos (business logic) pathos (in this case creating a strong sense that you're on the right track) and ethos (credible, ethical and aligned with the company's goals and values) into your approach.

Both external and internal analyses are needed if you want to create a winning business proposal, based on information that makes sense to the client. After all, you're telling their story.

Analysing the External Environment

In this section we showcase external customer analysis (i.e. customers of our clients) and the use of a PESTLE analysis (Political, Economic, Social, Technical, Legal and Environmental) to complete a holistic external scan.

An Overview of External Customer Analysis

Effective external customer analysis is a key to organisation success – no exceptions. Understanding your client's customers' unique needs and expectations ensures your analysis and recommendations target prioritised needs. 'Customer analysis includes researching and analysing customers to create a profile of them and their behaviour.'[14]

> **Top Tip:** Make sure you ask whether the client has already conducted customer analysis and whether they already understand their level of satisfaction or whether they have any under-serviced or unexplored segments.

From system and process solutions to marketing campaigns or onboarding programs, targeting product and service experiences to your client's customers improves your ability to prioritise solutions that will increase satisfaction and help improve business outcomes.

Let's take a closer look at what customer analysis is, its purpose and value, and how to get started. The goal of customer analysis is to establish:

- Who the client's customers are, how they are segmented, what they have in common and what makes them unique;
- What your client's customers' needs are, whether there are un- or underserviced customer segments, what influences each segment's decision-making and how long their decision-making takes;
- Any price sensitivities and how much customers are willing to spend;

- Whether and how often the customer might make repeat purchases or service requests; and,
- What content, products, services or campaigns resonate best[15].

Table 6-1 provides some ways to explore these goals and better understand who your client's existing customers are, using the APV – Attribute – Purpose – Value approach to expressing the information.

After completing a customer analysis, you are better prepared to have a dialogue with your client about customer impacts, and how these influence any solution priorities. You can also identify new or unexplored opportunities or can create user personas based on real customer traits to help make sure you target and focus your solutions. Further you can build a customer journey map to make sure your solutions are hitting all the touchpoints and to understand how customers engage with your client's brand[16] - their products and services and the promises your organisation makes.

The timing of this analysis will depend on whether you plan to ask these questions in your initial, 'kick-off' meeting with the client. You also have the option ahead of your first client engagement meeting to conduct external analyses such as PESTLE or Porter's 5 Forces.

Table 6-1 identifying, segmenting, and understanding customers

Attribute	Purpose	Value
Segment existing customers and identify their distinguishing characteristics	To separate different customers into groups that share common characteristics	Helps target each segment based on their unique needs, interests and preferences
Identify under-serviced or unhappy customers	To understand any issues causing dissatisfaction within current segments	Can help prioritise actions and solutions
Identify unexplored customers	To understand whether solutions proposed offer opportunities to currently un-tapped customer segments	To provide services to a more representative audience. To potentially generate revenue from new markets.
Leverage product analytics	To do a customer behaviour analysis to better understand how customers interact with your product	Identifies patterns, trends and customer behaviours, usage and preferences in person or online

Attribute	Purpose	Value
Gather insights about customers from internal teams	To understand how segments are currently defined and elicit info about known issues	May highlight existing, current research. Make sure you ask if any department (e.g. marketing or web team) have created any customer profiles or personas – time savers!
Conduct 'social listening'	Reviews social media and search sites to obtain an unfiltered look at what customers are saying about the client's products, services and experiences	Can be a useful measure of product, service or organisational performance. Check whether the organisation monitors social media for this purpose.

PESTLE Analysis

The Political, Economic, Social, Technological, Legal, and Environmental (PESTLE) framework is used to analyse and monitor macro-environmental factors that may have an impact on an organisation's competitive position, strategy, performance, or decision-making.

By understanding the external environment, an organisation can better position itself to meet a wide variety of challenges and capitalize on opportunities.

> **Top Tip:** set up and use a dedicated SWOT or GAP run-sheet to capture insights from your PESTLE analysis.

Assign different parts of the analysis to team members and discuss. Or schedule a meeting with your client to share your insights and ask further questions.

Political factors

These are the external political forces brought on by the government or politics affecting the organisation, including governmental policies, government leadership, foreign trade and foreign relations, political issues and trends, regulations, and de-regulation trends.

A few examples might include current moves to change the retirement benefits age, changes in education policy, tariffs on imports from another country, or wars and conflicts.

Questions to ask:

- What shifts have occurred in the political climate?
- What is the potential impact of any upcoming elections?
- How might those shifts impact the client organisation?
- Are the impacts likely to be short- or long-term?
- What are the political threats you should monitor?
- Are they barriers, or enablers?

Economic factors

Economic factors consider rising inflation rates, changes and shifts in consumer spending on goods and services, changes in the supply chain, demand curves, and the health of the global economy. Analysis can be applied to local, national, and global economies.

Questions to ask:

- What is the current health of the economy? How might that impact the organisation?
- Are there any issues in the client supply chain?
- What local economic factors might impact our business? For example, Interest rates (affecting corporate loans), Government spending (for government clients), tax changes etc.

Social Factors

Social factors are about your organisation's customers and include changes in the greater social environment. These can vary widely, but include social trends like changing opinions about relationships, social justice movements or changing population, employment and demographic trends.

Questions to ask:

- Are there changing trends or disruptors in the client's industry, demographics or population? What are the possible impacts of any trends?
- How are changing social factors likely to impact the short-, medium- and long-term?
- What shifts can be observed in consumer or user behaviour, sentiment, or opinion?

Technical Factors

Changes in technology can affect a business's positioning, its competitive advantage, its efficiency and effectiveness even its survival as a sector.

Some recent examples are the rise of cryptocurrency (which can also fall into the economic category), Web3[17] development, the emergence of popular work-from-home technology, rapid adoption of electric vehicles, e-learning, AI developments, and concerns about cyber security.

It is important to consider how technology can prove to be a strength or an opportunity for your organisation, or a weakness and therefore a potential threat to it.

This technical factor analysis is perhaps the most important for a consultant / BA to undertake if the solution under consideration involves a change or addition to the client's system landscape.

Questions to ask:

- How has technology in the client's market changed? Is that an pportunity or threat?
- Is the client using available technology to its full advantage?
- Is the client leveraging the full value and usage of existing technology? How are they adopting Artificial Intelligence?
- How much does emerging technology impact your organisation?
- Are there key people amongst the client organisation likely to resist a new technology or application because they are 'married' to the existing one?

Legal factors

Legal factors look at the practical application of the political factors into rules and regulations that may affect your business or customers. These can include the laws and regulations of overseas customers.

This could include updated laws, new regulations, or abolishing laws. Depending on your business, local, state, and federal laws and regulations are worth scrutinizing.

Questions to ask:

- What changes in our international, national, and local legislation impact the client organisation?
- How are these legal changes going to impact the client organisation positively or negatively?
- What legal or regulatory changes are there on the horizon?

A great example of this might be analysing the impact of the General Data Protection Regulation for the client. This widely recognised regulation adopted by the EU, has:

- Legal - it is a regulation being adopted by many countries:
- Technological - it has significant impacts for data strategy – creation, access, storage, retrieval, and disposal;
- Political and social - access such as whether data can be stored offshore presents significant challenges around cloud suppliers and data sovereignty; and,
- Economic implications - financial impacts of previous factors and cost of compliance.

Environmental factors

Environmental factors are affected by weather, geography, climate change, and health crises. In addition to the public health crisis caused by the COVID pandemic, the world has also been impacted by wildfires, earthquakes, volcanoes and increasingly unstable weather across the globe.

Organisations should consider the short-term and long-term impacts of these accelerating changes, e.g., rising ocean levels, drier and warmer seasons affecting crop yields, and yearly weather conditions such as hurricanes and typhoons.

Questions to ask:

- What environmental factors are impacting us right now?
- What environmental factors might impact us in the future?
- What environmental factors do we need to monitor?

A PESTLE analysis is often used in tandem with a SWOT analysis to capture the results. These two analyses will also help you complete other sections such as impact and risk analysis (see later in the chapter).

Other tools for analysing the external environment

Porter's 5 Forces

Porter's Five Forces[18] is a framework for analysing the level of competition within an industry during business strategy development. The five forces are:

- Threat of new entrants into the market – think disruptors! and competitive rivalry, is it easy or hard to enter the market?

- Bargaining power of suppliers – think supply chain and resource costs;
- Bargaining power of buyers – think customer power – how easy is it for them to shift to a competitor;
- Threat of substitute products or services – think innovation of unique products and services. The more unique the harder to substitute; and,
- Rivalry among existing competitors – think brand power.

The framework is used to identify an industry's attractiveness, how easy it is for competitors to enter the market and profitability, and competitive positioning within an industry.

Top Tip: "What If" Scenario planning can be used to identify future potential risk and opportunity and identify potential solutions.

When to use External Analysis Tools

The industry and sector your client comes from will determine your decisions about when and whether to use analysis tools such as PESTLE and Porter's 5 Forces.

PESTLE works particularly well for government organisations but can also work well for the for-profit and not-for-profit sectors. Porter's Five Forces, also called competitive analysis, works best for commercial (for-profit) organisations. Next, we analyse the internal organisation.

Analysing the Internal Environment

Internal analysis enables an organisation to determine what they can do to increase their productivity and profitability. It is also useful for identifying change capability. This helps practitioners to identify, prioritise and recommend strategies for change. The goal is to thoroughly analyse the current state.

Through the internal Situation Analysis process, practitioners help clients examine their operations effectiveness and efficiency, internal structures, systems and processes.

Depending on the problem or issues, this can include analysis of resources, assets, characteristics, competencies, capabilities, technology, policies, systems and ways of working (processes).

The Goal of Internal Situation Analysis

The overarching goal is to help management during strategy formulation, decision-making, and execution processes by identifying the organisation's strengths and weaknesses, opportunities, and barriers to success.

So simply put, an internal analysis in strategic management should serve as the foundation of any business strategy.

Common Internal Situation Analysis Tools and when to use them

There are several frameworks used by practitioners for internal situation analysis. As already introduced in the previous section, a simple SWOT analysis and Porter's Five Forces can be good starting points, with the impacts of the external analysis conducted in either framework continued into the internal capability to respond to the findings.

Other frameworks that can be employed include Strategy Evaluation, Capability and Competency Analysis, TOGAF, Gap Analysis, and Process Analysis.

Strategy evaluation

Situating your analysis in strategy and success measures from the business plan provides a foundation for communicating from a logos perspective. If your client can see a clear alignment with strategy, and any of your suggested measures align as well, your recommendations will be more logical and potentially agreeable.

This means for every client engagement we strongly recommend obtaining a copy of the current strategy and business plan early on.

These key documents provide useful context for both the external and internal analysis and enhance the practitioner's ability to ascertain the current state and results of an organisation's performance against plan.

> Top Tip: With a view to the practitioner taking a holistic systems approach, strategy analysis is useful when conducted in parallel with simple frameworks such as SWOT and GAP analysis as a 'first cut' way of capturing the data you are discovering in a systematic way.

Strategy evaluation involves looking back at the goals and measures of the client's strategic plan to assess how well (or not) their current initiatives are tracking, whether the goals and measures are being monitored and reported on and identifying barriers and enablers to achieving them.

The goals of strategy evaluation include:

1. Identifying how the organisation is tracking against its current strategy and plans;
2. Evaluating whether monitoring and reporting is aligned with what the strategy and plans are trying to achieve;
3. identifying gaps, barriers and enablers (especially people, capability and culture); and,
4. identifying where and how specific issues or challenges can contribute to strategy and plan achievement.

The evaluation process involves answering questions such as:

- What has the external environment analysis revealed? Are the organisation's strategic focus areas still relevant?
- Which objectives have been completed and were these successful: how does the client know? How are other objectives progressing?
- Where did the organisation fall short of goals and objectives, and why did this happen?
- Are there any redundant objectives or objectives that need re-prioritising?
- Do we have sufficient projects to deliver incomplete objectives? How well aligned and integrated are these projects?
- Are the organisation's KPIs (Key Performance Indicators) still effective for measuring progress towards the objectives?
- How or where does the current identified problem align and integrate with, support or enable strategy?

Strategy and business planning are a circular process of constant iteration and evolution. A good strategy never really 'ends'. Rather, it should morph into something more ambitious and sophisticated as goals are met and the external environment changes.

However, achieving strategy and realising expected returns requires a deep understanding of the organisation's capabilities and core competencies.

Capability and Competency Analysis

Capability analysis is an evaluation of an organisation's abilities and resources to determine its potential for strategic success[19]. It is common for this analysis to be undertaken after a competitive analysis such as Porter's 5 Forces, or when completing a new product or system analysis.

As introduced in Chapter 2, capabilities are clusters of competencies, so the two analyses are often used in tandem to identify areas where the organisation needs to improve, or be more agile, to develop or maintain competitive or operational advantage.

For example, an organisation may develop an ambitious digital transformation strategy. However, do the senior leaders have the combined capability and associated individual competencies to lead the transformation, and realize the anticipated outcomes?

Core competency analysis[20] is a specific type of capability analysis that focuses on identifying the unique, important, and difficult to replicate skills and abilities that a business or organisation needs to do well to achieve strategically. Such core competencies are fundamental to helping the organisation develop new products and services that are difficult for competitors to copy. In other words, a capability analysis is a broader evaluation of an organisation's abilities and resources, while a core competency analysis focuses specifically on identifying the unique and important sets of competencies (skills and abilities) that give the organisation a competitive (or in the case of government, operating effectiveness) advantage.

Overview of how to conduct a Capability Analysis

A capability analysis is a systematic assessment of your organisation's strengths and weaknesses in delivering value to customers and/or shareholders. It helps to identify the gaps between the organisation's current and desired performance and prioritise the areas that need improvement.

Some tools that can be used for a capability analysis include:

- Capability Maturity Models (CMMs) to benchmark the organisation's current state and set realistic goals for improvement;
- Capability maps can be used to align capabilities with the organisation's strategy; and,
- Needs analysis and planning, which helps further refine professional development and training needs where competency gaps are identified. An outcome may be recruitment of professionals with specific capabilities.

Both GAP and SWOT analysis can be used in parallel to evaluate internal and external factors and prioritise areas that may affect the organisation's capability to achieve its strategies, goals and objectives, and performance.

Similarly, it is important to consider and prioritise whether information and technology capability is a risk to be mitigated.

TOGAF

The Open Group Architecture Framework (TOGAF) is a standard and proven enterprise methodology and framework used to analyse business efficiency[21] and build technological capability.

The goal of TOGAF is to improve the efficiency and effectiveness of an organisation by taking a structured approach to aligning business goals and objectives with information and technology (I&T) capabilities. Analysis follows an Architecture Development Method (ADM) which provides a structured approach for aligning strategy and business goals with I&T capabilities.

To achieve alignment and project integration, during the initial phases of the ADM, the business strategy, goals and drivers are used to define the scope and vision of a project. This helps ensure that the I&T architecture is aligned with the strategic direction of the organisation.

The subsequent phases of the ADM involve developing architecture models for each of the business, data, application, and technology domains[22].

ADM also helps provide a common language and methodology for designing and managing the architecture of an organisation. The process includes several phases that help organisations understand their current architecture, define their target architecture, and develop a roadmap for transitioning from the current to the target architecture. This process helps ensure that the organisation's I&T capabilities are aligned with their business goals and that their enterprise architecture supports their strategic direction.

While not a formally mentioned part of the TOGAF framework, our experience suggests conducting a detailed parallel analysis of all relevant Technical Debt within the client organisation.

Technical Debt Analysis

Technical debt can be critical to an organisation's success or failure -- and many don't even know it exists![23]

Technical debt refers to the costs associated with fixing or improving legacy systems, eliminating suboptimal coding, and reviewing and fixing inefficient or 'clunky' applications. It also applies to remediating other technology decisions that were made in the past, but which endure and affect performance in a modern, digital context.

A good starting point is to evaluate key user challenges with current information and technology systems. System performance metrics can help find bugs, usability problems, security risks, and performance problems arising from technical debt.

This data is relatively easy to obtain from user feedback and testing, surveys, and analytics tools. Common signs of the symptoms of technical debt include system or software issues in the following areas:

Bugs and Issues

Numerous bugs and problems with software could be a sign of technical debt. This is especially true if the bugs and problems are hard to fix or keep happening repeatedly. Perhaps the software is no longer supported: perhaps the application does not integrate with other information management systems. Perhaps the software or code was developed in-house, and the 'expert' has left the organisation without quality documentation of the development and maintenance of the item.

Slow Performance

If software is slow, 'clunky' to use or doesn't work as it should, this can be a sign of old or bad code, shoddy systems, or old infrastructure. Slow performance impacts work productivity and user / customer experiences.

Difficulty in Making Changes

If making changes to your software is hard, this could also be a sign of technical debt. This can happen if the code isn't organised well, there isn't enough development or maintenance documentation, or the infrastructure is old. It can also be because key influencers are 'married' to a particular piece of software because that's what they are familiar with and have used for a long time.

Take the example of a tertiary education provider. Students and some teaching staff satisfaction with the usability of the online Learning Management System (LMS) was exceptionally low.

The system had been in place for over 12 years. The user experience was described as 'so 90s' and 'clunky, and not intuitive' by users.

From a management perspective it was also very difficult to derive student performance and achievement data from the system, so nigh impossible to easily integrate into Data Management or Business Analytics initiatives.

However, a small but influential group of senior academics and the Teaching and Learning management team refused to consider moving to a modern platform, despite clear evidence of brand-eroding student and faculty experiences with the old LMS, and significant ongoing costs to maintain the platform.

Deeper analysis revealed that these sentiments were based on familiarity with the old LMS, convenience and personal preferences rather than factors such as cost, security, user impacts or brand erosion.

High Maintenance Costs

If it costs a lot to keep your software up-to-date, or the organisation is investing heavily in bespoke functionality within a platform or within an instance of complex commercial systems such as ERPs, this can also be a sign of technical debt. This generally happens because of old / bad code, badly designed and implemented systems, or old infrastructure. The latter can pose high system and data security risks.

It is not unusual for an organisation to implement an Enterprise Wide System, procured from a commercial vendor, and rather than adopt the best practice processes upon which the software is designed, make bespoke changes to align it with current practice and processes. Organisations take this path because, for them, it is easier to change the system than change the processes and thereby create less change impact upon the personnel. What this means, however, is that when major upgrades occur, the bespoke changes need to be re-implemented at significant cost – leading to technical debt.

It is also important to evaluate the currency and maintenance status of all software and hardware to identify vulnerabilities that may not yet have any visible symptoms of age or dysfunction, but which might present other security or commercial vulnerabilities if not detected and fixed.

Technical Debt Analysis helps build the Business Case for change

No matter the reason, with rapid change in information and technology systems now a normal part of digital business, this type of analysis will help practitioners build a logical (logos / facts and data) approach and business case for ensuring that the architecture is modern, secure and optimized to support the organisation (from both a data strategy and user experience perspective) to achieve its strategies and plans, and to operate in more agile ways.

Potential Risks and Costs of not understanding Technical Debt

To make sure that information and technology systems will work in the future, it is important to find and deal with technical debt. If you don't, it can lead to high maintenance costs, less work getting done, and bad user experiences.

Technical debt needs to be on every organisation's risk register, to help ensure that ongoing remediation activity and the associated budget are considered each year and monitored via governance.

GAP Analysis

GAP analysis is a simple, practical approach to help identify performance deficiencies and internal weaknesses.

GAP analysis helps practitioners and the client to identify where the organisation is performing to its potential or not, and if not, why, at a very focused level. It is a good framework for fine-tuning a single process (or a selected few) instead of the organisation as a whole. In addition, it helps to pinpoint flaws in resource allocation, planning, production, processes, systems, information access etc.

Practitioners can work with the client to compare the current problem and opportunity and the desired future state and identify and understand the gaps between the two states. This is very useful in the ideation and solution development (Plan / Design) phase of the lifecycle because the goal is to create solutions then recommend a plan to bridge those gaps.

Process Analysis

Business Process Analysis (BPA) is an approach to analysing business operation processes. It is a detailed, multi-step examination of each part of a process to identify what is working well in your current process, what needs to be improved and how any necessary improvements can best be made. BPA is a subset of Business Process Management (BPM), a much larger framework and long-term strategy that seeks to manage an organisation's processes for optimal performance.

The goal of BPA is to help organisations improve the efficiency and effectiveness of their operations - how the organisation runs and how it can improve. BPA can allow companies to:

- Gather in-depth data on how processes are currently performing;
- Increase the efficiency in existing processes;
- Identify areas for potential process automation and data collection;
- Clarify policies and rules by properly documenting processes;
- Spot which user actions are hindering processes;
- Identify cost savings by revealing redundancies in tasks and labour; and,
- Expose communication gaps and resolve approval problems[24].

By examining each part of a process, practitioners can identify potential improvements and suggest changes that can lead to cost savings, increased revenue, and better user and customer experiences.

Other common tools

In this section we have highlighted some useful tools. However, there are many more commonly used tools, which (akin to the parallel use of SWOT or GAP Analysis) can be used at the same time as the more complex models. These include: The Five 'Whys', Ishikawa / Root Cause Analysis, UX (User Experience) Analysis and so on.

Chapter Summary

There are many more tools and frameworks available online, that also provide step-by-step instructions. A skilled practitioner will automatically begin to consider the use or modification of these models as they plan and prepare a proposal. With skill and practice practitioners increasingly understand which tools and frameworks are best for each situation, and how each relates to the stages of the consulting and engagement lifecycles.

This is why we call it a consulting toolbox! When used to enhance the quality of the project research and proposal stages, each framework guides both the analysis as well as the communication of your findings in ways that many clients are already familiar with. This builds logos (facts, data and logic), pathos (problem solving with alignment and value) and ethos (building trust and confidence) and provides an excellent foundation for the client-centred story you will research (chapter 7) and write (chapter 8).

Endnotes

14. How to Conduct An Effective Customer Analysis in 8 Steps (userpilot.com)

15. https://www.glew.io/articles/how-to-conduct-effective-customer-analysis

16. https://www.glew.io/articles/how-to-conduct-effective-customer-analysis

17. Web3 is the adoption of blockchain technology to enhance data security and increase disintermediation. Web3 development agencies such as

Labrys.io are creating blockchain applications across a wide variety of clients all over world. As Greg is a co-owner and strategic advisor, they use the techniques outlined in this book.

18. Porter, M. E. (1980). Competitive strategy: techniques for analysing industries and competitors. Free Press.

19. Barney, J. (1991). Firm resources and sustained competitive advantage. Journal of Management, 17(1), 99-120.

20. Prahalad, C. K., & Hamel, G. (1990). The Core Competence of the Corporation [Article]. Harvard Business Review, 68(3), 79-91.

21. From <https://pubs.opengroup.org/togaf-standard

22. TOGAF Series Guide: Business Modelling - The Open Group. https://pubs.opengroup.org/togaf-standard/business-architecture/business-models.html Accessed 24/04/2023.

23. https://www.techtarget.com/searchitoperations/tip/6-technical-debt-examples-and-how-to-solve-them

24. https://www.indeed.com/career-advice/career-development/business-process-analysis

Chapter 7 – Research and Proposal Planning

Chapter guide

In this chapter we introduce how to conduct background research, analysis and planning essential to creating a business report or proposal. This is where systems thinking (see chapter 2) i.e. your ability to think in holistic and integrated ways really matters.

The guide steps you through the basics, so you are encouraged to add your own questions and considerations as you work through the process of exploring each section, and how each builds towards a client-centred view.

We focus our approach on research that in turn will help you provide targeted business communications. **We introduce a bespoke IS Consulting / BA proposal planning canvas process.** This approach helps practitioners to focus client engagement and communications based on the information gleaned from meetings and research and uses the canvas as a type of journey map.

Our goal is to boost even the most seasoned practitioner's capability in proposal writing to the level where your ***clients want to read your proposal*** because of the way they are structured and written. We cover:

1. Planning in the context of business communication, and specifically the background research required to write a professional-quality business proposal or report; and,
2. How to use a Business Analysis research and planning canvas.

Introduction to Planning Business Communications

Consulting proposals and presentations are business communications that require high levels of professionalism. Each provides the means for you to outline and discuss what you, as a practitioner, understand about the client and their problem, and then propose how to solve their identified issues. While we provide detailed business writing tips in Chapter 8, this chapter provides a foundation from which to build professional quality business communications.

Planning is essential. Although you will have gathered a lot of information from your initial engagements, all practitioners need to be able to turn this client information into clear, concise, compelling proposals and presentations.

In Chapter 4, we discussed the engagement phase of the IS consulting lifecycle. These key activities identified the client's needs and requirements (dialogue / diagnose) and prepared us to respond to the client in the plan / design phase. This is where planning for a quality, written proposal comes in.

The models and processes described in this chapter enable both the client and consultant to agree on outcomes, scope, stages, approaches, measures of value, reporting and governance before creating a final proposal.

There are multiple tools and models to help achieve this. We covered some of these in Chapter 6. Sometimes consultants make up their own models and tools. But the goal is still the same: to provide a relevant, consistent framework for conducting and communicating the various phases of the lifecycle in ways that make sense to the client. Until you become very experienced, we recommend using the canvas approach to structure and order your thinking, to plan how to do a quality job, and to develop your responses.

The information you are seeking is used throughout each client project's lifecycle. You can add to the information you gather throughout the project. It's wise to do this because quality background research and analysis are the basis of engagement planning as well as drafting your proposal and presentation. Targeted and focused communication becomes achievable when you consider all the requirements as part of a communication package.

As shown in Figure 7-1, and covered in-depth in Chapter 8, the basic proposal scaffold that we recommend for professional proposals has four sections.

The four main sections to a business proposal or report are:

1. The **Front End** – the Executive Summary, Table of Contents and Introduction. These focus the reader's attention and help them find the information they seek. They should always be written in a very sharp and compelling style to create interest and encourage them to read more. Many proposals do not make it past this stage in large responses.
2. The **Background / Problem Identification** sections demonstrate that you understand the client's issues, their sector / industry, external factors and trends and introduce why and how their challenges can be resolved.

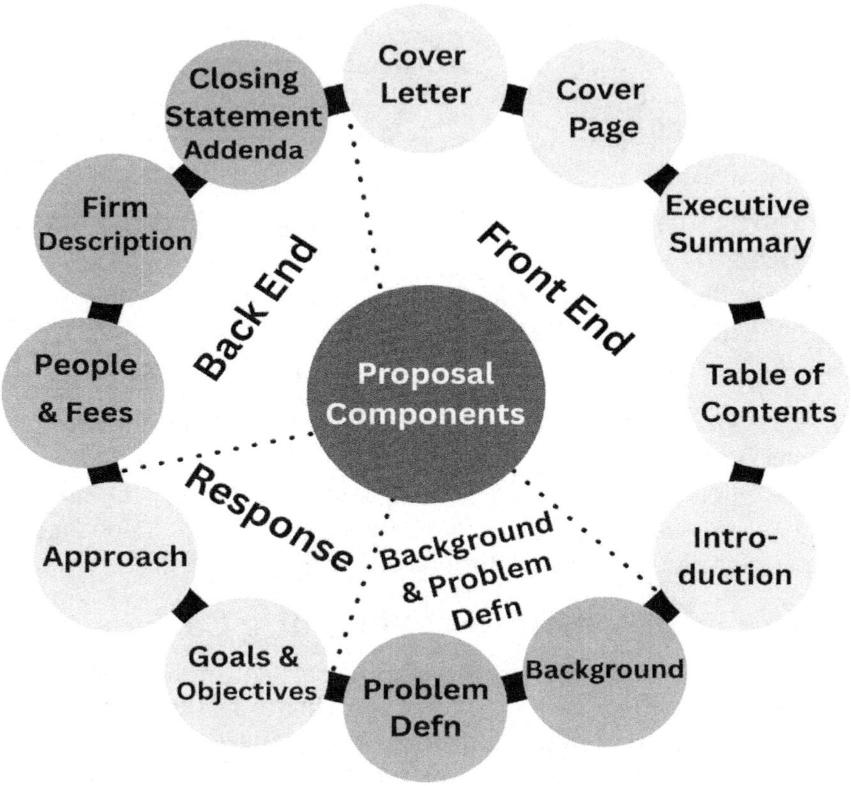

Figure 7-1 Overview of the proposal 'package' and summary of proposal contents

3. The **Response** sections outline options, your recommended solutions, and the approach you suggest to implementing the solution. The section outlines considerations such as project methods and timeline, change impacts, risks and mitigations, project communication and governance.
4. The **Back End** - Here you suggest the people who will work on the engagement, what role each will fulfil including the client, how much you estimate the project including resources will cost and talk about your firm. This finalizes the document and appends additional material.

Additional components of the proposal package not covered in this chapter are meeting communications (Chapter 5). We also cover Proposals and Business Writing in Chapter 8, and Presentations in Chapter 9.

Use the bespoke canvas provided in this chapter to plan to achieve a great client outcome with objectives to:

- Convince the client that you understand their organisation and the identified challenges
- Demonstrate how your approaches will provide the outcomes the client seeks
- Advise what activities are required to create outputs and where these will take place
- Acquaint the client with whomever will provide the expertise to effectively deliver the required outputs
- Suggest a timetable of when these activities will occur
- Provide an estimate of how much the client will pay for your services.

Any canvas should be treated as a living document. It can be added to or amended as you engage with the client. The purpose is to help you focus on and prepare for meetings, presentations and to write reports and proposals.

Working with a Proposal Planning Canvas

Having decided to invest in writing a proposal, you now double down on the client problem, the core issues you are trying to resolve, what additional research you need to conduct, information you need, steps you will take to resolve them and subsequently, what resources you will invest in this resolution process.

Canvases are planning tools that can help you compile a plan on one or two pages to target and focus you and your team's research and writing efforts. A canvas can help you focus on what's really going to drive a great client outcome while not getting too bogged down with non-essential details and content at the planning stage. The more care you take in undertaking this initial due diligence, the less likely you are to present work that does not meet your client's needs.

The Outcome, Purpose, and Benefits of a Planning Canvas

For proposals, the communication outcome is to make a compelling case for the client to proceed with your project recommendations. The purpose of using a proposal planning canvas is to make sure you have sufficient, targeted information to create a compelling, client-centred story from beginning to end. There are three benefits to working with a proposal-focused research and planning canvas:

1. **Speed**: It's obviously a lot faster to compile a plan based on one or two sheets than it is to make sense of lengthy written notes that are not organised to support efficient proposal writing. If you complete other complementary analysis tools (such as SWOT or GAP as covered earlier) alongside your canvas, you can optimise your effectiveness.
2. **Usability**: The step-by-step approach of a canvas allows you to focus on what's really going to tell a great story and provide a logical flow. It also helps highlight where you need to do more research or where you might need to clarify matters with the client.
3. **Collaboration**: The model can be used as a tool for communication and collaboration between team members, stakeholders, and key client employees. Different subject matter experts can see what they need to contribute and where their needs and interests are catered for.

To provide more detail, we have separated out the sections of a consulting proposal into the components of the canvas to assist you to create a logical flow in your analysis and your proposal or report writing. The process prompts you to ensure you have essential background data to:

- Provide context within which the business operates, including external factors or trends that could impact future goals and objectives;
- Provide a high-quality analysis of the client's business;
- Clearly state the problem and highlight underlying causes; and,
- Provide examples of excellence or highlight industry disruptors to set the scene for your goals, objectives and recommendations.

In short, research and planning bring the future into the present so your client can do something about it now, starting with quality research.

Sample Research Planning Canvas

Getting started with your canvas is relatively straight forward. Read each row from left to right of Figure 7-2 (on the next page). Complete the first 6 steps, making notes or action points in steps 8 and 9 to help you determine and prioritise your research.

With Figure 7-1 in mind, for the rest of the chapter we provide guidance on each canvas section, and, where useful, provide suggestions about analytical models and tools that help focus your research and writing. Make client-relevant notes as you go to help complete a usable canvas based on quality research.

Figure 7-2 Proposal Background Research and Planning Canvas

<table>
<tr><td colspan="4">FRONT END</td></tr>
<tr><td colspan="2">1. Consulting / BA group name

Team member name</td><td colspan="2">2. Client name: Industry / Sector:
Key info about client organisation e.g. name, approximate number of employees, location/s</td></tr>
<tr><td colspan="4">PROBLEM DEFINITION AND BACKGROUND</td></tr>
<tr><td>3. Problem Definition –
What problem/s have the client identified?
Why is this important to the client / industry or sector to solve the problem/s now?
Any unique circumstances?
What factors from the external and internal environments may be driving the need for change?</td><td>4. Client requested outcome/s –
what end-result is the client seeking?
What are the expected benefits to the client from solving the problem?
In what ways do the expected outcomes and benefits align with the organisation's strategy and business plan (or not)?
Inter-dependencies?</td><td>5. What are other similar organisations or sectors doing?
What opportunities does this represent?
Where is there technological disruption relevant to the client?
What barriers or hurdles will the client need to overcome?</td><td>6 Determine how you'll conduct the research.
Based on your answers to 1-5:
What issues or aspects of the problem need to be researched in depth to provide quality background insights?
What is your individual research topic and what is your group research plan? NOTE: You might also answer this after step 7.</td></tr>
<tr><td colspan="4">RESPONSE</td></tr>
<tr><td colspan="4">7. Client Project Outcomes Outputs, Goals and Objectives (OOGOs)</td></tr>
<tr><td colspan="4">8. Indicative measures of value / client success-measures - (such as MOV CCV or UCV)
(Top Tip: make sure you have a measure for each goal and objective.)</td></tr>
<tr><td colspan="2">9. Approach - Solution options and priorities</td><td colspan="2">10. Project approach, milestones and timeline</td></tr>
<tr><td colspan="2">11. Impacts / change to be managed</td><td colspan="2">12. Risks and Mitigation</td></tr>
<tr><td colspan="4">13. Project Reporting and Governance</td></tr>
<tr><td colspan="4">BACK END</td></tr>
<tr><td colspan="4">14. People and Fees: costs / budget, Team Information, a Closing Statement and Addenda.</td></tr>
</table>

Top Tip: In Step 14 make sure you have identified approach costs associated with Steps 9-12.

The Front End - Steps 1 and 2

In this section we consider the research you need to complete for the Introduction section. Other parts of this section (as shown in Figure 7-1) such as the cover letter and Table of Contents and Executive Summary are completed during the proposal writing stage (see Chapter 8).

Information for the Introduction Section

Step 1 is all about your BA or consulting team and you. Enter your consulting or BA Team name, and your name/s. This helps if you're working in a group, as you can use the canvas process to determine which team-member will research and write about the different issues that form the background.

Step 2 is all about the client. And remember, in our approach, the client is always the 'Star of the show!' Enter your client's organisation name and correctly identify the sector and industry and key information about the client organisation.

We introduced the concepts of sectors and industries in chapter 2. Sectors describe a large segment of the economy (e.g., Government, Farming or Education), while Industry refers to a specific sub-sector - a group of similar types of companies (e.g., Immigration as part of Government, Dairy Farming or Tertiary Education). Being clear about the sector and industry can be invaluable when hunting out information from Industry Peak Bodies (e.g. industry associations and institutes) or best practices in the same or similar organisations later in the canvas.

Step 2 is also about getting to know the client's business at a high level. This provides initial insights into the establishment, purpose, size, location/s and possibly key information about leadership or issues associated with factors such as:

- Being large and complex or a small, under-resourced organisation;
- Whether geographically dispersed or located in one place;
- The number of employees;
- Unique capabilities (see chapter 2);
- The types of products and services provided, and the main customer segments currently serviced; and,
- Overall maturity of the organisation.

You will usually find these sorts of information on the client's website, in their latest annual report, via an online media search or by asking the client. Size and location are particularly important. A distributed, national organisation will have very different process, staffing and technology platform requirements than a small enterprise with a single building in one location. If available, you can also find any other relevant information such as product or service volumes, production or perhaps ways of delivering those products and services. Are they delivered face-to-face or online for example? How are these goods and services supported? This information helps provide the context of the client problem.

Problem Definition and Background – Steps 3 to 5

The purpose of these three key steps is to get you and your team to the point where you are clear about the problems that need solving, how to align the problem with your client's strategies and plans; where the potential project may have interdependencies with other organisations and where there could be examples of successes in similar circumstances elsewhere.

Define the Problem - Step 3

In **Step 3**, provide a brief statement of the **problem, opportunity or issues** as described by the client. Using the client's description of the problem is important. It helps build the ethos and pathos aspects of your relationship with them. However, here is where you need to consider what type of internal or external analysis tool or framework will best help you to thoroughly explore and check the problem. This is the true art and skill of a top practitioner.

Whether or not you agree with the description of the problem from the client, at this stage you may not have had the opportunity to explore the problem more deeply with them.

As early as possible in the relationship, and specifically through an engagement meeting, you need to explore whether the problem, as stated, is the actual problem, or a symptom of the problem. Your goal is to establish this and the root cause of the problem.

From a research perspective, in step 3, you are also looking for strong logos indicators: facts and data to help you provide the details for the background section. **By conducting the appropriate combination of analyses, you set the context for the entire proposal.** There is more detail in Chapter 8 – Proposals. To complete the introduction, you must be able to very briefly summarise the information in Steps 1 – 3 in a way that sets the scene for the Background section.

Information for the Background section

Taking a disciplined, professional approach to **Step 4 provides the strongest possible foundation for the rest of the project**, including your engagement communication at later stages of the project. Getting this critical step right will affect your ability to accurately and cohesively present your findings and recommendations to the client, and your ability to write compelling proposals.

Your goal is to create a logical and well-researched basis to test the client's understanding of the problems they face, determine their resolve to complete the project and add measurable value.

In **Step 4**, and keeping all information at this stage at a very high level of detail, complete the information about your understanding of the **outcome or end-result the client is seeking**. If you are unable to do this with reasonable confidence, you'll need to engage with the client to clarify!

Also in step 4, identify the high-level benefits to the client of seeking assistance to solve the problem **now**. Try putting yourself in the client's shoes and 'crystal-ball gaze a little. This enables you to help imagine the client benefits of solving the problem. This important step is fundamental to identifying **measures of value** such as cost savings, improved efficiency, improved customer or staff satisfaction for example.

Take a pathos approach here - imagine the relief or excitement or sense of achievement the client would experience when the project is successful, and their problems are resolved.

An essential component of any background analysis is the client's **external and internal environments**. Use internal and external analyses to explore and record any initial insights that may play out later in your proposal.

This helps build the foundation for identifying and justifying options, solutions, approaches, impacts, importance and urgency in this section. You're looking for any **opportunities associated with solving the identified problem/s** for the organisation.

Provide any insights you may have gathered about the client's unique current circumstances, and your understanding of the importance (to the client) of solving their identified problems now. And you need to:

- Record any initial insights about why this is a problem within their stated timeframe and explore whether others in the sector and/or industry are also experiencing similar problems.
- Identify whether this has been a problem over time i.e., establish how long this has been a problem.

- Identify what the likely impacts of not solving the problem might be for the client. This latter information can also be useful when establishing value measures, flagging risks and recommending a timeline.

While we introduced some key analytical models in Chapter 2, refer to Chapter 6 to expand your toolbox of internal and external analysis methods. Understanding how the elements of your canvas relate will help you ask for the information you need as well as help you write a proposal that flows logically (logos) and aligns with the client's strategies and priorities.

Strategic Alignment as Background Context

Establishing a foundation of **strategic alignment** is essential when gathering background materials. Strategic alignment is the process of taking a systems thinking approach to ensure that all aspects of an organisation, including its goals, resources, and activities, are coordinated and in harmony with its overall strategy. This helps plan and determine project and investment priorities as well as measures of value.

You may have received some background information from the client at this stage to identify where and how the client's desired outcomes align with and support the organisation's current strategy and/or business plan. Alignment provides practitioners with the ability to integrate planned activities and is a very useful way of demonstrating measurable value.

Top Tip: If you do not have the client's strategy and/or business plan, take an immediate action point to ask at the next engagement meeting. You need it – urgently!

Finally, find out whether there are any other projects or important transformation activities happening within the client organisation to **determine any interdependencies.**

Determining and Prioritising Interdependencies

Practitioners need to be aware of several common, important interdependencies which (when planned for) help to effectively bridge the gap between business needs and technological solutions. Here are some of the most important dependencies that can, and do have significant impacts especially on strategic alignment:

1. **Stakeholder Relationships**: BAs and consultants must manage relationships with various stakeholders, including executives, project managers, developers, suppliers and end-

users. Effective communication and collaboration are central to ensuring that all parties are aligned and that requirements are accurately captured and understood.

2. **Business Processes and IT Systems:** Understanding how business processes interact with IT systems is essential. BAs need to ensure that any changes to business processes are supported by the right IT infrastructure and vice versa. Failing to conduct impact analysis to understand (in detail) how systems and processes are impacted by change, invariably ends in cost blow-outs and project delays. Here is where business architecture can be reviewed.
3. **Data and Analytics:** BAs often work with data analysts and data architects to interpret data and derive insights that inform business decisions. Practitioners need to understand how data flows throughout the organisation, what data the client currently collects or needs to collect to manage performance and provide insights, and how to leverage data to improve business outcomes. Understanding where there are data gaps, and what the organisation currently measures and reports on, as well as how your proposed project will be included in future planning, is central to ensuring strategic alignment. Here it is useful to understand whether the client has a data strategy and the relationship to any formal data architecture.
4. **Regulatory and Compliance Requirements:** BAs must be aware of relevant industry regulations and compliance requirements that affect their projects. This includes understanding how changes in regulations can impact business processes and systems.
5. **Market Trends and Business Strategy:** Keeping abreast of market trends and aligning project goals with the overall business strategy is vital. BAs need to ensure that their projects support the strategic objectives of the organisation.
6. **Technical Constraints and Opportunities:** BAs should understand the technical constraints of the systems they work with, as well as any opportunities for leveraging new technologies and applications to improve business processes.
7. **Interdepartmental Dependencies:** Projects often require collaboration across different departments. BAs need to manage these interdependencies to ensure smooth project execution and to avoid bottlenecks.

By being aware of these interdependencies, practitioners can better navigate the complexities of their role and deliver solutions that meet the needs of the business. Now let's look at other sources of inspiration, disruption or best practice.

Opportunities from Similar Organisations – Step 5

The considerations in Step 5 can be very insightful. This step is all about encouraging you to think about where disruptions are happening anywhere in the world and locally. Changes and opportunities for learning can be in related and even unrelated sectors and industries that are grappling with the same or similar problems. Here the focus is to identify opportunities as well as potential barries, or internal or external hurdles the client may need to overcome for their project to be successful. The goal is to Identify whether there are any valuable lessons or good practice examples applicable to solving your client's challenges.

> Early in Elizabeth's career she worked on the transformation of a consumer (retail) bank. The chief executive recruited people into the leadership team with significant experience in retail to complement and sometimes counter the 'old' ways of thinking of the experienced bankers on the team. This was because he wanted to transform retail banking. He wanted to build a whole new way of providing banking products and services to ordinary people. At the time, much of the daily processing of transactions happened behind the counter. His vision was to digitize and centralize as many transaction processes as possible, to enable front-line tellers to concentrate on engaging with customers rather than processing paper.

The key is to look for early indications of disruption in a segment. For example, Tesla has taken lessons from online shopping in transforming the process of buying a vehicle as well as managing inventory. Tesla's approach has disrupted the old model of car dealership networks while carving significant costs from the process to the benefit of customers.

Plan how you'll Conduct the Research – Step 6

In **Step 6** and especially if you are working in a team, you determine how you are each going to conduct in-depth professional quality research. This essential background helps you keep the client at the heart of your analysis and planning. A quality job of this informs and provides gravitas to your engagement, your presentations and your reports and proposals.

This step is about a conversation if you're working in a group, or, if working individually, a time to reflect on what information you need to find in your research.

The goal is to also put a simple research plan in place to ensure you obtain quality information to present and discuss with the client, or to write a draft proposal.

> **Top Tip:** A good place to start is a discussion to identify what information you already have (what has the client already given you or what have you already discovered through online search) what information you need and where the information gaps are.

Types of Research

Here are a few ideas about the kinds of research you may need to conduct, and how, if you are working in a team, you can divide up background research effectively to help ensure thorough coverage and efficient use of resources.

1. **Define clear research objectives** – doing this makes it easier as a group or individual to make quality decisions about the focus and priority of the research, how to conduct it and who will do what. Remember that the research must be highly relevant to the client problem, their industry and sector. An example might be: determine and prioritise AI uses in professional services firms. Or, identify All of Government digital transformation initiatives where data transformation is central. The trick is to make your research objective relevant to the sector, the problem to be solved and any identified disruptions or trends.
2. **Segment by research type:** Divide the research into different types, such as market analysis, competitor analysis, regulatory requirements, internal process analysis or technology reviews. Each team member can take responsibility for one type or a combination of research areas.
3. **Leverage individual strengths:** Assign tasks based on each team member's strengths and expertise. What are the

capabilities and experiences within the practitioner team? What unique aspect of the problem will each team member research? This helps in assigning tasks that are aligned with the overall goals as well as with each team member's skills and experience. For example, someone with strong data analysis skills might focus on quantitative research, while another with excellent communication skills might handle stakeholder interviews.

4. **Geographical or Functional Segmentation:** If the project involves multiple regions or departments, assign team members to specific areas. This ensures that each segment is thoroughly researched and understood.
5. **Use Collaborative Tools:** Utilize tools like shared documents, project management software, and communication platforms to keep everyone informed and organised. This helps track progress and ensure that all research is accessible to the entire team.
6. **Document and Share Findings:** Ensure that all research findings are well-documented and shared with the team. This is done through reports and presentations, or through developing a shared knowledge base.

> **Divide up the research.** If a client is struggling with declining sales in a retail chain, one consultant might analyse consumer behaviour trends, another could assess sales data and dealer network or store performance, while a third investigates competitor strategies and a fourth might investigate internal operations associated with service delivery. The team then synthesizes findings to present a cohesive solution or proposal tailored to the client's needs.

Again, if you are working as part of a BA or consulting team, we strongly recommend you agree on what aspect of the problem you are individually going to work on.

By following these strategies, a BA team can efficiently divide and complete the background research, ensuring a comprehensive understanding (pathos) of the client's needs and building their credibility (ethos) through the project.

Plan your Research Approach and Timeline

Once you understand the way to get the best value from your research efforts, put a simple plan in place based on whatever deadlines you need to meet. These are usually related to the preparation for a meeting or for drafting a report or a proposal.

This is where your earlier analysis of what information have you got, what information you need and the likely sources of information will inform both your research planning and your engagement planning.

Response Section – Steps 7 to 12

This part of the process covers your planning around the outcomes and outputs the client expects and the associated goals, objectives and measures of value. Doing a thorough job here means better clarity and justification when it comes to options and the approach you will recommend to the client later in the proposal.

Outcomes and Outputs, Goals and Objectives – Step 7

In **Step 7**, we summarize the difference between Outcomes and Outputs. Then we focus on how to complete section 6 of your canvas with quality goals and objectives.

The hierarchy, differences, and important roles that Outcomes and Outputs, Goals and Objectives (OOGOs) play in telling your story is an essential lesson for those aspiring to be top practitioners.

It is important to understand the distinction between outcomes, outputs, goals and objectives so you can decide what to promise the client, how this aligns with their vision, strategy and business plans, and what it will take to achieve the proposed change you are recommending.

Outcomes and Outputs

In a consulting proposal, **outcomes** describe the result the business wants or needs to achieve based on your initial research and problem definition. Outcomes are also the (future) impact on a client-organisation of performing a set of consulting activities.

Outcomes are frequently dependent on the behaviour of client leadership capability, other managers, team members, customers and suppliers, and external forces. Outcomes may either be easy or difficult to measure.

Examples might include 'Launch new tax calculator' or 'Increase online customer satisfaction' or 'Implement a chat-bot to support online shopping experiences and provide data query insights'. Other examples might be more efficient transaction processing, increased revenue or profits, or increased customer traffic on a company website. **They're high-level, but descriptive** – your client will know whether the outcome has been achieved!

Top Tip: Knowing how to think in terms of outcomes and end results, impacts, risks, and benefits are core competencies of practitioners who write proposals.

Outputs are deliverables with a tangible dimension that contribute to achieving an outcome. An easy way to think of this is that outputs are the tangible project deliverables and include products, systems, processes and project documentation.

It could be a new 'live system', intranet feature, organisational restructuring, report on network traffic or an information systems audit report. The delivery of an output is normally tangible, measurable and identifiable.

For example, a business outcome could be 'increased customer satisfaction'. Outputs that might help achieve this could be 'Customer satisfaction monitoring report', or 'Responsive online ordering system options identified'.

Outcomes can be both qualitative and quantitative and more challenging to verify, while Outputs are usually quantitative / tangible and easy to measure. Clarify these before completing project goals and objectives

Goals

Goals are broad, high-level categories of what needs to be done to achieve the outcomes and outputs. They add a layer of detail, providing insights into the categories of activities that need to be undertaken.

Goals can range in scope and feasibility, but mostly goals are a 'stretch'; they are ambitious but achievable. 'Think of goals as guiding principles that will give direction and focus [to the] work'.[26]

In consulting and BA assignments and projects, a single project might have multiple goals. It depends on scope. For an outcome such as 'business sustainability' or 'increased revenue', goals might include 'growing the customer base', 'improving the user experience of the website', or 'increasing the efficiency of an online ordering process'.

Goal Alignment

We recommend aligning **outcomes** and **goals** with the organisation's strategy and business plan. In your early client engagement, it is extremely useful to understand the project sponsor's project goals and how these relate to their **Key Performance Indicators (KPIs).** This means that any goals you propose as a practitioner clearly align with those of the organisation and show how your recommendations will help the sponsoring person achieve in their role.

Senior executives might have broad goals amongst their role accountabilities, such as improving profits, becoming more sustainable, or creating a more inclusive work culture. These high-level goals can often be found in the annual business plan and commonly have category measures as part of the goal, for example, improve manufacturing productivity by 5% by 2030.

If the practitioner engagement goes well and the desired impact of the recommended activities are realized, then a client should get a strong sense (pathos response) that the work is moving towards goal achievement. A strong positive pathos response creates feelings of trust and increases relationship bonds.

Objectives

Objectives are measurable outputs or outcomes to help achieve a project or program of work.

Whereas goals are broad categories, objectives are the smaller, more measurable steps taken toward each goal. Objectives are usually narrower in scope, easier to measure, and are essential to the achievement of each goal. In other words, you can see them playing out in your (or your team's) day-to-day work and can easily translate them into action-oriented tasks, sprints, or individual accountabilities. No matter how small, a good objective will contribute to moving the project towards a desired goal, output, and outcome because they are generally more task or activity orientated. Objectives also provide granular details against which project and governance reporting can be provided.

We recommend practitioners become familiar with three main types of objectives: strategic, operational, and tactical. Strategic objectives are long-term and can resemble goals. Tactical and operational objectives are shorter-term.

Strategic Objectives

Strategic objectives are specific and measurable. As with goal alignment, strategic objectives further contribute to ensuring that a consulting or BA assignment aligns closely with the organisation's strategy and business plan.

Of the three types of objectives, strategic objectives are the most like goals. They are usually established by senior leaders within the organisation and contribute to a longer-term goal that is aligned with the company's overall vision.

For example, a strategic and measurable objective might be to increase revenue by 10% as part of achieving the desired long-term profitability goals, and financial sustainability outcomes. Strategic objectives are commonly measured and reported through senior management reports and are usually

Top Tip: Strategic objectives provide an ideal opportunity to evaluate capability requirements and the associated building blocks, competencies (see Chapter 2.)

included in governance reporting to the Board of Directors. Strategic objectives are achieved through a combination of tactical and operational objectives.

Tactical objectives

Tactical objectives are specific and measurable. These are task-focused, relating tightly to achieving a measurable component of a goal. Tactical objectives are more commonly set by business unit managers or team leaders and program or project managers. Tactical goals can appear as contributors to strategic objectives. Tactical objectives are the most tightly focused, short-term actionable tasks that support high-level objectives and goals.

Tactical objectives are commonly reported through manager's monthly reports to their senior managers, and contribute to governance reporting, especially if risks, exceptions or variances against strategic objectives and goals have become obvious during the reporting period.

Operational objectives

Operational objectives are also specific but tend to be easier to monitor and measure. They are short-term activities that break down large tactical goals into smaller tasks. Project and operations managers, team leaders, and business analysts typically set operational objectives. Of the three objective types, these are the most task orientated and usually have the shortest timeframes.

Operational objectives focus on daily, weekly, and monthly tasks that, when taken together, ensure that a business is operating smoothly, and that teams are making progress toward larger, more strategic objectives and goals. Each goal usually has multiple operational objectives to help plan, resource and monitor the work that needs to be done to achieve the tactical or strategic objective, the associated goal, output or outcome. Operational objectives are typically the most closely monitored and reported during a project because they provide the clearest evidence of current performance against plans. Operational objectives are most commonly the focus of agile sprints and stand-ups.

Understanding and using the types of goals and objectives correctly provides an excellent example of integrated, holistic thinking in practice that builds capability and value.

Top Tip: Operational performance planning is also an excellent time to evaluate specific competency gaps and skill requirements, and to turn these into part of your change management or capability development planning.

A simple example

Here's a fun, non-IT example so that you're very clear of what they are and the level of each.

Imagine it is Harry's 6th birthday. You have ordered a Spiderman-themed cake for the party. You ask a group of colleagues what they believe the outcome of this transaction is. Surprisingly, too many answer that the outcome is the birthday cake. That is not correct.

The **outcome** will be a super happy birthday boy and happy guests, filled with delicious but healthy cake, and therefore happy parents.

The **output** is the cake. The **goal** is a healthy cake that caters for all attendees' dietary requirements.

The **objectives** might include:

- Present and confirm cake design and costs (strategic)
- Confirm all dietary requirements 1 week prior to delivery date (tactical)
- Bake and ice cake 24 hours prior to delivery date (operational)
- Package / deliver cake by 10 am on required date (operational).

If the cake had not been tasty, or if the bakery had delivered a wrongly-themed cake instead of the promised Spiderman version, at a price that didn't match expectations; or if they had provided a cake containing ingredients incompatible with dietary requirements, or late, then the desired outcome—happy kids and happy parents — may not have been achieved!

Why it is important to get this right

Proposing to deliver tangible outcomes, outputs, goals and objectives that are mostly within the practitioner's control, helps create measurable and achievable expectations with the client.

Top Tip: Not only does clarity and specificity help define and agree project scope with the client, it also can make it easier to monitor and pinpoint when the engagement is completed satisfactorily, or if things are getting off track.

Clarity facilitates monitoring and reporting (and therefore governance). These in turn help reduce potential disputes about outcomes, payment for promised performance or variances in deliverables. It is often difficult enough just to deliver on promised outputs that require defined input and commitment from the client.

Practitioners who promise to meet client goals or post engagement outcomes that are outside their control are taking avoidable risks. Practitioners need to decide, before committing themselves to a proposal, exactly how they can assist the client in meeting their goals and objectives. Remember that these are the client's goals and objectives. The consultant's role is to assist the client.

No matter the type of objective, the key to writing good objectives is the extent to which they are measurable. Here is where the well-known acronym SMART (Specific, Measurable, Actionable, Realistic and Timebound) comes into play. This is primarily achieved through providing measures that align with strategy and add measurable value.

Determining Value Measures - Step 8

You and your team have determined outcomes, outputs, goals and objectives and identified how and who will conduct each part of the research.

We now return to the components of your report or proposal with Step 8 to determine measures of value. You have already gathered information that can help inform this exercise, especially in Step 4. You've also determined your OOGOs in Step 7. In this section you are guided in how to determine generic measures as well as strategically aligned Measures of Organisation Value (MOV) and Measures of Client Calculated Value (CCV) or User Calculated Value (UCV).

Generic measures used in setting Objectives

Generic performance measures include QQCT (Quality, Quantity, Cost and Time):

- **Quality**: does the product or service live up to quality standards or brand promises of quality. Measures include: product recall levels, product fixes under warranty, customer complaints or satisfaction and the volume of negative or positive social media commentary from customers or users (Logos, Pathos and Ethos).
- **Quantity**: these are generally quantitative measures around volumes against a target, or an indication of growth or decline against a product or service level target (Logos).

- **Cost**: these are generally quantitative measures of actual cost against budget, or calculated costs in budget forecasts (Logos).
- **Time**: these are generally quantitative measures indicating planning periods, or 'by when' measures for milestones or project completion (Logos).

Each of these generic measures can be used to create SMART objectives. However, we encourage practitioners to think more strategically and holistically about measures in terms of the specific value they add to the client, as well as the consulting firm or BA team.

It is interesting to note that when time or cost targets are exceeded there is often an emotional reaction by stakeholders. Be aware of this, as a logical explanation will rarely ameliorate an emotional response.

Measurable Organisational Value (MOV)

MOV objectives and measures help organisations determine if their strategy and business plan have been translated into action and if their projects are being executed to deliver value to the organisation and its stakeholders.

MOV should be used as part of project development, portfolio management, and project execution. It helps organisations determine if their projects are delivering the bottom-line impact needed and the outcomes promised.

The skill for practitioners is to create measures that provide indicators of achievement in the short to medium-term as a contribution to the client's annual business plan, and longer-term to their strategy achievement.

Client Calculated Value (CCV)

CCV is a measure of all the costs and benefits associated with a product or service. Measures can be quantitative or qualitative. In proposals, CCV refers to the anticipated benefits that a client will derive from the solutions proposed and the services practitioners suggest, to support decision-making and project delivery.

According to McKinsey 'In many cases the customer—not the competition—is the key to a company's success'.[27] We explored this in detail in Chapter 6.

CCV can also refer to third party value such as the impact of internal organisational improvements proposed around external customer value or service experience improvement.

Generic, **quantitative** examples include price, quantity, cost and time. Generic **qualitative** measures might include quality, effort, satisfaction or dissatisfaction or the emotional costs or impacts of a proposed transformation. The more value a client perceives in a recommended approach compared to its cost, the more likely they are to adopt the recommendation.

User Calculated Value (UCV)

UCV refers to the benefits that a user derives from implementing and using a product or service. Measures are most commonly qualitative, however can also be quantitative.

User value elements depend on the product or service considered. The more value a user perceives in a product compared to its cost, the more likely they are to adopt that product in their lives and recommend it to others. In marketing terms, UCV is understood from three main perspectives:

1. The product or service is identified by clients as adding value. Such measures can fall into simple categories as better, faster and/or cheaper, or these days, greener / more environmentally friendlier (Logos, Pathos and Ethos).
2. The product or service relieves some type of challenge or pain i.e., the product or service solves a problem (Logos, Pathos, Ethos).
3. The product or service creates unique capability and is therefore a 'gain creator' – it either creates a new market or improves user volumes and therefore sales volumes or market share (Logos and Ethos).

More than financial measures, there are also functional, social and psychological measures of value to consider.[28]

Quantitative measures might include surveyed satisfaction or dissatisfaction with a product or service (here a survey using a Likert Scale can be useful). Another very useful quantitative measure and one that can demonstrate Return on Investment (ROI) from the implementation of a new system or software, can be user uptake (volume: how many are using a product, system or service, and how long for)[29].

An associated qualitative measure could be checked via a survey or tracked via system usage data. Here, uptake, usage, confidence and competence could be built into the AI or Machine Learning (ML) tracking capabilities of the new system's software.

Being clear about what measures best align with your client's current strategies and plans and what measures of value provide the greatest levels of overall confidence in what you are proposing to your client, sets the foundation for the Approach section.

Determining Options and Approaches – Step 9

In Step 9 we consider the process of identifying and prioritising solutions and options to present to the client, before recommending a project approach.

Identifying and evaluating solution options

There are many tools available that can help you gather and analyse information when conducting research for potential solutions. Some of these tools include:

Search engines: Search engines such CoPilot or Google can help you quickly find and evaluate relevant information from a wide range of sources.

> **Top Tip:** If using AI such as ChatGPT or CoPilot, always review the findings with a critical eye, and further explore the sources. CoPilot provides good references / sources. Make sure you use citations in key places and disclose when using AI when required.

Online databases: Online databases such as JSTOR or ScienceDirect give access to academic journals and other scholarly publications that can provide in-depth information on a wide range of topics. If you don't have access to such academic databases, you can use Google Scholar to find open-source

Industry 'peak' or representative bodies and associations and government organisations can also be rich sources for industry-specific research and information, white papers and case studies, as can the major consulting firms.

Survey tools: Survey tools such as SurveyMonkey or Microsoft Forms can help you gather information directly from your target audience by conducting simple surveys or polls. Make sure you research how to write effective questions to ensure you obtain quality, credible data

Data analysis software: Analysis software such as Excel can help you organise, analyse, and visualise data to identify patterns, trends, and relationships. Other visualisation software tools such as Tableau and Google Charts are also worth exploring.

By using these tools, you can gather and analyse information more efficiently and effectively, helping you identify potential solutions that could address the problem or meet the need you are trying to address. These tools can also help you visualise and present complex information to clients in clear and understandable ways.

Evaluating Solutions

The following table provides some steps to evaluate what you have identified.

Table 7-1 Evaluating solutions

Step	Actions / Benefits
Revisit the problem statement	This will help you focus your research and identify relevant information.
Identify sources of information	Here you are looking for insights into effective ways to address the problem or meet the need. Identify best practice examples based on the type of change, transformation, or implementation etc. that your client is trying to achieve. This could include industry publications, academic journals, case studies, or consulting with experts in the field. Look for disruptors, where people in other sectors have solved similar problems (or organisations within the same sector).
Analyse your findings	Sort through your findings identifying potential solutions that are worth evaluating. We like to use the APV approach – Attribute (description of the solution features) Purpose (the purpose it serves in solving the problem and Value (the benefits and measurable value the solution might achieve relating to the outcomes and goals the client has expressed.
Evaluate potential solutions	Evaluate the potential solutions you have identified based on their feasibility, effectiveness, and alignment with your goals. Guide your evaluation approach based on factors such as cost, time, resources, and potential risks or opportunities.
Rank and rate your findings	Identify your top 3-4 findings and make notes about why you have chosen these potential options. If it is important to demonstrate to the client why you have made a recommendation, you can weight your criteria, create an evaluation table for each solution and conduct an evaluation using the weighted criteria. This approach can be useful for presenting your proposal as you can honestly say that you evaluated X number of options and recommend Y for the reasons noted.
Assess feasibility	Evaluate based on your established criteria such as cost, time, resources, and potential risks or opportunities when evaluating solutions. (Check against your SWOT / GAP / Risk analyses for deeper insights.)

Determining options and solutions includes using a range of common tools and methods - some you will have found while completing the initial steps of your canvas. Start by checking and discussing the following :

1. **Review and agree root causes**
   Use tools like root cause analysis, fishbone diagrams, or the "5 Whys" technique to ensure the problem is fully understood before exploring solutions.
2. **Generate a range of options**
   Encourage brainstorming sessions within your team and with stakeholders to develop a broad set of potential solutions. Include both conventional and innovative ideas to ensure a diverse range of possibilities. Here is where it is useful to refer to industry and sector disruption from technology including new business models, innovation in product design, production and service delivery, and the likely impact of AI and robotics.
3. **Assess feasibility and impact**
   Evaluate each option against criteria such as cost, time, resource availability, risk, and alignment with business goals. Tools like SWOT analysis or a decision matrix can help prioritise effectively. Refer back to steps 3-5 for insights.
4. **Engage stakeholders (or take a client-centred view)**
   Involve key stakeholders in reviewing and refining options. Their insights can highlight practical considerations and increase buy-in for the final solution.
5. **Document assumptions and dependencies**
   Clearly outline any assumptions, constraints, and dependencies associated with each option to support transparent decision-making.
6. **Recommend a preferred solution**
   Present the most workable option(s) with a clear rationale, including how it addresses the problem, supports project objectives, and delivers measurable value.

By following these steps, you can evaluate potential solutions to determine which ones are most likely to address the problem or meet your client's needs. Now it is time to evaluate risks and opportunities.

Review Team Members' Research Responsibilities

Once you have determined and prioritised options and landed on a preferred solution you can evaluate potential approaches and methodologies. We recommend you also check and clarify which aspects of the research each team member has taken responsibility for to ensure the focus and priority remains relevant. This ensures that the approach to completing the research and how your individual contributions will be brought together remain focused on a single, cohesive report or proposal.

Project Approach, Milestones and Timeline – Step 10

Step 10 determines the approach and what project method will work best for the specific type, size and scale of project required. With the client's problem clearly defined and project goals and milestones established, to complete Step 10, we review and summarize the problem, remind the client of the recommended solutions, and evaluate potential project approach. This involves assessing the complexity of the problem, identifying whether the client has any preferred project methodologies and software including their reporting and governance requirements. You might also discover whether they have expectations of stakeholder involvement, timeline constraints, and the need for flexibility.

> **Top Tip:** These considerations provide rich engagement planning opportunities at every step of the project. Chapter 8 provides detailed guidance on writing this section. Each project is different.

Therefore, the **outcome** of the approach section is to demonstrate clarity of the problem, the connection between the problem and proposed solutions, and to provide a clear indication of **how** the client can implement the recommended solutions. This activity includes providing project milestones which, done well, act as both a timing and reporting framework.

How to get the approach off to a good start

When writing any consulting proposal, it's important to identify solutions that address the needs and goals of your client. If you have done a thorough and professional job of completing all parts of your canvas so far, you should have a reasonably clear idea of both the client problem and a solution or solutions. In this section we cover planning to use your insights, data and analysis.

You have researched your client's organisation, their external and internal environment, and engaged with them to develop a clear understanding of the problems they are facing and what they hope to achieve by working with you. Your client may already have suggested solutions to you, and you will have explored the underlying causes and potential best-practice solutions relevant to the outcome the client wants.

You will be increasingly clear about your client's goals and expectations for the project, and you may have already been able to derive some measures of value or performance standards. If you have not completed these steps, go back and do so, otherwise your solutions and approach may miss the mark.

Well done if you have done a complete and comprehensive job! If the summary above has highlighted any gaps in your research, consider going back and completing it.

Review the data gathered so far

What you have probably discovered for yourself is that Information Systems projects and transformations are invariably about a combination of People, Process and Technical systems. To make sure you design a comprehensive set of solutions and approaches, now is the time to ask / remind yourself whether your proposed solutions and approach will:

1. Be strategy and/or business plan-aligned;
2. Provide an integrated blend of outcomes, outputs, goals objectives and measures;
3. Be easily measured and reported on and,
4. Add tangible client value.

In the remainder of this chapter, we will continue to help you answer these questions.

In Chapter 2, Table 2-1, we introduced Kast and Rosenzweig's socio-technical systems approach to analysis. Reviewing this table can help you determine where best to target the approaches you will recommend in your proposal.

Before determining the project approach to include in your proposal, first **refer to the outcomes, outputs, goals and objectives** you have established. Review the top options and the recommendations you are making. We also recommend considering the project's context and culture.

Evaluating these factors will help to provide an approach that is a good fit for your client. We suggest aligning with project methods your client is familiar with, and that they trust the method or they want to embrace it.

Top Tip: If you have carried out a parallel SWOT or Gap analysis alongside PESTLE (or separately) now is the time to review it to make sure the content is relevant to the problems identified by the client, and progress to researching and evaluating potential solutions. Before determining your project approach

Project Approach

Once you have considered these factors, it is time to determine your project approach—e.g., Agile, Waterfall, Hybrid i.e., the project methodology.

The project approach will, to a very significant extent, be determined by whether your client has already adopted a preferred project methodology. Larger organisations may have a Program Management Office. It is important to choose a method that will further the project's overall outcomes and goals and ensure that the practitioner or practitioner teams have the required capabilities, competencies, and skills (see Ch 2).

These are major considerations for your approach and costings, as well as identifying risk around people, process and systems. **Explore these questions early in your engagement with the client.**

Determine your Project Methodology

In this section we summarize nine common approaches to consider when deciding on the best project method for a client project. These include:

1. **Waterfall:** This approach is often called the "traditional" project management approach and involves completing projects one stage at a time and in sequential order.
2. **Agile**: is not a methodology per se but is the catchall term for the collection of process frameworks that start with eliciting user needs and splitting project scope into smaller more realistically completable work packets. Agile methods rely heavily on frequent user feedback and cross-functional collaboration over top-down plan design and sequential execution. Agile covers Scrum, Kanban, Lean, SaFE Less, DAD Crystal and XP, some of which we highlight below.
3. **Scrum**: This framework was created to tie together the most successful of the practices within the scope of agile, and while highly flexible, it takes time to reach its full potential. This is because teams need to learn about key roles and culture for it to be effective. The best agile teams are long standing, stable, and cross functional. They understand other's roles but have deep specialization in something relating to the product or change outcome to be valuable contributors. There is a strict role separation between discovery and delivery. Importantly, teams are encouraged to fail fast and often to facilitate swift knowledge acquisition that can be implemented in future iterations.
4. **Kanban**: Kanban is a visual project management methodology that promotes continuous delivery and workflow efficiency.

It uses a Kanban board to represent tasks as cards, moving through columns that depict stages of work (e.g., "To Do," "In Progress," "Done"). By limiting work in progress (WIP), Kanban enhances single-piece flow, reduces cycle and lead times, and improves team collaboration. This approach allows teams to quickly respond to changes and to optimize processes for better efficiency.

5. **Six Sigma:** This method focuses on improving the quality of project completion. Teams classify any problems and then remove them during the project process. The goal is to do so without increasing waste. This type of project management features quantifiable results. It works to achieve high financial returns. It also focuses on improving customer satisfaction by using data analysis.
6. **Lean:** This method mainly centres on the mindset of the customer. It then uses plans to achieve the best results while being affordable. Additionally, this method tries to deliver results as quickly as possible. Lean tries to minimize problems along the way and focuses on providing results with a minimal number of materials, employees, and suppliers.
7. **PRINCE2™:** This method focuses on delivering efficient results while reducing risks. The method separates projects up into smaller jobs to be finish one at a time, helps provide complete results against contract, and minimizes mistakes.
8. **Systems:** This approach focuses on understanding the interactions between different components of a system.
9. **Critical chain and critical path:** This approach focuses on identifying the longest sequence of dependent tasks and managing resources to ensure that the project is completed on time.

Next, we provide the client with an indication of how the project will play out and set the milestones and timeline. These then enable practitioners to establish budgets and finalise the proposal. But first, how do we make sure the project details align with, and solve, the identified problems? To answer this, we suggest clarifying the scope of the project.

Top Tip: A note of caution. If, for example, the client has recently embraced more Agile methods, you will need to determine how advanced their implementation is, how well supported the methodology is, and whether, in your judgement, the method has become part of the organisation's culture.

Determine Project Scope

Determining project scope for a proposal is an exercise in translation and judgement. You need to translate what you know about the problem, requirements, outcome, outputs, goals, objectives into a project scope statement that outlines what the project will provide (or, just as importantly, will not provide).

Identify and be able to specify what is in and what is out of scope; Identifying what is in and what is out of a project scope is crucial for setting clear expectations, managing resources, and avoiding scope creep. Here is an example of how to define both:

✔ **What's In Scope (Inclusions)** - These are the elements the project will deliver or address.

Table 7-2 Inclusions

Guideline	Explanation	Examples
Define deliverables	List all products, services, or results the project will produce.	A new website, a marketing campaign, a training program.
Specify activities	Outline the tasks and processes that will be performed.	Design, development, testing, deployment.
Include timelines	Clarify the duration and deadlines for each phase.	Project runs from Sept to Dec, with milestones every 2 weeks.
Identify stakeholders	Mention who is involved and what their roles are.	Marketing team, IT department, external consultants.
List resources	Include tools, budget, and personnel allocated.	$50,000 budget, 3 developers, Adobe Creative Suite.

✗ **What's Out of Scope (Exclusions)** - These are elements that will not be included in the project, even if they seem related.

Table 7-3 Exclusions

Guideline	Explanation	Examples
Exclude unrelated tasks	Clearly state what will not be done to avoid assumptions.	No mobile app development, no international marketing.
Limit deliverables	Define boundaries around what will be delivered.	Only English-language content; no e-commerce integration.
Clarify stakeholder roles	Note who is not responsible or involved.	Finance team not involved in decision-making.
Exclude future phases	Mention if future work is outside current scope.	Phase 2 (maintenance) is not part of this proposal.
Avoid scope creep	Prevent additions without formal change control.	Any new features must go through a change request process.

Tips for Scope Definition

- **Use a scope statement:** A formal document section that outlines inclusions and exclusions.
- **Consult stakeholders:** Ensure alignment and avoid misunderstandings.
- **Review regularly:** Revisit scope during project milestones to ensure compliance.
- **Use critical thinking and judgement:** you can use scope to set boundaries on the project and define exactly what goals, deadlines, and project deliverables you are proposing. A clear and agreed scope ensures the achievement of project goals and objectives without unexpected delays or overwork. This is called scope creep.

Watch out for scope creep

Scope creep is what happens when project deliverables exceed the project scope. Any added work that your project team was not expecting or prepared for could cause unnecessary stress or even delays with your project's original deliverables. Creep can also cause overwork, or low-quality deliverables. Scope creep elicits both a logos and pathos response in stakeholders.

While scope creep tends to be incremental, scope leap occurs when a client wants to add significant functionality or change direction mid-project. Scope creep and scope leap may lead to changes to project timelines and contract re-negotiations.

That is why it is important to ensure the scope of any project is agreed with all key stakeholders before commencement. That way, everyone is on the same page about what your project does—and does not—cover.

> **Top Tip:** To cover this contingency, and depending on how complex your project is, you may also want to define a change control process. This process defines what happens when things change outside of what is described in the project contract or brief, or when the client wants to add in additional outcomes. Project management methodologies such as Prince2 usually include change control processes and governance.

In general, milestones are an important way to clarify scope detail. As well, milestones provide the basis for project monitoring and governance and are a useful source of headings for your proposal communications section.

Establish Milestones

Milestones are important because they help you focus on the project management aspects of writing your business proposal. The Project Management Institute[32] found that "organisations that invest in project management waste 13 times less money because their strategic initiatives are completed more successfully."

Project milestones help you break down a project into smaller sections, so you have a clear idea of what tasks need to be completed and by when.

A project milestone marks a significant point in time. You can use milestones in your projects to represent events such as key deliverables received, project kick-off completed, final plan approved, requirements gathering, design approved, project phases completed, and much more.

Milestones provide the outline of the project roadmap, showing the main 'chunks' of the project's bigger picture. They are specific, measurable outcome categories that help practitioners, and their clients track progress and manage responsibilities. They can either mark the major progress points or can be broken down into smaller objectives. Either way, project milestones are important for measuring progress – in both chunks, or smaller pieces.

Thus, milestones are used as a method for defining important phases in a project. They are also essential for determining and allocating budgets and other resources for the various phases, and form the basis of monitoring, reporting and project governance. (More on this later in this chapter). Let's walk through four examples of how milestones can work for you and the client. Use milestones to:

1. Mark critical tasks that must be completed at a specific time or the project will stall. For example: 'complete requirements gathering' or 'develop concept for approval by XXX'.
2. Highlight the end of a phase or stage such as 'Obtain sign-off from all stakeholders by 30 June'.
3. Focus on a major event or deliverable such as 'implement and test software'.
4. Focus on hitting goals, objectives with milestones expressed as key results, such as meeting a launch date, providing the means to measure a service improvement, revenue or efficiency outcome etc.

Now that you know why milestones are important, next we provide the steps to creating them.

Steps to Creating Milestones

The secret to establishing flow is taking a logos (logical) approach when defining the major 'chunks'. These become your project milestones with an associated timeline.

Establishing milestones and a timeline that align with project goals and objectives is essential for ensuring structured progress, reporting and governance. Here's a step-by-step overview:

1. **Break down project objectives into key deliverables**

   Start by checking that each goal is expanded with sub-outcomes and therefore broken down into high level objectives and tangible, measurable results. These deliverables form a foundation for defining milestones.

2. **Identify major phases of work**

   Segment the project into logical phases (e.g., relate them to the project or life cycle phases that work for you such as discovery, design, implementation, testing, deployment). Each phase should have a clear purpose and outcomes.

3. **Define milestones for each phase**

   Milestones are checkpoints that mark the completion of critical tasks and contributing sub-outcomes, and frequently represent key decision-points in a project. They also provide the framework you will use for engagement and reporting, and therefore project governance. Examples of milestones in the discovery phase, expressed as outcomes or measurable results might include:

   - Complete all key stakeholder interviews
   - Approve project outcomes
   - Approve reporting and governance framework.

   Milestones for the design phase, expressed as outcomes or measurable results might include:

   - Approve draft system
   - Design and agree Minimum Viable Product (MVP)
   - Launch MVP and monitor
   - Review and adjust
   - Approve design and architecture
   - Approve implementation plan
   - Monitor and review.

4. **Consider interdependencies.**

   If your client has a Project Management Office or similar, it is advisable to check with them to identify any project dependencies.

5. **Consider stakeholder needs**

   Every effective project has stakeholders who are in total control of its execution. These stakeholders are important in this step of project milestone writing because they are responsible for bringing aspects of the project to completion. If appropriate and time permitting, we recommend seeking their feedback and input as they are crucial to project success.

> **Top Tip:** Here is a good place to check in with your risk notes. You can use milestones to categorize risks and issues in the project. See Step 12.

Once you have determined your milestones, you have the foundation for developing a timeline.

Timelines- an Essential Visual Tool

A well-crafted timeline provides a visual representation and roadmap for your client. It aggregates and highlights much of the data you have been gathering. The content for each timeline depends entirely on the focus and outcomes of the project. They visually list key information for your project approach, the goals, milestones, objectives and resources assigned.

An accurate time estimate of the duration of each task is essential for planning, scheduling, and creating project management timelines. The Program Evaluation and Review Technique (PERT) is a useful method to estimate the duration of tasks. This technique was developed for the first moon landing.

Depict project phases, milestones or key tasks or activities in chronological order. This helps the client and allows the project manager to view the entirety of the project proposal and an overview of the plan, in one place. At the same time, identify and estimate resource requirements. This will assist you in calculating the costs of executing the tasks and producing the deliverables.

Resources can be people, materials, tools and other supplies. A project plan timeline can also incorporate the resource requirements, i.e. when you need them, the outcome they are needed for, and so on.

PERT, Gantt charts, critical paths and dependency identification are amongst the most common considerations in project planning. Many tools for these techniques are readily available online.

Software such as Microsoft Project, (project management software that is part of Office 365), offers simple, powerful tools. These tools help you organise your tasks, show when they start and finish, view task deadlines, and link dependent tasks.

Use milestones and the development of your timeline to develop the critical path. A critical path defines the shortest time that a project can be completed based on task dependencies. This is important because it identifies and helps you check you have covered the critical activities that determine the duration of your project timeline.

All aspects of the timeline, especially resource allocation, are essential for estimating costs. You can also use milestones to schedule deposits and release partial payment of funds.

The important thing is to make these connections and the logic-flow obvious in your planning. Choose your methodology carefully then use project phases expressed as milestones to create a visual of your approach using tools such as a Gannt chart. Irrespective of project approach, a simple **Gantt Chart** helps the client to visualise the project timeline and sequence.

The Promise of Success

Done well, this simple sequence will also help you determine and recommend a project approach to your client. It is important that the client understands how the approach that you develop will get them to the outcome they desire. The work that we do relies on keeping our promise to the client that our actions will result in the beneficial outcome they require and expect. If they accept that the path we suggest is the best one, you should expect the client to award you to project. Often we work in a world of competitive forces so if a competitor presents a better path they will get the project, assuming that the cost to the client is similar. We will address cost / price in Step 14.

Check Alignment

The approach needs to provide focus and clarity, facilitate iterative development, and enable continuous stakeholder feedback. This crucial Approach section provides for adaptive planning, ensuring alignment with client expectations and the timely delivery of value. The approach must be clearly tailored to the client's operating environment, their organisational culture and to maximize impact as well as minimize risk.

The approach is also the perfect opportunity to double-check the alignment of your work with the client's strategies and annual plans. If you have done a good job of finding out how to strategically align your project outcomes, outputs, goals and objectives, establishing your project milestones should be relatively easy. Figure 7-3 illustrates how this process can become a kind of journey map that also helps you present your work to the client in a logical sequence.

Figure 7-3: Aligning strategy, annual plans with project outcomes and approach

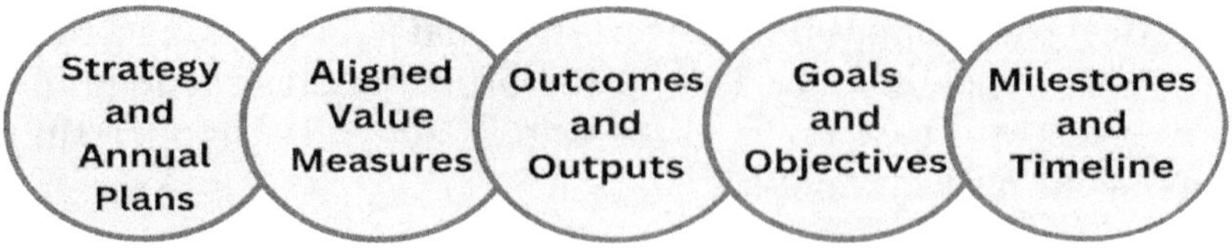

Having determined your milestones and timelines based on your planned approach, you are now in a position to determine and outline change impacts on the clients and risks that may arise during the projec.t

Impacts, Change and Risks – Steps 11 and 12

Step 11 employs a quick check to identify any known or likely change impacts. If impact analysis is coupled with agreement with the client about urgency, BAs are better equipped to cross-check timelines and adjust if necessary.

Step 12 entails analysing risk and suggesting mitigation. This analysis also depends on the goals and objectives, project approach and timeline. This important analysis step will inform or act as a cross-check for your implementation phase of your project plan. Chapter 10 provides comprehensive guidance on dealing with the impacts and practicalities of change. Here we provide insights into the information derived from impact analysis.

Impacts to be managed

While originally developed to analyse the impacts of software development, testing and implementation, our experience is that this important tool can easily be modified to analyse most types of change impacts.

Impact analysis is a systematic approach for evaluating changes to a system or process. It involves examining the possible consequences of a potential change to the organisation.

Also known as a change impact analysis, the approach can also help identify issues and risks of an unexpected event or 'ripple-on' effects from changes to a system, process or procedure.

> **Top Tip:** You can conduct impact analysis at any time when completing your canvas. We recommend, at a minimum, that you evaluate and capture impacts when setting outcomes, goals and objectives, and again when determining your approach to the engagement.

The technique is designed to unearth the "unexpected" negative effects of a change on an organisation and is important for practitioners to consider when crafting solutions and determining project approaches. However, not all impacts are negative.

> **Top Tip:** Make sure you identify "positive" impacts or consequences at the same time, as these can be useful candidates for demonstrating and even quantifying the value of what you are proposing.

For BAs in particular, impact analysis is a critical component of responsible requirements' establishment and management because it offers more accurate knowledge of the consequences of a proposed change, allowing everyone concerned to make informed decisions. Here are five steps to consider:

1. Identify how your recommendation and the steps you suggest for implementing might impact other surrounding / associated systems or processes, policies, roles and responsibilities;
2. Establish how the change could impact the project's critical path. Be specific: identify how the change might impact on the organisation, people, technology systems or processes and the potential risks or threats.
3. After the two steps above, establish how likely it is that the impact will occur (High / Medium / Low) and the significance for each (Severe / Moderate / Low).
4. Evaluate the impacts on the project's completion time frame and cost, and provide an estimate of the proportional benefit, penalty, cost, and technical risk of the change.
5. Document your findings to show you have considered the implications of what you are recommending, ensuring the client can use the data to establish whether to progress or decline the proposal.

Depending on your findings, you may either discuss your analysis with your client or modify your recommendations and approach to overcome negative impacts and promote positive ones. Much of this analysis can be used for completing the next sections – solution options and risk analysis.

Conducting a Risk Analysis

Knowing how to perform a risk analysis is useful for almost any kind of decision-making and business communication process—no matter what your professional role or sector. When you analyse risk, you develop essential skills such as critical thinking and problem-solving.

> **Top Tip:** Create a project-specific SWOT analysis alongside client research, to identify potential strengths, weaknesses, opportunities and threats as you go.

These can be evaluated as potential items to include in the risk and mitigation section of your proposal. Another source can be your impact analysis. All strengths, weaknesses and threats can also become candidates for opportunities. Follow these steps to capture a basic analyse risk for most situations:

Identify the Risks

Be thorough when you analyse risk. If using a SWOT, be mindful that problems can occur at any stage of a project and therefore impacts and risks have a wide variety of possible sources.

Evaluate identified weaknesses and threats, and brainstorm potential risks with team members who may have different perspectives. Consider different phases of the engagement as risks can vary across phases and activities. Ask for input from the client, especially teams or individual roles that will be impacted or practitioner teams who have experience in dealing with similar situations.

Positive factors should be evaluated to see if they will help you reduce identified risks, or whether, given the impacts or risks identified, each could turn into a risk. For example: you might have identified that your client has unique competence in a mission critical area. However, if the proposed change might negatively affect the key person's role, they could become a 'flight' risk and leave!

Define Risk Levels and Impact

Once you have identified the potential sources of risk, the next step is to understand the likelihood of the risk occurring, and therefore how much uncertainty surrounds each identified risk. Your analysis can be calculated as an estimate of High / Medium / Low or calculated more precisely if you can estimate and quantify it.

The easiest method is to calculate the probability of the event occurring as a percentage then multiply it by the event cost.

Risk value = Probability of Event as a % x Cost of Event.

Example: Let's say you want to assess the risk that the cost of producing a promised 1000 widgets will increase substantially. You estimate that there is a 55% chance of the event happening based on current supply chain problems. The cost to your business will be approximately $250,000 if the price of the implementation increases. You would calculate the risk value as follows:

Risk calculation	=	**0.55 x $250,000**
Risk value	=	**$137,500**

Gather as much information as possible about the potential costs and the probability of different events occurring, that way you can make an accurate estimate of possible losses. Historic data may be a useful guide if you do not have access to current information or forecasting.

A matrix approach can help you identify, rate or rank those identified risks, and prioritise how to address them. In the example above, numbers in the boxes will relate to the items listed on your risk list or register.

Mitigate Identified Risks

Risk management processes seek to minimize the likelihood of incidents occurring. Risk mitigation is an element of risk management that aims to minimize the impact of identified risks on the organisation or risks to the success of a strategy or project. Mitigation helps organisations prepare for, and minimize, the impact of unavoidable risks.

Put simply, mitigation attempts to resolve or avoid the problem or reduce the likelihood or impact of identified risk. Risks can take many forms, so mitigation will also take many forms. Each depends on the type of industry, the type of business and the nature of the identified risk. Categories of risk include:

- **Strategic risk** – the result of a company's flawed business strategy or lack of a clearly defined strategy, high level measurable goals and priorities.
- **Operational risk** – The efficiency and effectiveness of the way an organisation goes about its business can have serious impacts on operating costs and can potentially drain its profits. Both internal systems and external factors can cause operational risks (hence the usefulness of a parallel risk 'run sheet')[30].
- **Compliance risk** – this represents risk to a company's reputation or finances when the company violates external laws, regulations, or standards. This is becoming a more complex area, with compliance of standards such as GDPR[31] meaning different things in different countries for people transacting business online.
- **Legal risk** – this is a type of compliance risk that happens when a company breaks the government rules for companies or industry standards. When companies face legal risks, they can also get caught in expensive lawsuits.
- **Reputational risk** – All risks can negatively impact the company's standing or public opinion. Reputational risks can result in loss of profit and decreased confidence among

company shareholders, suppliers and customers.As a final check we suggest using the People, Process, Technology and Data categories to prompt critical thinking around both impacts and urgency risk and opportunity.

Now that you have researched most of the critical components of your proposal, you can plan the approach and back end of your document, depending on the solution/s you have recommended to the client.

Project Communication, Reporting and Governance – Step 13

Depending on the size and scope of the project, how, when, with whom and how often it is prudent to communicate during a project is best agreed with the client to meet their expectations.

Project Communication

Project communication needs to target each identified key stakeholder, their reporting needs, timeframes and expectations. These must be established via the client engagement process.

For example, Table 7-4 provides an example of targeted communication for a large, complex, high-cost project.

As table 7-4 clearly illustrates, project communication is a crucial component of project governance, as it ensures that all stakeholders are aligned with the project's goals and kept informed of progress as well as challenges as they occur.

Table 7-4 Sample communication schedule for proposal

Stakeholder	Type	Frequency / how
Project Manager	Reports against goals, objectives and milestones, risk register and exceptions	Stand-ups as agreed. Weekly email against plan and Sprint. Weekly meeting. Monthly report
Project Sponsor	Report against contract, goals, objectives and milestones, risk register and exceptions	Monthly / email and meeting
Chief Executive or President	Report against contract OOGOs	Monthly summary for inclusion in board report
Board of Directors	Report against contract OOGOs	Board report as per board timetable.

Project Reporting as a component of Project Governance

Here are some key ways in which project communication forms part of project governance:

- **Stakeholder Engagement:** Effective communication keeps stakeholders informed of project progress, issues, and decisions. IT also facilitates collaboration and engagement (Logos, Pathos and Ethos).
- **Transparency and Visibility:** Regular and transparent communication enhances project transparency, allowing stakeholders to monitor and control the project's direction, as well as detect problems early (Pathos and Ethos).
- **Decision-Making:** Clear communication channels support informed decision-making by providing timely and accurate information to the right people at the right time (Logos, Pathos and Ethos).
- **Risk Management:** Communication is essential for identifying, assessing, and addressing risks, ensuring that potential issues are managed proactively, and, with planning in place, responsively (Pathos and Ethos).
- **Reporting:** Regular reporting through meetings, status updates, and documentation ensures that everyone is aware of the project's status and any changes that may occur. It is a mechanism for holding people accountable and a key means of governing change (Logos, Pathos and Ethos).

By integrating effective communication into project governance, organisations can reduce risk and improve project success rates, stakeholder satisfaction, and overall project performance.

We recommend aligning your project communication and reporting with the project milestones you have created. This will help to show how the client can track progress and demonstrate the project's status to stakeholders.

Project Governance

Project governance refers to the framework, functions, and processes that guide project management activities to ensure successful project delivery. It involves defining roles, responsibilities, and decision-making structures to align project objectives with organisational goals.

- **Alignment with Organisational Goals:** Ensures that projects are in line with the strategic objectives of the organisation.

- **Decision-Making:** Provides a clear structure for making informed decisions, which is crucial for project success.
- **Accountability:** Establishes accountability by defining roles and responsibilities, ensuring that everyone involved knows their duties.
- **Risk Management:** Enhances the ability to identify, assess, and manage risks effectively.

The importance and benefits of including at least an outline of project governance in your proposals cannot be overstated.

Benefits of Project Governance

As a practitioner, the benefits of good project communication and establishing a project governance framework not only enhance the Logos, Pathos and Ethos of your client projects, they enhance your professional reputation because of:

- **Improved Project Success Rates:** By providing a structured approach, project governance increases the likelihood of project success.
- **Stakeholder Engagement:** Keeps stakeholders informed and involved, leading to higher satisfaction and enhanced stakeholder support.
- **Effective Resource Management:** Ensures optimal use of resources, reducing waste and improving efficiency.
- **Transparency and Visibility:** Offers greater transparency and visibility across the project lifecycle, facilitating better monitoring and control.

Understanding and implementing robust project governance is essential for business analysts to ensure that projects are delivered successfully on time, and within budget. This knowledge will be invaluable as you advance in your careers and take on more complex projects.

Creating a client stakeholder approach to project reporting provides the basis for project governance. It also means that the client has the means to update the project plan regularly to ensure it reflects the latest status of the milestones.

Down the track, this also provides the client and practitioners with an opportunity to celebrate milestones as they are achieved to keep the team motivated. Next, we complete one of the most important section – the one that can make or break a proposal!

The Back End – Step 14

Completing the back end of a proposal does not normally require a great deal of research. This is because it is largely about people who might undertake the work and how much their efforts and your proposed solutions will cost the client. However, if there is anything you need to research or discover to complete your canvas, here is where you would review and complete that task. We also cover the details of the closing part of the proposal in detail in Chapter 8.

People and Fees

When thinking about the people, cost and fee impacts you are calculating budget considerations in proposals, there are many factors to consider. Essentially your calculations are about time and materials. These include the type of resources, salaries, research and development costs, travel costs, operational expenses, and any software or hardware, plant or equipment that might be part of the project. Costs are unique to every project. Table 7-5 illustrates the types of costs you may incur and provide a guide to what fees you may bill your client. As an IS consultant, you would calculate the profit margin you seek from project work on clients. Keep in mind, when considering profit margins, to include an amount for contingencies - to cover project overruns from unexpected issues arising that you can't directly pass on to your client.

The principal resources, in every case, are the people who perform the project activities. Clients may be charged on a time and materials basis i.e. the price to the client varies according to how long the assignment actually takes, or a fixed-price arrangement, where the consulting firm assumes the risk of overruns and benefits from efficient delivery. Other contemporary charging arrangements include risk and return sharing, capital sharing and bonus schemes. Whatever the arrangement, the client is seeking value from the application of consulting resources.

Depending on the type of project, you may be required to provide calculations of value or return such as Net Present Value, Payback Period, or Return on Investment. These financial management measures are useful if your proposal has a strong focus on providing a business case or if you need to add more financial details to support the client in getting internal approval for the work your proposal recommends.

Along with measures of value (MOV, CCV and UCV as discussed earlier in this chapter) carefully thought through costings provide an essential indication of investment and contributes financial measures that feature in project communication, reporting and governance.

The people you assign to the project will normally include the partner or senior BA who engaged the client, a senior person to manage the project and an appropriate team of specialists to perform the work. For the purpose of the proposal, it is common only to name key personnel. The next chapter (8) provides a guide to conveying this information.

Table 7-5 Estimating Costs

Category	Description	Examples
Direct costs	Expenses directly tied to the execution of the project or delivery of the product/service.	People: Salaries for project staff (internal); hourly rates for consultants and consulting firm oversight; Raw materials (e.g., steel, fabric); Equipment rental; Manufacturing and packaging costs
Indirect costs	Support costs that are not directly attributable to a specific activity but necessary for operations.	Fixed costs - Prorated amount of: Office rent and utilities; administrative staff salaries; IT support services; Insurance premiums.
One-time costs	Initial or non-recurring expenses required to start or complete the project.	Variable costs: short-term expertise; business licenses and permits; consultant fees for market research; staff training programs; Initial software setup
Contingency and risk costs	Budget set aside to cover unforeseen expenses or risks that may arise.	Emergency repairs; Cost overruns due to delays; Legal fees for unexpected disputes; 10% contingency buffer
Recurring costs	Ongoing expenses that continue throughout the life of the project or business.	Monthly software subscriptions (e.g., AI or CRM tools); Equipment maintenance; Internet and phone services; Lease payments
Cost of finance	Costs associated with borrowing or securing funding for the project.	Interest on business loans; Loan origination fees; Credit line maintenance fees
Opportunity costs	The value of the next best alternative foregone by choosing this project.	Lost revenue from postponing another project; Time diverted from core business activities
Cost Breakdown & Timeline	A phased view of when and how costs will be incurred over the project lifecycle.	Phase 1: Setup (€10,000); Phase 2: Development (€25,000); Phase 3: Launch (€15,000); Monthly operating costs (€5,000).

Competing on Price

When you submit a proposal and enter negotiations with a client they may want you to reduce your price. We deal with negotiation in Chapter 10. Bear in mind that if you pursue a fixed price approach, and reduce that price, you are bearing more risk should the project go overtime. At some point in this price negotiation you will risk making a loss on the job.

If they want to reduce the charge-out rates you can counter by offering them less qualified personnel but point out that doing so will potentially increase the time period of the project. A competitor may be offering a lower price and this is prompting your client to put pressure on your price points (fixed price or charge-out rates if you are charging on a time and materials basis).

So sometimes it is better to walk away from a cost-conscious client and let the competitor take the risk.

> **Top Tip:** If you walk away from a client, make sure you communicate your willingness to step in at a future date should the client be unhappy with their choice of consultant. It is not unusual for a consultant who competes on price to abandon a project once they realise they will make a considerable loss.

Team Information

Chapter 8 sets out a table that describes the key personnel who will be involved in the project. You can also talk about your firm's capabilities more generally. Having said that, make sure that the information in this section is directly relevant to the client's project. You will have plenty of opportunity to cross-sell other firm services during the engagement.

Closing Statement

This statement re-iterates your willingness to work effectively with the client to ensure they get the beneficial outcome they expect. It provides another opportunity to the client to reach out to the principal BA or Consulting Partner to discuss any aspect of the proposal.

Addenda

The most powerful addenda items are **glowing references** from past clients who have had you perform similar services and that they took the journey (Approach) with you to achieve the outcome that they wanted. Remember, you are relying on the **promise of success** and third-party references will solidify your chances of engaging the client.

Chapter Summary

This chapter provides essential processes and tips for completing the research and planning for the creation of a professional quality consulting or BA proposal. Once you have completed your canvas, you have largely gathered the information you need to write the proposal.

With practice, taking the very structured approach to this exercise that we recommend, the approach and skills required will become your automatic way of thinking and working. The approaches highlighted are what top professionals around the world use to win work and deliver great results for clients.

As you will learn through the remaining chapters, many of the skills are applicable to other types of business communication.

Endnotes

25. While it is common for consulting and BA work to address discrete problems, a lot of your work is the design of new systems and processes. This is where the People, Process, Technology and Data model is useful as a cross-check.

26. Eby, K. (2022) Goals vs Objectives. Web page: https://www.smartsheet.com/content/goals-vs-objectives

27. Delivering Values to Customers Web:https://www.mckinsey.com/capabilities/strategy-and-corporate-finance/our-insights/delivering-value-to-customers

28. Customer and User Perception of Value and What it Means to Designers | IxDF (interaction-design.org)

29. Marchand, D. A. (2005). Reaping the Business Value of IT. Business and Economic Review, 51(4), 21-24.

30. A run sheet is a list of procedures or events organized in temporal sequence. It is a type of schedule that people use to help them know how to run an event or program. As it relates to television or the stage, a run sheet breaks the show up into segments and lists which guest will appear when, for how long, and when breaks will take place. (Source Bing ChatGPT search June 2023, which cites sources as Sweetwater.com, template.net and sample.net).

31. The General Data Protection Regulation (GDPR) came into effect in May 2018. It is a regulation in EU law that sets guidelines and obligations for the collection and processing of personal data from individuals in the EU and the EEA but has international impacts and implications. It aims to give consumers control over their own personal data and to hold companies responsible for the way they handle and treat this information. (Source: Bing ChatGPT search June 2023, which cites Wikipedia.)

32. The High cost of Low Performance | Pulse of the Profession 2016 (pmi. org)

Chapter 8 - Writing a Proposal

Chapter guide

In this chapter we discuss how to write a professional proposal. We follow a structured approach that translates the information you gleaned from your client engagement meetings, research and canvas analysis and planning, and turns this into a clear, concise client-centreed 'story'.

Each part of the story is intended to flow from, and build on, the crucial Front-End - the Executive Summary, Introduction and Background.

Our goal is to boost even the most seasoned practitioner's capability in business writing to the level where your clients want to read your documents because of the way they are written and structured. We cover:

- The purpose and benefits of proposals
- How proposals help consultants and analysts
- Translating your canvas into a client-centreed story
- Targeting your communication to the audience and writing effectively
- Structuring the proposal
- Conveying complex information
- Measuring value
- Identifying and mitigating risk
- Proposing communication and governance approaches
- Proposing a team
- Costing a client proposal
- Chapter Summary.

Introduction to Proposals

A consulting proposal is a document that outlines everything that you, as a practitioner, would deliver for a potential project or client assignment. It also works as a marketing proposal that showcases why and how your consulting firm or BA team's experience, competencies and skills are right for the client.

In Chapter 4, we discussed the activities of the engagement phase of the IS consulting lifecycle. These key activities identified the client's need

(Dialogue / Diagnose) and prepared us to respond to the client (Plan / Design). A proposal may recommend the execution of a Diagnose / Dialogue phase or a Plan or Design phase. Or, having already executed these phases, it could set out what will be accomplished in the Perform phase. It may also be a proposal for an initial Review of some kind or a response to a tender or request for information. It just depends on what the client problem is, and what will ultimately work best to solve it.

The Purpose and Benefits of Proposals

Proposals help to clarify and negotiate a specific course of action. They outline how the practitioner recommends completing the lifecycle including how the work might be undertaken (performed) and how success will be measured (reviewed). So, proposals have two functions.

The first is to set out, in a structured and influential manner, the business case for, and activities of, the proposed approach and how these activities will lead to beneficial client outcomes.

The second is to form the basis of a contractual arrangement, should the client or project sponsor (for BAs) proceed with the engagement.

Experienced practitioners carefully consider both functions when drafting a proposal. For consultants, maintaining balance between the two functions is recommended because:

You don't get to do the job unless you win it first!

Writing proposals can be a time consuming and sometimes thankless task. While proposals might not always be work-winning for BAs, they are most definitely career enhancing. Done well, however, these key professional documents can be one of the very best ways you can secure new clients, make sure you're the right BA for a task, and continue your development as a professional practitioner.

Proposals are Targeted Business Communications

The outcome of a proposal is to win work (as a consultant) or have your ideas and solutions implemented (as a BA). There are two outputs – a cover letter (or internal memo) and a proposal document.

By the time you draft the proposal, you have already identified your client and you have some understanding of that client's needs. Your proposal goal is to demonstrate the depth of your understanding of the client's business and to present strategy-matching, actionable solutions to their identified challenges and opportunities.

Your communication objective is to persuade the client or project sponsor to act on your proposal and either procure the services of your consultancy, or to assign you onto the project team as a BA. To achieve this objective, you must:

1. Convince the client that you understand why they want or need to engage your assistance;
2. Demonstrate how your approach will provide the outcomes the client seeks;
3. Advise what activities are required to create required outputs and when these activities will take place;
4. Acquaint the client who will provide the expertise to effectively deliver the required outputs;
5. Suggest a timetable of activities; and,
6. Provide an estimate of how much the client will pay for your services.

Proposals are fundamentally about persuasive communication and are also a key marketing tool that makes promises to the client. They set the foundation for what the client can expect from the service that your firm or team will provide. These expectations include the six points listed above and include the quality of the service as well as the style of your firm and competencies of the individual consultants or BAs delivering the services.

If you have done work for the client previously and have built operational trust, then your path is possibly more assured but not necessarily guaranteed. Operational trust arises when both parties operate in a predictable and reliable manner to benefit each other.

Use Logos, Pathos and Ethos to build Trust

In the absence of an operational trust relationship with the client, the proposal must provide surrogates to operational trust. These surrogates include the logical process and methods (logos); key personnel with applicable experience (ethos and pathos); dependable technical and information artifacts (ethos); past examples of successful similar engagements (pathos); and, third-party references (ethos).

Expressing all this material in a written proposal also forces the practitioner or team to reflect on their ability to deliver on the promises and market their services to the client.

Why Proposals help Practitioners

Proposals are pre-planning exercises for practitioners. A hastily written proposal without due consideration can lead to undeliverable promises, unrealistic or mis-aligned solutions, under-pricing and poor marketing outcomes.

To avoid the displeasure of a loss-making assignment or the embarrassment of a misguided proposal, use the proposal process as a due diligence and internal planning process.

A formal, properly managed proposal process forces the practitioner to understand the client and the objectives they are seeking to achieve from the engagement based on mutual understanding.

Capability and Ethos Alignment

When reviewing the assignment and the outcomes, goals and objectives that the client is seeking, it is recommended that you conduct a team (or personal) capability analysis and reflect on the alignment between your firm's (or BA group's) capabilities and the capabilities required to complete the proposed assignment. You may be proposing a solution that will require the development of new capabilities for the team, or at least some members of the team. Some reflective questions include:

- Does this engagement help the IS consulting firm / me as a BA build capability and competency?
- Is this work well aligned with our current capabilities and value proposition?
- Will it challenge those who need to be challenged in the team?
- Will it train and broaden developing consultants or BAs?
- Does the client have the potential to request more work?
- Is the client a good and ethical reference site? Is reputational risk a possibility if we undertake this work?[35]
- Are we providing services that are in decline in the marketplace?
- What expectations do we have from this engagement?

Constant reflection of these issues will assist your consulting firm or BA team to continually enhance their internal and market capability. Other factors you might consider are:

- Do we have an existing relationship with the decision maker or their influencers?
- Did our network sources inform us of this opportunity, or did we find out about it using public information?

- Who are our likely competitors and what strategy would they use to bid for this work?
- How is the client likely to select a practitioner or consulting firm?
- How do the timing and capability requirements of the potential engagement fit our forward schedule and resource availability?
- What are the risks involved in this engagement?What is the likelihood of our winning this work?

Having decided to make the investment of writing a proposal, you now double down on translating the research you have completed in your canvas: the core issues you are trying to resolve, the approach you recommend and subsequently, what resources will be needed in this resolution process.

Due diligence and care up front are essential

The more care you take in this initial due diligence, the less likely you are to under-price your efforts, propose work that does not meet the client needs, or find yourselves working in an industry that may not share the same ethics and values as your firm or you personally.

Top Tip: For larger engagements, you might consider drafting an internal business case before deciding to write the proposal.

Remember, the second function of a proposal is to form the basis of a negotiated contractual arrangement. This holds true for BAs as well, though the agreement document might be in the form of a Memorandum of Understanding or Letter of Intent[36]. These documents are a baseline in the event of future disputes. Clarity and agreement are essential.

Additionally, proposal writing is an exercise in integrated thinking and expression. It sharpens the mind and hones communication skills. Clear thinking is a precursor to clear communication. Junior staff should be included in proposal writing at the earliest possible opportunity to develop their consulting and business communication skillset. That's why it is so important for practitioners to continuously improve their professional communication skills, especially engagement, interpersonal (see chapter 2), professional writing and presentation skills (Ch. 9).

But, before we get started, let's make sure you know how to set up a proposal template and use the efficiency tools built into most software.

Learn to write efficiently

As you learned earlier, there are ways you can use readily available applications to make the process of writing and editing your proposal efficient and effective. In appendix 1 we provide tips to help you set up, design and write your document to a professional standard.

Learn to write effectively

Business writing is an essential skill for all practitioners. This competency-set encompasses the ability to communicate clearly and concisely through all written, visual and spoken mediums. Learning effective techniques to strengthen your business writing skills can help you succeed in your career. Here are some tips to help further develop effective business writing skills :[37]

Set clear communication goals and objectives for each section

We have spent a lot of time demonstrating OOGOs (Outcomes, Outputs, Goals and Objectives), so it will come as no surprise that we recommend using goals and objectives to help the structure and flow of your business communications.

For example, if the communication is an email, what is the purpose (goal) of the email and what outcome do you want from it (the objective) – this is a call to action (more on this later).

Generate ideas and key points for each objective

You may already have captured some key points in your planning canvas. It can be helpful to generate key point ideas before writing because it helps you be clear about what you want to say. Creating or adding points to your canvas may also help you identify themes within the topics, which you can then use to develop topic paragraphs or segments in your document. Taking this step helps you design the flow of the communication.

Use the Active Voice

Using the active voice provides clarity to writing and avoids wordiness. In the active voice, the subject of the sentence performs the action, but in the passive voice, the subject is acted on by the verb.

For example, "The dog was walked by his owner" is a passive sentence. "The owner walked the dog," which puts the idea in the active voice. This is more concise and comes straight to the point of the sentence. In business writing, using an active voice may also help sound more professional, increasing the influence and authority (ethos and pathos) to the reader. People tend to read the active voice more quickly and absorb the content more easily.

Use Headings and Subheadings

Create sections in your writing by using easily identifiable headings. Headings and sub-headings make it easier to scan and navigate the document for the reader (see previous section on using headings in 'Styles'). Headings usually comprise the main section topics, while subheadings can break the main topic down into further, digestible sections for organisation and clarification. These sections can be used to identify where key materials or points are and make it easier to break up long text sections in written communications.

Break up big blocks of text (particularly if the document is going to be read online). Keep key points together and use segues to help the writing flow and readability. Numbering your sections allow you to reference particular points more easily when discussing the document.

Create Logos

Begin a paragraph with a main idea statement. This sets the communication objective and opens the door to supporting it with facts and data. When the opportunity arises, expand on any information you provide by using examples, figures or statistics. This practice can help add more validity (logos) to information you introduce to the client. This practice emphasises it's relevance and promotes understanding in a context. One strategy you can use is to apply the Five Whys[38] approach as a simple Root Cause analysis. This can help check if you have answered the questions or objective from the client's viewpoint.

Watch out for Jargon and Waffle

It is too easy for technical specialists to assume that everyone understands technical jargon and acronyms with which you are familiar. Replace jargon with simplified word choices, and write acronyms out in full at least the first time they are used. To avoid waffle, use universal language to make it easier for the reader to understand your writing. It might be helpful to use a thesaurus to help you find simple words to replace more technical terms.

Another good practice is to have a colleague critique your draft.

> **Top Tip:** Read your work out loud when you are editing. If it doesn't flow or comes across as complicated, wordy or pompous when read out, it's probably worse for the reader! Our 'acid' test is to ask, 'would you write this way for a trusted colleague?' If the answer to any of these questions is NO... time to edit your proposal further!

Include a Call to Action!

A call to action encourages the reader to take immediate action after reading the document. Doing this helps provide relevancy about why they're reading the piece and how they can use the information when they're finished with it. A call to action is aninvitation to take a particular action or next step. This can include a short statement designed to receive an immediate response at the end of the communication. For example, in marketing campaigns, 'click here' or 'call us for more information' are calls to action.

Using Transitions or Segues

A transition, or segue, in writing can be made in several different ways. A segue is a transition or connection between two ideas in writing. It is used to move smoothly from one point to the next and give your writing cohesiveness.

The choice of words you use and the context in which you use them, gives your writing cohesiveness, helps organise sequences, and signals to the reader that you are moving from one point or section to the next. Here are some examples of segues in business writing:

Using transitional words or phrases: Words like "however," "in addition," "furthermore," and "therefore" can be used to connect ideas and create a smooth transition between them. For better readability, don't use the words 'therefore' and 'however' (and similar words) as the first word in your sentence.

Start with the subject of the sentence, follow it with the transitional word, and then complete the sentence.

> **Example**: "The situation, therefore, needs further exploration." This emphasises the subject. Compare the readability of this to "Therefore, the situation needs further exploration." **Note** how the first example emphasises the subject of the sentence.

Using signals: Writing a short sentence that highlights what you will cover in the next section. This helps your writing to flow by connecting one section, or chapter, or even paragraph to the next. You may, for instance, want to signal a forthcoming anecdote.

Using anecdotes: An anecdote can be used to illustrate a point or create a connection between two ideas. Anecdotes usually relate to the subject matter that people are discussing to make a point or share a relevant story.

Using repetition: Repeating a key phrase or idea from the previous paragraph can help create a connection between the two paragraphs. You can indicate a new idea is coming using the signal technique, then repeat it

Example: During a meeting, one of our managers wanted to stress the importance of meeting deadlines. She told a story about a time when she was working on a project and her team missed a crucial deadline. As a result, they lost the contract, and the company suffered financially. The manager used this anecdote to illustrate the consequences of not meeting deadlines and to motivate her team to work harder to meet them.

later on as a reminder or to emphasize the idea. Movie script writers do this all the time.

Using questions: Asking a question at the end of one paragraph can help lead into the next paragraph. For example: "Is it a good idea to use summaries?"

Using summaries: Summarizing the main points of one paragraph at the beginning of the next paragraph can help create a smooth transition.

Segues can be an invaluable writing tool for maintaining interest and creating flow. You will find we have used segues at the end of many sections and chapters in this book. We cover segues again in Chapter 9.

Use citations to add credibility

The best way to add credibility to your proposal is to support the forecasts and ideas presented with data provided by credible sources. These can be found in authoritative books, industry papers, credible websites, journals and government and trade publications. In other words, cite your sources. If you don't it's considered plagiarism, which looks (and is) unprofessional.

Citations are a way of giving credit and adding emphasis, confirming a key point and adding gravitas. They provide your readers with the information necessary to find that source again to explore the topic more deeply or check the facts. In business proposals, citations can be used to add credibility.

There are multiple ways you can do this. In this book we have used Endnotes40. For larger publications you can automate the creation of a Bibliography or similar. Again, go to the **References** tab, and capture, then insert citations, and create your reference list. This is good practice, as it keeps sources for citations in one place, and means, once set up, that you have a fast and efficient way of citing while you write. There are many sources of tips for writing business communications clearly and concisely.

Above all, proof, proof, proof, edit, edit, edit! Savvy clients always pick up mistakes and may ask 'does this consultant have an eye for detail?'

Using graphics to convey complex information

Even skilled graphic designers can struggle with creating effective proposal graphics. While the usual rules of good graphic design still apply, proposal graphics come with their own unique set of challenges and requirements[41].

Your goal is to communicate complex, interrelated information in a creative yet business-appropriate way. Your objective is to choose, then create an effective way to convey this information in ways that are relevant to the client or situation, so that they will make sense to the client. But first, let's dispel two common myths.

Myth 1: Creating proposal graphics requires special software.

This is a common misconception. Many effective proposal graphics are made in widely available programs like Microsoft's PowerPoint, Word or Visio. For graphics requiring more precision, Adobe Illustrator or even subscribing to an online graphics provider may be a better choice. The key is to use something with which you're competent.

Myth 2: Proposal graphics need to be flashy.

The truth is that clarity is much more important than flashy or fancy, overly complicated images. For instance, a simple organisational chart using only straight lines, rectangles, and a couple of well-chosen colours conveys the orderliness and elegance of your solution. Conversely, a chart with a rainbow of colours and lines zigzagging everywhere suggests that your solution is convoluted, confusing and potentially high-risk.

> **Top Tip:** Think of this as a Business Process Mapping exercise where 1) simplicity, 2) just enough material 3) logical flow, and 4) connections - are the goals of the diagram.

Here are some additional tips:

Only use graphics for important points.

Nearly anything in a proposal could be represented with a graphic (including photographs), and since very text-heavy pages can look pretty boring, it can be tempting to fill a proposal with graphics. The trick is to balance the need for a graphic to illustrate or educate, with efficient, effective use of space. When using a graphic, make sure that it is illustrating a key point or is relevant to the information you are summarizing.

Graphics attract attention to themselves, so make sure you're using them to highlight major challenges, opportunities, approaches, process etc.—those essential points you most want the reader to understand and remember.

Top Tip: Always start thinking this through by having a clear communication goal and objective for any graphic – it is, after all, a form of business communication.

Another device is the call-out box (akin to the Top Tip boxes in this book.) Callouts catch the reader's attention and provide a highlight for key points without sacrificing much page space.

Top Tip: All of the graphics (tables and figures) in this book were created in PowerPoint and Canva, saved as PNG files and copied into the book-publishing software. Printers have guidelines about formatting e.g. all the diagrams must be a maximum of 300 points per inch (ppi).

Make sure the graphic stands on its own.

If your proposal graphic requires a lengthy explanation, you may need to re-think its effectiveness. Whenever you include a graphic, ask yourself, *'If I saw this graphic alone, with no other text, would I understand it?'*

Remember, your readers are busy people. If you need a block of text to explain what the graphic is supposed to show, then the graphic is wasting space—the text could do that work alone.

Top Tip: Aim for self-evident graphics that can be interpreted in 10 seconds or less. Any longer and the reader is likely to give up and move on. The body text around the graphic should elaborate, not explain.

Carefully craft your action captions.

A major solution to supporting your graphic in 'standing alone' is to carefully craft captions (below for figures and above for tables). You busy reader, skimming the page, will likely pay more attention to the graphic and its caption than any one sentence in the body text. For that reason, you want to make sure your captions effectively present your graphic purpose and key point.

For example, consider these two possible captions:

1. Company X's proposed digital transformation. Our proposed transformation shows decision-makers key project review points.
2. Company X's Proposed Organisational Structure. Our proposed transformation shows decision-makers key project review points, reinforcing the organisation's agile methodology and providing governance checkpoints.

The first option is a missed opportunity. Anybody looking at an organisational chart should be able to tell immediately that it is a project roadmap —if not, there's something wrong with the graphic!

The second option is an effective, targeted communication. It calls attention to a feature of the graphic, explaining why that feature is beneficial to the customer. It employs the Attribute-Purpose-Value (APV) structure we discussed earlier.

> **Top Tip:** An easy way to add a benefit statement is to start the thought with, 'and the client benefit is...'. You probably won't write that, but it prompts the thought...

Pay close attention to fonts.

Here is where using a style guide really comes into its own. Many Requests for Proposal (RFP) have strict templates or requirements, so make sure you check that you meet the potential client's requirements. For example, 'all text must be Calibri 11-point'. Unless the RFP specifically states otherwise, these restrictions apply to graphics as well as body text. In other words, if you reuse an old graphic and forget to convert it from Times New Roman 12 to Calibri 11, your proposal is non-compliant and could risk rejection.

> **Top Tip:** No matter how good your proposal is, if a client receives, say, 50 proposals, any excuse to reject one, based on non-compliance, makes the selection process easier for them. Generally, they are looking for a short-list of 3 to 5 proposals and only one winner. Non-compliance of just a font, although minor, is a sign that you have not demonstrated an eye for detail, generally a must to win an assignment.

There's also another reason. The random use of fonts and highlighting can be visually unappealing. Create a style and stick to it, using CAPITALS, italics and bolding carefully and sparingly.

Make sure your graphics are readable

The most common compliance problem isn't using the wrong font when building the graphic, but rather, accidentally making the text too small after the fact. Inexperienced proposal graphic designers will often create a graphic using the correct font size in the PowerPoint or Illustrator source file—but when they go to move the graphic into the proposal document, they find that it's too big. So, they shrink it down to fit the page—and now the font is too small, rendering the graphic non-compliant. Of course, if compliance is not an issue, you can resize your graphics but do make sure that anyone can still read them easily i.e., that the font size is still reader friendly.

Consider the size of the screen that a reader might be using. When screen-sharing on a video call, everything gets smaller.

Top Tip: To avoid this problem, always design your graphics at actual size. For instance, if your proposal has 8.5" x 11" pages (21.6cm x 27.9cm) with 1-inch margins (2.5cm), you have a maximum of 6.5" x 9" (16.1cm x 22.9cm) of usable space. Make sure you set your slide (PowerPoint) or artboard (Illustrator) to those dimensions before you start building the graphic. When you insert it into the proposal, it will be exactly the size you need, eliminating the compliance risk.

As a rule, don't shrink graphics to fit into a proposal document. Conversely, do not expand small graphics to fit the page either—this can lead to blurry, 'stretched' graphics. Instead, go back to the source file, where graphics can be resized without loss of quality.

Finally, designing your graphics at actual size has the additional benefit of making it clear from the beginning how much page space the graphic will take up. In severely page-limited proposals, shaving that extra half inch off the side of the graphic can make all the difference.

Provide a key

If you use colour or numbering within the graphic, be sure to include a 'key' so that the reader can quickly and easily decipher the meaning.

Next, we turn our attention to the structure of the proposal – what goes where, and how to tell the story.

Structuring the Proposal

As you have already been made aware through the Proposal Research Canvas, professional consulting proposals have four sections:

1. **The Front End** – the Executive Summary, Table of Contents and Introduction focus the attention of the reader and help them find the information they seek. They should always be written in a very sharp and compelling style to create interest and encourage them to read more.
2. **The Background / Problem Identification** sections that demonstrate you understand the client's issues and explain why their challenges need to be addressed and how each can be resolved.

3. **The Response** sections outline your recommended solutions, and the approach you suggest to implementing the solution. The section outlines considerations such as project methods and timeline, change impacts, risks and mitigations, project communication and governance.
4. **The Back End** - Here you suggest the people who will work on the engagement, what role each will fulfil including the client, how much you estimate the project including resources will cost and talk about your firm. This finalises the document and appends additional material.

Our suggested structure should not be regarded as a template but rather a guide. You can change the structure to suit the client, size of the engagement and requirements of the project.

The goal is to create a scaffold for holistic, integrated, professional document 'front-to-back' professional flow, as shown in Figure 8-1. We saw this figure back in Chapter 6.

To create a story that flows in a client centred way, you translate the information from your analysis and planning canvas into the various sections of the proposal, applying logos (logic), pathos (emotion) and ethos (trustworthiness) to add influence and emphasis, and build a compelling business case.

As you can see in Figure 8-1, proposals are comprised of 'package' of professional quality content divided into the four parts described above.

A proposal is an integrated description of what the consultant is going to do and how they are going to do it. In writing the document, you will constantly be aligning activities with staff capabilities, staff capabilities with individuals, individuals with their availability, the cost to the firm of performing the project and ultimately the profit margin that the consulting firm wishes to achieve.

At its heart, the proposal must be client-centric. You must continually express that the project is important to the client and you are a trusted partner in making sure that the project is completed effectively, while managing the expectations of the client and their stakeholders.

When things to wrong, delays happen, unintended consequences arise, key personnel become unavailable and all the myriad of roadblocks that occur during complex transformation projects, a consultant must be able to fall back on the proposal and show that they have considered all of (or at least most of) these risks and what will happen should they occur. This comprehensive approach is a demonstration of your professionalism.

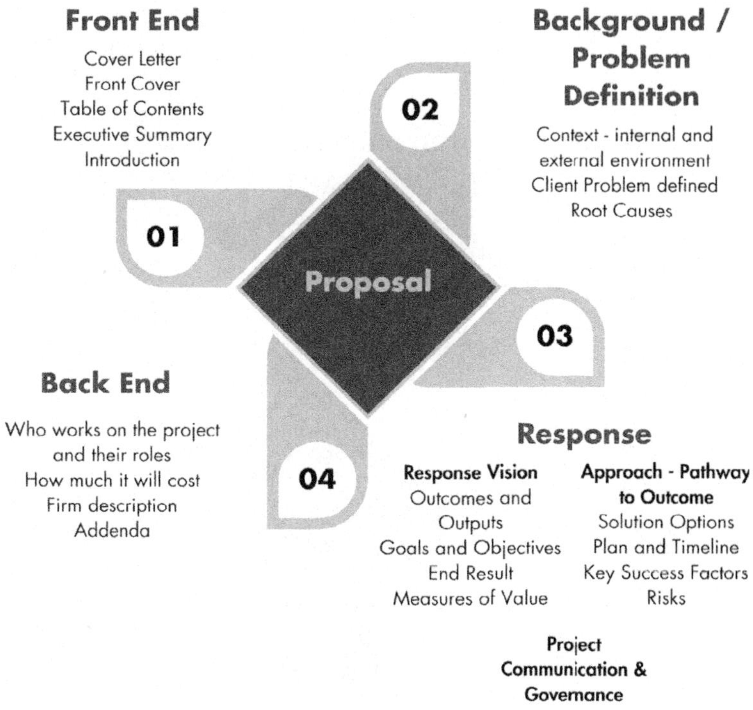

Figure 8-1 Structure of a Proposal

Figure 8-2 also illustrates the flow of a proposal, with one section setting the scene for the next, until, in the back end, your proposal is finalized, and the client is equipped to make a decision.

The Front End

As you can see in Figure 8-2, the Front End of a proposal consists of four items. These are the Cover-Letter, Cover-Page, Executive Summary, Table of Contents and Introduction. We will examine each item in turn.

The Goal of this section is to provide a targeted, compelling snapshot of your proposal. The objective is to pique the interest of the executive management or proposal review team such that they want to read the proposal because it appears to meet their needs or selection criteria.

The harsh reality is that the people who receive consulting and large BA proposals are probably receiving multiple other proposals at the same time.

They are busy people who will skim these front sections and decide whether to invest the time in reading your proposal. Failing to do a top, professional job of the front end risks your proposal missing the mark from the outset, or worse, ending up in 'file 13' – the trash.

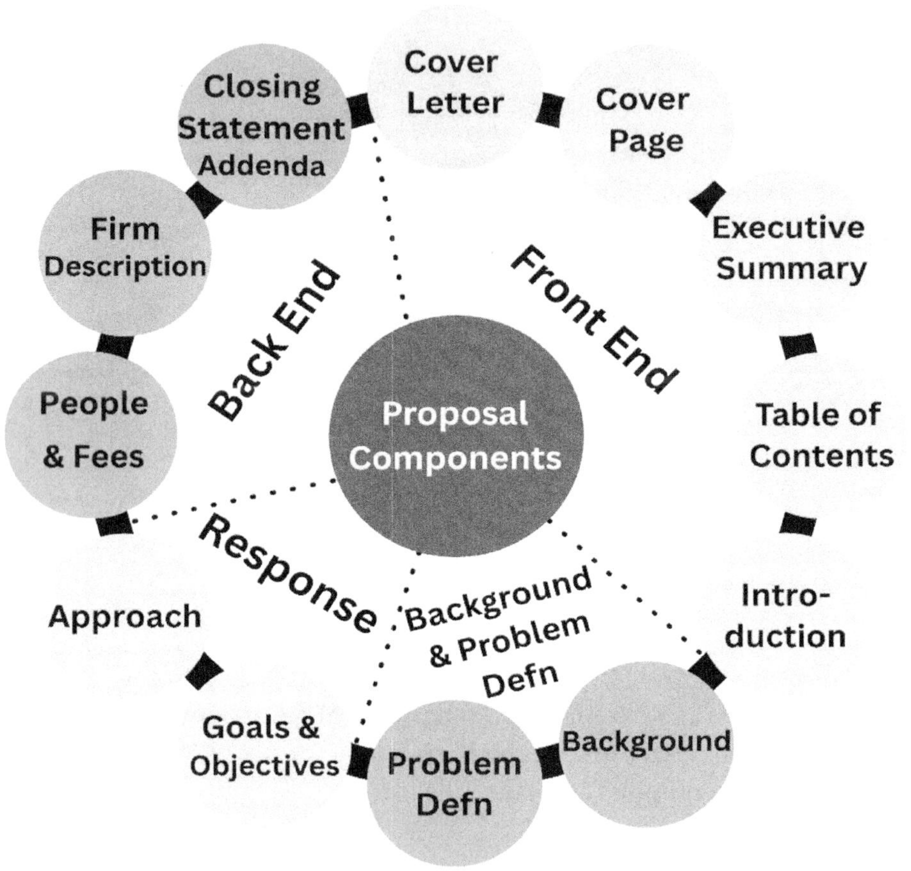

Figure 8-2 The Elements of a Proposal

Cover Letters

Cover letters are a separate, loose sheet attached to proposals. As you can see in Figure 8-3, a cover letter forms an essential part of the package you will send to the client, so should be clear, and to the point. The cover letter is a personal communique from the principal consultant or senior BA addressed to the principal client. It is normally very short; usually one or two paragraphs, formal business letters have a specific structure. Traditionally, cover letters are attached by a paper clip, slipped inside a plastic cover visible to the person receiving the proposal, or appended to an email as a separate document. They should always be branded. A well-crafted cover letter is a sign of professionalism.

Figure 8-3 provides a general template for a professional cover letter.

Another common practice is to address the client formally and then cross out the formal attribution and write their Christian (first) name in ink above it. You would only do this if you have met the person and have established a personal relationship with them. For example:

Aggie

Dear ~~Ms Christie~~

The cover letter is a traditional addendum that gives the proposal a little extra polish. It is commonly the first item your client reads, so following the suggested outline will get your proposal off to a good start.

The cover letter has two essential features:

1. It outlines the benefits of your solution and the benefits of using your consulting service i.e., your firm's value proposition.
2. It has the contact details of the consulting / BA principal – this must be easily found and should appear in more than one place in your proposal.

Place and Date

Firm Name

Client Name
Client Title
Address

Dear [client name],

RE: Proposal to ....

[ISCON Firm name or BA Team] is please to present this proposal to [describe project outcome].

[Our value proposition is...]

Should you have any questions please do not hesitate to contact me [or my associate]. We look forward to working with you on this critical project.

Sincerely

Signature

Title
Phone

Figure 8-3 Cover Letter format

Cover Page

Cover pages are also important branding artefacts that should include the following:

- Title: Proposal to [create project outcome by performing set processes] or whatever the title the client uses. Interestingly, in our experience, proposal titles often describe the process not the outcome. Using the outcome in the title sets a positive and beneficial tone. Use the APV technique at every opportunity.
- Name of the Consulting Firm
- Name of the Client
- Date
- Logo: proposals usually include the logo of the consulting firm.

It is common to see the client and consulting firm logo-s side-by-side, creating the impression of a future partnership. These client logos are often taken from the client website or printed materials without permission. A logo of a company forms part of its intellectual property and may be legally protected. Normally, you would seek permission to use a logo from its traditional guardian, the marketing division.

You might also include a relevant or stylized picture on the cover-page.

> **Top Tip:** To format the recommended content as outlined above, you will find excellent document templates for professional proposals online. Create a template to maintain consistency of your brand.

Executive Summary

An Executive Summary is a one-page snapshot of the proposal. Depending on the size and complexity of the proposal, these summaries may extend to two or even three pages. But less is better if it is targeted and focused.

The communication objective of the Executive Summary is to give just enough information to pique your client's interest, persuading them to read further. This critical section creates an important first impression of your ability to communicate in writing, formally and effectively.

Consider this: Imagine a busy executive, time-poor, who has not read your proposal. This person is meeting with you, the consultant, or internal personnel to discuss your document and perhaps other competing proposals in a few minutes. To save face and not look unprepared, they quickly scan each proposal.

Your Executive Summary is where they hope to get the important information to participate in the discussion and decision-making process. If you don't provide the pertinent information, they have to sift through the document to find it. An effective Executive Summary could give you the edge in a competitive situation.

Why you should write the Executive Summary last!

Practitioners who write the Executive Summary before writing the proposal tend to write an Introduction rather than a summary.

Our advice is to write it last. Take the key points from each of your major sections and put them in the Executive Summary.

What to include in an Executive Summary

As a guide it might include:

1. A statement that demonstrates your understanding of the client or context. Why is this project happening? What insights, customer feedback, product plan, or other need caused it to come to life?
2. A statement that demonstrates your understanding of the problem the client wants resolved;
3. Briefly outline the recommended solution, or the project's objectives. Then a very high-level description of your approach towards a solution and what benefits or desired outcomes this approach will bring. How is the project going to solve the problem you established in the first part? What are the project goals and objectives?
4. Explain the solution's value. Once you've finished your project, what will happen? How will this improve and solve the problem you established in the first part?
5. Provide indicative costs.
6. Wrap up with a short conclusion about the importance of the work. This is another opportunity to reiterate why the problem is important, and why the project matters. It can also be helpful to reference your audience and how your solution will solve their problem. Finally, include any relevant next steps.

Unless the Proposal is extremely complex, your goal is to write no more than one page for your Executive Summary, two at the absolute maximum.

You will adjust the style and content of the Executive Summary to meet the individual needs of the target reader at the client firm. If you find yourself repeating the Executive Summary in the Introduction section, then you probably need to re-write it.

Table of Contents (ToC)

A detailed Table of Contents (ToC) is like a road map for the client. It is positioned after the Executive Summary for a reason! If the reader cannot find what they are looking for using the ToC, then they may not persist in their search. Remember that the ToC is just a reflection of the document structure. A ToC does not fix poor structure.

Automate your ToC

If you use a document template and styles (see earlier section), the headings are automatically captured when you create a ToC. For example, Microsoft Word has functionality to automate the creation of a Table of Contents.

Why it is important to do a good job of headings and your ToC

In a proposal, the ToC is not just a document afterthought, automatically generated by word processing software. It is a strategic guide for key personnel to find information critical to decision-making.

The super-users of the ToC are client personnel tasked with reviewing and applying selection criteria to several proposals to make a recommendation to the principal client.

If a poor ToC does not guide them to the information they need, they will grow frustrated with your offering. Sometimes, a selection panel will miss important information because it is buried in a section poorly named or not reflected in the Table of Contents.

Additionally, if the proposal is large and complex, you might find it useful to include a separate ToC for diagrams and tables. Using Styles in Microsoft Word for these features of your document can also be automated.

In concert with the Table of Contents, use document headers and footers to further guide the reader. Section headings repeated in the header can be useful. This allows you to use continuous page numbering throughout the document.

Now, we turn our attention to the Introduction.

The Introduction

The goal of the Introduction is to invite the reader to invest the time to read your proposal. The client will only invest this time if they believe the proposal will address their pressing issue(s).

It is important that the Introduction is client centric. Too often practitioners, especially smaller consulting firms, start with a description of their operations, clients, services, and history. Leave this for later. Remember, this is all about the client.

The objective of the Introduction, in general terms, is to communicate that the client's issue and circumstances are unique and important, and that their decision to seek assistance to resolve their challenges was the right thing to do:

- Communicate your main idea(s) to resolve the client need briefly and at a very high level in this section so that you can build on each later in the Approach section.
- You can briefly state that your firm is able to assist with their issue because you have the right experience and capabilities to both understand and address it. An expression of your firm's principles and values may be appropriate here too; aligning your values with your client's values can assist.
- Invite the client to contact you should they have any questions or need clarification on any points in the proposal (yet another place to insert contact details).

Then use a segue sentence to move to the next section, which describes the background to the project.

For example, your segue might be: 'In the following sections we provide our summary of the problem, background research on the issues and impacts of your challenges remaining unresolved.

Background and Problem Definition

The Background section is the story of how you came to be writing this proposal. The client is the main character in your story. Providing some background to their situation, how it came to be, demonstrates your understanding of the business and the context in which the issue has arisen. Remember, do not point fingers or blame the current management for the issue(s) that may have arisen

The goal of the section is to concisely define the context for the issue that the client wants addressed. Here you might cover the most pertinent findings from your PESTLE or competitive analysis, providing the external and internal circumstances under which this issue is occurring and the impact it is having on the client.

> **Top Tip:** Beware of long descriptions of the client's business - the client already knows their own business!

Rather than just repeat back what the client has described, you have an opportunity to reframe the problem in a context and promote your initial thoughts and insights into their issue. This might include identified root causes of the issue and the current and future impacts. This means the primary objective of the section is to set up the context for the client story in such a way, that everything else in the document has relevance to, and flows from, the Introduction.

To do this, the secondary objective is to demonstrate your knowledge of the client's internal operation and your understanding of their external environment (industry and marketplace, trends, disruptors etc).

Here's where you use the facts and data (logos) you have discovered while completing Part One of your canvas.

As a guideline, be sure the facts you present are accurate and relevant. This shows you have been listening and that you understand the client and their problem. If you are responding to a written document, such as a Request For Proposal (RFP), you might reference your understanding back to the document the client has supplied to you.

If you have experience with this type of engagement, now is the time to mention how you have helped prior clients with similar issues. It's best not to say that your past clients' issues are the same as what your prospective client is experiencing. Each client generally believes their issue is unique because of the context in which it is occurring.

Be careful about commenting based on personal assumptions; if you are wrong then your credibility will decrease.

> **Top Tip:** Each section should flow in a logical way into the next, so it is critical to craft your story with future sections in mind. Creating key points to expand on, or provide solutions to, while researching your canvas can help with this. Use section introductions and segues to assist with creating flow in the document. A flowing document is easy to read so prospective clients are more likely to continue reading.

Figure 8-4 demonstrates the flow of your proposal. As mentioned earlier, writing a proposal is an exercise in integrated thinking. The way in which a proposal unfolds to the reader will influence their decision to act upon what you propose.

Following the flow in Figure 8-4, after establishing what the problem is, and why it's a problem, the goals and objectives section clarifies the desired end result, and the approach section introduces your recommended solutions and how these might be implemented.

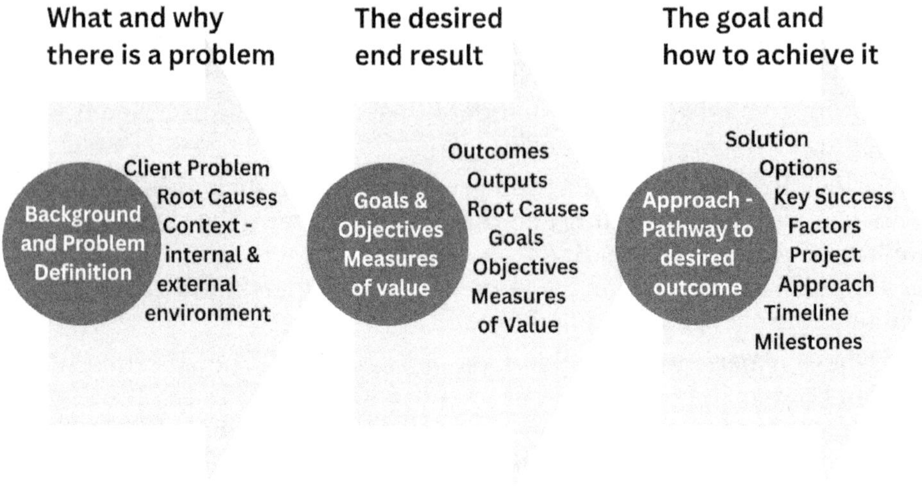

Figure 8-4 Flow of the Proposal

Furthermore, an accurate definition of the problem provides the basis for scoping the engagement.

Scope

The scope of the assignment sets out what will be included and what will be left out. Scope can also be conveyed singularly or in combination. In Table 8-1 we illustrate a variety of scope alternatives.

It is impossible to create a model of the different social, business and technical issues that an information systems consultant or BA will face in an engagement. However, we have a few suggestions, based on our prior discussions in the book, that you may find useful. They are presented to encourage practitioners to broaden their considerations when looking at a client issue before narrowing their focus. This assures proper scope definition, focus and management.

Check the Focus of your Scope

Information systems consultants and business analysts look at the relationships between people and technology, processes, and data. As introduced in Table 8-1 and shown in Figure 8-5, scope issues, particularly scope issues that require a technical solution, may occur in any one of multiple areas of business operations, technology infrastructure, data, business process or people and culture.

To reiterate the importance of holistic thinking Figure 8-5 illustrates the complex relationships that these factors have and how they are increasingly dependent on quality data. For example, no matter what analysis approach or model you have used in your background, when crafting your proposal, be alert for how changes to any one part of the system will impact another.

Table 8-1 Scope Alternatives

Scope	Description
Issue	The issue at hand defines the scope. All activities required to resolve the issue are within scope, e.g., decision to outsource technical services.
Function / organisational unit	The scope only applies to a certain function or organisational unit e.g., service desk efficiency, intranet management, maintenance programme.
Location	The scope is limited by location e.g., head office, branches, international offices, or whole of organisation.
Technology	The scope applies to existing or planned technical upgrades e.g., retiring technical debt, moving to the cloud, integrating AI or ML into data strategy.
Business process	The scope encompasses an existing, new or one-off process, e.g., transaction processing, inventory or supply chain management, new stock processing, ERP systems selection.

Top Tip: Considering data as an asset to support agile methods and quality decision-making is especially important with the rapid growth of AI and Machine Learning. Data and its use for BI are rapidly becoming a source of competitive advantage, if not survival in many industries.

If you are looking to understand impacts more widely, consider impacts across Kast and Rosenzweig's sub¬systems view of an organisation (as discussed in Chapter 2).

The consulting lifecycle model is another way to consider what scope, and activities should be considered in the analysis of a client issue and focus of a client engagement. While the sub-systems model considers the scope and issues from the client perspective, the lifecycle model considers the engagement from the consultant's perspective. You're seeking a balance between the two.

In Figure 8-5, we have expanded the classic People Process Technology model[42] to include data and its uses within BI (Business Intelligence) as central to change.

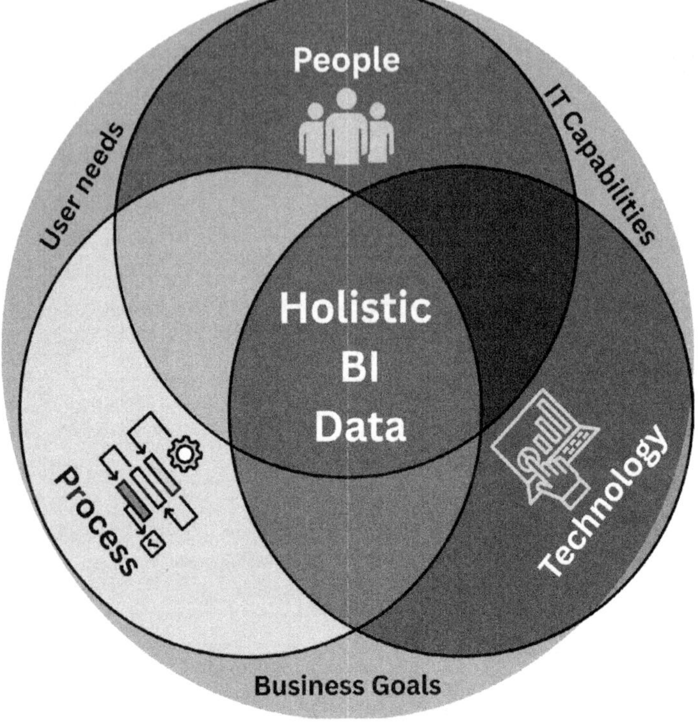

Figure 8-5 People, Process, Technology and Data

The models described in the book are there to assist information systems consultants and business analysts in managing scope, thus enabling both client and consultant to agree on when the assignment is satisfactorily completed. This question is further determined by the next section of the IS consulting proposal, the *Response*. This includes Goals and Objectives, Outcomes and Outputs and your Approach to solving their issue.

Response

Goals and Objectives

In this section of the proposal, you should clearly state the goals and objectives of the project. Before we start discussing this section, we expand on outcomes, outputs, goals and objectives. It is important to have a practical understanding of the distinction between these terms so you can decide what to promise the client. Practitioners should only propose what they can deliver.

If you analyse the impacts of these using People, Process, Technology and Data (or any other impact analysis model) will the OOGOs solve the client problem in a holistic and integrated way?

Top Tip: Now it is time to return to your canvas. What Outputs, Outcomes, Goals and Objectives (OOGOs) have you drafted? Have you discussed these with your client?

By proposing to deliver tangible, achievable outcomes and outputs the practitioner is creating measurable and achievable expectations with the client. It is easier to pinpoint when the engagement is completed satisfactorily, and it reduces the risk of potential disputes about payment for promised performance.

Practitioners who promise to meet client goals or post¬ engagement outcomes that are outside their control are taking avoidable risks. It is ofen difficult enough just to deliver on promised outputs that require defined input and commitment from the client.

All practitioners must decide, before committing themselves in the proposal, exactly how they can assist the client in meeting their goals and objectives. Remember that these are the client's goals and objectives. The Practitioner's role is to assist the client in agreeing to these goals and objectives for the assignment. Return to your canvas and check that you have defined Measurable Organisation Value and either Client, or User Calculated Value.

Check that these measures provide:

- The outcome the client needs;
- Measures that can flow into milestones in your approach as well as indicate completion as specified in the scope; and,
- The foundation for project communication and governance.

Consulting OOGOs should scaffold the value the client wants. Ensure they can be achieved in both principle and in practice.

Tips for writing this section

The skill in writing this part of the proposal is to clearly draw a link between the issue impacting the client, the outcomes and outputs, goals and objectives of recommended project activities, and goals and desired outcomes of the client.

These links are best described using positive, benefit-oriented language. Here is an example of benefit-oriented language:

Example: "We recommend [performing this consulting process] [resulting in this output] thereby addressing [this part of the issue] and creating [this benefit]."

The client needs to be consistently, but gently reminded of what value your services provide and how this will be beneficial in meeting their overall business goals. In other words, benefit statements help highlight what's in it for them. Having said that, often it is up to the client to apply the new technology or process introduced during an IS engagement. Post engagement activity is where the benefits are realized. If the client has internal resistance to the change and the benefits are not realized, remember that this is often out of the control of the consultant or BA. The proposal writer must be cognizant of this when making promises relating to outcomes. Your promises in the proposal should extend to those activities over which you have control. Where you mention benefits arising from those promises, these must be made contingent on the client's adoption and perhaps other market forces.

The more you know about the client's motivations, business objectives, plans, modus operandi (how they operate) and personal style, the better you will be able to communicate appropriate goals and objectives for a consulting engagement.

Top Tip: If the engagement entails an Expertise, Experience or Efficiency approach (see Chapter 2), you might consider mentioning successful outcomes from prior clients. Highlight where you have encountered similar issues (never exactly the same issue because every client thinks they are unique), where you have assisted past clients using a similar approach and the measurable value that your particular solution added.

This is a time to introduce the specific expertise and experience of the practitioner or team who will be working on the project. Capable, competent practitioners are the centrepiece of your practice or BA team. Recruiting the right people, developing their skills, balancing their personal needs with the needs of the practice or team can be a challenge. It is a difficult and rewarding road to travel.

Communicating professionally, respectfully and in a positive light conveys self-confidence to the potential client. The client needs to know they can rely on you and your people to help them succeed, to overcome their issue and move their company towards a better future.

Practitioners need to convince clients that the recommendations they make will lead the client to the beneficial goals, objectives and outcomes they are seeking. This is communicated in the Approach section.

Top Tip: Too often, partners and principal consultants will engage with the client to win the work, then use less experienced people to develop their skills. This can lead to poor experiences for clients unless the junior or less experienced practitioners are carefully supervised. Clients expect the personnel to be 'job-ready', possessing all the skills necessary to perform all necessary tasks and deliver the outputs. They certainly do not expect to pay people to learn on the job! Junior personnel who are still training need to be carefully supervised on jobs to which they are assigned so they appear to be competent in their roles.

Practitioners need to convince clients that the recommendations they make will lead the client to the beneficial goals, objectives and outcomes they are seeking. This is communicated in the Approach section.

Approach

The approach to an assignment is best communicated as a unique solution to a unique problem. This section is where you describe how you will solve the client's problem. It should be clear and concise, and should include:

- A quick summary of the problem (this could be a sentence in the intro to the section);
- Your proposed and justified solution/s;
- A list of deliverables;
- A detailed explanation of how you will implement your solution (to achieve the deliverables);
- A timeline for the project;
- Key success factors;
- What success looks like;
- Risks and mitigations; and,
- Project reporting and project governance.

Therefore, the outcome of the approach section is to demonstrate clarity of the problem, the connection between the problem and proposed solutions, and how to implement the solutions. The objectives are to provide:

- Strategy and business plan-aligned solutions to the identified problem/s or opportunity;

- An indicative project method that suits the client;
- A road map and timeline
- Change impacts including risks and mitigations.

Different styles of clients will be interested in different parts of the proposal. Clients who are goal-oriented will look carefully at the Goals and Objectives section. Clients who are people-oriented will be very interested in the consultant Personnel Pages in the back end of the proposal. Clients who are process-oriented will focus on the Approach section.

Success factors for the Approach section

The main success factors for the 'Approach' section are that they are clear and concise, demonstrate your understanding of the client's problem / opportunity and their organisation, and show how you will solve the problem / realise the opportunity. This means finding ways such as the appropriate use of tables, charts, diagrams etc. to convey complex and interrelated information.

Therefore, the goal of approaches is to convey a 'current state – future state' view of how the client can get from where they are now to the end result. It must be written in a way that is easy for the client to understand. If the client can see how the solution moves the organisation from the current state to the future state, you have achieved your goal in this section.

Distinguish between Method and Approach.

A method is a pre-prepared or well-developed technique to order or arrange your activities for an assignment. The Approach, as we describe it, may apply such a method or employ a model, as a guide for diagnosing, planning, or executing a specific type of engagement. An Approach section, therefore, may require you to craft your proposal as a unique application of that particular method.

A practitioner's methods and approaches can define their value in the marketplace. IS Consultants and BAs often employ methods without recording them as a process. As a consulting practice or BA team grows, however, the passing of knowledge from practitioner to practitioner will vary.

To maintain the corporate memory, and exploit the experience of past engagements, your organisation may invest time in recording a method, especially if the process has been developed in-house. The goal is to create a process that guides future assignments, with the aim of maximizing client benefits and instituting quality standards across the client portfolio.

Such proprietary methods represent valuable intellectual property for the consulting firm and should be protected carefully. Consequently, when presenting your approach in a consulting proposal, you must provide sufficient information to prove the method is effective, without giving detailed information about its specific features or application.

Balance brevity and depth with complex information

Often the client does not want detailed information about your methods unless they are very process oriented. Clients, particularly executive management, are generally more interested in the outcome, how the solutions will 'take away the pain' or 'create a better future', how to get there, what to invest and the anticipated value.

While we cover these matters in the rest of this chapter, here it is useful to bring the Goals and Objectives into this section. The way to use goals and objectives in your approach section will vary. Commonly, practitioners take a very visual style when suggesting their approach. A simple example is to create a table with your goals and objectives as milestones, shown here in Table 8-2.

Table 8-2 Example of goals and objectives used in approach

Goal	Objectives (used as milestones)	Actions
Provide sales monitoring plan by 30 June.	***Determine fit between new reporting requirements and current system by 31 March.***	• Confirm Executive reporting requirements to meet governance. • Identify current system capabilities for automated reporting. • Identify gaps and assess criticality.
	Determine new data compliance impacts by 30 April.	• Analysed US and offshore customer / supplier GDPR requirements. • Determine risks and mitigations.
	Provide analysis report and recommendations by 31 May.	• Draft to manager by 15 May. • Edits completed for manager sign-off 25 May. • Report and slide deck to manager 29 May.

You might decide to add another column to cover Resource Requirements or Key Success Factors or dependencies. These choices depend on what you are trying to communicate.

As you can see, the example in Table 8-2 includes time indications, but not a formal timeline such as a Gantt Chart. Again, this is a choice. High-level Gantt Charts show broad tasks, their timing and dependencies and can be very useful alongside a table such as 8-2. The trick is to modify devices such as tables, charts, and diagrams to suit the situation.

If, in a large project, your table includes a summary of outcomes, outputs, goals and objectives, the actions column could be higher level and provide a summary of the approaches for each outcome. This is another example of why and how it is important to consider your communication objective and strike a balance between brevity and depth.

By using tables, charts, and diagrams to summarize complex information, you can communicate clearly what the pieces of the solution are, what you recommend, how these relate and how each will benefit the client. These devices allow you to mix and communicate important concepts and provide an overall message of communication competency and professional confidence to the client.

Top Tip: Not all clients behave ethically. Consultants in particular need to provide a client with sufficient detail about the approach, but not too much. Giving too much can result in the client using your ideas to carry out the work themselves. In essence, you have provided free consulting!

This has happened to both authors: our well researched and carefully crafted proposal was used as an RFP to another provider who quoted a lower price! While the other provider was unlikely to be able to fulfil the assignment in the way we intended, the client risked wasting time and money.

Essentially, the approach section is a roadmap to the client's destination, so any diagram should include the important signposts, forks in the road, interim stopovers, the destination, and consequent key outcomes from making the journey.

The Approach section should be more than just a description of the process: it should also emphasize other elements to demonstrate your broader capability and sensitivity to client needs, and to establish the project for success.

Ultimately, every Approach is a description of how consulting skills, experience, tools, processes and information products will enact beneficial change within the client organisation. Of course, all approaches contain some element of risk that requires mitigating.

Risk and Mitigation

The risk and mitigation section in a consulting proposal should include the main risks that could arise during the project and how you suggest the client might mitigate them. You can also include a risk assessment matrix that shows the likelihood and impact of each risk. We covered how to conduct an analysis in Chapter 6.

However, here we cover how to include this in a proposal. When writing your proposal, how you convey risk and mitigation is a prime candidate for a table.

Table 8-3 Risk Table format commonly found in reports

Risk List	Likelihood	Impact	Mitigation	Owner / Date
Risk Description	High, Medium or Low (H,M,L)	High, Medium or Low (H,M,L)	How to address the risk	Name / Date
Senior leaders not being available to make decisions	M	H	Ask CEO to support requirement for on-time action from senior leaders	Senior BA Dec 28

What is Project Governance?

Project governance is an oversight function that is aligned with the organisation's governance model and encompasses the project and consulting life cycle. Good governance guides the project decision-making process and determines what will happen within the life cycle of a project and when it will happen.

The interdependence between Governance and Reporting

A stable foundation of project governance has three key pillars – structure, people, and information.

- The structure of a project must be supportive of the organisation's overall structure including those leading various workstreams, committees, and governance oversight teams such as audit and risk.
- Successful project governance arrangements mean having the right people in place, and roles and responsibilities for decision making are clear.
- The foundation of governance information is the reporting schedule your project requires. Such a schedule identifies key stakeholders and their communication type, frequency and communication responsibilities.

Consider this: Project governance and reporting are interdependent. Taking this approach ensures that projects and the reporting agreed are aligned with the organisation's strategic objectives and that the overall combination of governance structure, arrangements and reporting of information to the right people at the right time delivers value to the organisation.

Understanding this is especially important in a proposal, which, as we have already introduced, is commonly the basis for a project contract.

A reporting schedule should have the attributes set out in Table 8-4. Each attribute may require different approaches depending on each stakeholder's needs and expectations.

In essence, this sub-section summarizes your proposed communication plan for the engagement, and at the same time puts a solid foundation and structure in place for project governance.

The principal practitioner assets are people's technical, business, operational and 'soft' competencies, knowledge, skills and experience.

The next section describes how these skills and experiences will be applied, both as individuals and as a combined unit within the firm. It looks at the role the client should play and provides an estimate of costs to the client. In the final sections we cover the Back End including people and fees, information about the practitioner/s involved and a closing statement.

Table 8-4 Considerations for reporting and governance

Attribute	Explanation
Who	Who will receive the communication? What are their needs, interests and ability to understand your topic and messages? Are there other primary or secondary stakeholders?
What	This is determined by exactly why you are communicating and what you are communicating about – what are the purpose and objectives of the communication? These could be a regular, scheduled update against milestones where you also highlight issues, matters arising, or next steps. You might be seeking sign-off, or permission to move to the next phase. You might be requesting action by the client or signaling an identified problem or risk. You might also provide working papers; end of life-cycle reviews, final outputs report etc.
How	How the report will be provided – written, electronic copy, verbally, in a meeting, via video conference, presentation, via email, in person.
When	Timings - frequency of reporting and delivery of outcomes – daily, weekly, fortnightly, monthly, end of milestone or stage. TIP: Always indicate How and When in proposals to gain agreement with the client.
Where - data	Where will communications, files and data be stored to meet data access, security and compliance requirements?
Why – the benefit	Agreeing project communication and reporting provides a robust foundation for project governance. It contributes to organisational governance (for larger projects) and provides assurance to the client and the practitioner. Good project communication planning is an opportunity for the practitioner team to demonstrate value. It is a means of pre-empting or resolving disputes if things change or if views of a deliverable differ.

Top Tip: You will almost certainly need a different communications approach for different stakeholders. For example, the project Sponsor may only require fortnightly updates via emailed memo, whereas the project manager might require a weekly update report, presented in person.

The Back End – The Firm, People and Fees

Consultants tend to structure this section moving from the general to the specific. This is your opportunity to provide information that traditionally assists clients to make their selection decision. Clients will only select you if they believe you will successfully complete the engagement. Because consultants and BAs provide a service, not a product per se, the option for clients to "try before they buy" is limited. What you are proposing is the promise of success. So, the client judges attributes of your promised service offering, and whether they believe there is business value in what you are proposing. They want to be able to trust that your firm or BA team has what it takes to support them as a client to deliver the promised result. To assist with this, you can use third party references (see References and Recommendations section). These are likely more appropriate as addenda.

This section starts off with a description of the People who will form the project team.

Personnel 'Pages'

In this section of the proposal, you introduce the consulting personnel or BA team who will execute the proposed project. This section should contain key personnel only. Normally you lead with your highest profile team member, which could be the partner, or a senior member of your team that the client already knows and trusts.

Personnel Pages usually include the identity, qualifications and level of individuals who will work on the project. Typically, a thumbnail photograph of the staff member is included. Make sure this photo is professional - avoid candid and out-of-date shots. Clients will expect you to look your age. Also note that black and white thumbnail photographs can age you. This can work for or against some people. The Personnel Pages should list individual consultants' experiences with similar projects. To create an integrated story, some of these similar, preferably recent, projects would feature in the references section (with permission from those clients). These are not meant to be complete resumes; in fact, complete resumes should be avoided. Personal contact details of employees should also be avoided: unethical clients can use these to headhunt firm staff.

The key message you are conveying in this section is that your staff and colleagues have the knowledge and experience to competently address your problem or develop your opportunity. The knowledge should encompass the specified function, client, their firm, industry, environment or technology associated with the engagement.

If the personnel do not have knowledge in any of these areas, then they are NOT key personnel and should be left out of the Personnel Pages section. Typically, their knowledge will come from experience in similar engagements, or work in firms prior to joining your consulting firm. Another message to convey in this section is that the consultant has had experience in assignments of similar complexity and duration.

The Personnel Pages in a proposal helps to justify the fees the IS consulting firms charge to clients or indicative costs in a BA assignment. An example of an entry in the Personnel Pages is contained in Appendix 2 at the end of this Chapter.

By describing the talents of the team, you are preparing the client for the fees that you will be charging for that team.

Fees and Indicative Costs

This section is where you turn what you have recommended into cost (or investment) considerations. Traditionally, the amount charged to a client for a consulting assignment is calculated by the following:

Price = (Estimated time spent by individual consultants) X (Salary costs + Profit Margin) + (Disbursements including travel and other administrative costs)

These guidelines are useful for BAs who might omit profit margin, but otherwise include all other aspects.

For consultants, clients may be charged on a time and materials basis i.e. the price to the client varies according to how long the assignment actually takes, or a fixed-price arrangement, where the consulting firm assumes the risk of overruns and benefits from efficient delivery. For internal BAs, your calculation of cost needs to be sufficiently accurate for the project owner and sponsor to be able to analyse budget impacts.

Other contemporary charging arrangements include risk and return sharing, capital sharing and bonus schemes. Many large firms no longer break up their costs, rather quoting one overall price to the client. Whatever the arrangement, the client is seeking value from the application of consulting resources. The principal resources, in every case, are the people who perform the consulting activities. So, the client often judges the people attributes of your promised service offering, loosely based on behavioural considerations. Like a job interview, the principle in play is:

Past behaviour is the best predictor of future behaviour.

Applying this to the proposal, the client uses specific examples of past behaviour and other information that substitutes for future behaviour.

What level of detail?

Some consultants believe this section should be very detailed; others believe it should just be an overview. Fee policy is something for your firm to decide early so that you give a consistent message to your existing and prospective clients.

Consulting firms have a myriad of ways to determine fees for consulting engagements. For the purposes of discussing the proposal, we will assume the use of the time-and-materials method, as this broadly applies to BAs determining cost considerations.

Traditionally, fees are made up of two components: personnel and non-personnel costs. Personnel costs are based on hourly or daily rates for differing levels of expertise and experience e.g. higher rates for partners, lower rates for junior consultants. Non-personnel costs include travel, materials, administrative costs and other non-time-based expenses.

Typically, you would calculate an estimate of fees by multiplying the hourly or daily rates of the specific personnel by the projected timeframe for the client. Short generic descriptions of the activities may also be included. An example is given in Table 8-5, for a simple project.

Note that only key or senior personnel have been named, allowing for flexibility in allocating staff to different client engagements. Non-personnel costs are included.

Table 8-5 Costing example

Staff	Practitioner Role	Daily rate	Estimated days	Totals
Jan McCarthy (partner or snr BA) Weekly meeting with client	Project overview and quality assurance	$3,000 Or Salary prorated	8	$24,000
George Wanaka (manager)	Project management	$1,400	20	$28,000
2 Analysts	Business and technical analysis	$800 x 2	50	$80,000
			Sub total	**$132,000**
Travel and accommodation				$2,500
Printing and admin				$1,500
			Total	**$136,000**

Mechanisms for Billing Clients

What many consultants fail to include when formulating their costs are the mechanisms for billing the client. In this section you need to include the following three pieces of information:

- How the fees will be billed: the extent of the information to be provided for each bill;
- What triggers full/part payment of fees e.g. stages completed or outputs delivered; and,
- How and when you expect the fees to be paid e.g. terms of 30 days, by direct deposit etc.

Variations and Exceptions

Additional information for the Fees section could also include what might contribute to a variation of fees e.g., delays by the client to deliver specific information and any assumptions built into your fee structure. For example, as highlighted in the risk register example in Table 8-3, availability of key client staff can cause risk and scope creep within the project. We recommend establishing the availability of key client staff, necessary for a timely completion of the assignment. If, for example, you need to engage with a person from the client at a particular time in the project, only to find they are overseas on leave for two weeks, this can impact your timeline leading to time and cost overruns.

If this is a potential risk, in the People and Fees section, it may be appropriate to outline the role of the client, should you depend on their involvement to reach your project goals. This is also an opportunity to outline the importance of their partnership in the achievement of the engagement objectives.

The amount of information that you supply about how you calculate the fees will be dependent on the type of client. This is a matter of judgement and worthy of discussion during the pre-proposal preparation.

Your proposal should provide sufficient information to the client, so they can make an informed judgement about the proposed investment and the benefits that will accrue from that investment.

Top Tip: It's all about how all the information flows to this concluding point. Detailed information about fees should align with key personnel descriptions and the proposed activities in the Approach section. The proposed activities should clearly lead the client to the project's anticipated beneficial outcomes.

Now you can talk about your firm!

This is the right time to describe the firm, its values, the client base, its successes and all the benefits that past and present clients have gained by using your people. You can link to your website and user stories to demonstrate your skills and experience.

Lots of consulting firms start their proposals talking about how great they are at the beginning of the document. But is that what you do in real life? Do you meet a client for the first time and spend 10 minutes telling them how brilliant you are and how great your firm is and then ask them what their issue is? Probably not, so why would you do it in writing? They will look you up - your website, LinkedIn profiles etc. This proposal structure is an integrated story that is client-oriented, starting with what the client issue is, analysing it a little, leading them on a path to a solution, showing you have the capability to assist and then outlining how much it will cost. Now you talk about your firm and its general capabilities - the purpose is to showcase all your services just in case they want more. But for the purpose of winning this job you focus on the issue and its solution, which may only be a subset of your firm's capabilities.

Firm Description (for consultants)

For consultants, the firm description section usually outlines how long the firm has been in business, how many branches there are, and how many consultants the firm employs. So, the implication is that successful past consulting behaviour drives firm growth and longevity (financial stability). Keep it fairly brief.

In proposals, some consultants provide a history of the growth of their firm; often expressed with great pride. Others provide detailed information of the structure of their firm. If you are going to do this, make sure you have a purpose for making the client read this additional material. For example, if you are trying to cross-sell other services, telling the client briefly that these services are available is purposeful.

Many consultants target well-known brands to boost their market credibility. They list their largest clients in this section, usually 'Top 100' firms implying that these large firms were willing to trust the IS Consulting firm to deliver consulting services to them. Use relevant past client experiences in this section. And refer to the client references in the Addenda.

The 'About' section for BAs

For BAs, professional reputation is also based on past behaviour, such as assignments completed for your current or past employer(s). All practitioners can use past successful behaviour at the appropriate time to expound on past successful assignments with similar clients or similar situations. Having set out this integrated story, it is time to wrap up your story by concluding and summarising.

Short Closing Statement

Don't let your proposal fade away at the end. You have an opportunity to summarize the important points made throughout the full proposal and conclude with the following points:

- Re-iterate the importance of the project and the 'good fit' that your firm has with the client/achievement of the project;
- Re-iterate in a couple of sentences the 'value proposition' / benefits of engaging your consulting firm;
- Again, indicate a willingness to answer any questions; and,
- Indicate a willingness to begin work within a certain timeframe. This is your call to action.
- Include your principal contact details again so if the client is ready to make a decision based on your call to action, they can get in touch easily.

This is not the end of the formal proposal. The last section is important additional information. The principal client might not read it but some appended documents will be very relevant to any team comparing proposals.

Addenda

There are several potential extra parts to a consulting proposal that will be appended to the main body. Where appropriate, some of these sections might be included in the main body of the proposal.

The addenda might include the following:

- Client References
- Legal Terms and Conditions or sample contracts
- Confirmation Letters for the client to agree and sign
- Assumptions
- Information about consortia - where a group of firms collaborate in a joint proposal and,
- Required statements or certifications.

Now we are done!

Chapter Summary

A formal consulting proposal is the centrepiece of communication about the engagement with your client. All future discussion will start from this document. It has four parts. The Front End includes a Cover Letter, Cover Page, Executive Summary and a Table of Contents. The Front End draws the attention of the reader and assists them to find the information they seek.

The Background / Problem Identification section introduces your proposal in the client's business context. It provides background, clearly and concisely conveying your understanding of the client issues and opportunities.

In the Response section, this understanding then flows into your recommended OOGOs (Outcomes, Outputs, Goals and Objectives) and measures of value. In this section, the Approach explains how the consulting engagement will resolve matters, describing what your proposal recommends and how this can be implemented. It details risk and mitigation and culminates in an outline of how reporting and project governance will provide assurance to the client throughout your recommended solution.

The Back End includes People and Fees section outlines the personnel who will work on the engagement, any required role for the client in the engagement and what fees will be charged. You talk about your firm more generally in this section.

This final part of your proposal finalises your document by providing a closing statement and provides Addenda (if required) to add other necessary material. Once you have developed the material for the consulting proposal, you will be in a position to summarise and present it in person to the client. In the next chapter, we explore the art of the consulting presentation.

With practice, taking the very structured approach to this exercise that we recommend, will become an automatic way of thinking and working. Top professionals around the world use a proposal structure to win work and deliver great results for clients.

Appendix 1

We acknowledge that professional writing deserves, and is the subject of, whole books as well as many blogs and YouTube videos. Here we provide a few brief tips about working efficiently as practitioners. Our intent is to save you time, effort and money!

Set up your document folder and collaboration space

Continuing the Microsoft Teams example from earlier chapters, (or working where you and your team are able to co-author your proposal in real-time) create and save your proposal template.

In Teams, you would do this under the 'files' tab. If you didn't set up a collaboration space for your research canvas, now is the time. In MS Word, click on File, then New, and a wide range of templates become visible or you can search for more via your favourite search engine.

Using styles within a document template

We recommend using styles in Microsoft Word to give your document a consistent and professional look. Styles are readily available in all Microsoft Word documents and available on the home screen as seen in Figure App-1. The following tips reflect the numbering on the figure:

1. The styles menu is on the Home screen in MS Word. You can work with styles from this drop-down menu or;
2. By clicking on the expander arrow the full styles menu will appear as a panel on the right of your screen.
3. One of the benefits of using Headings is these instantly appear on the left of your screen if you have 'Navigation' turned on. This can be found by clicking on 'View' tab on your menu bar and checking the 'Navigation' box.
4. To add a citation, footnote or endnote, click on the 'References' tab on your tool bar and add the appropriate citation. More on this under citations.
5. Turning on the 'Show / Hide' box is a personal preference. It is a more advanced feature useful in big documents such as proposals and assignments where advanced layout and formatting may be a requirement.
6. Finally, if you are working on a shared document in the Teams collaboration space, it is good practice for everyone to check that AutoSave is on. This makes sure the centrally held document is saving all work, including individual's edits and comments.

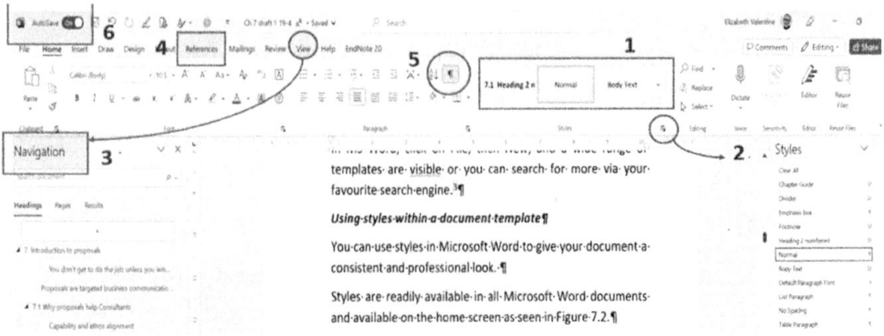

Figure App-1 Using available formatting tools to work efficiently

Applying styles and their benefits

To apply a style, select the text you want to format and on the Home tab, point to a Style to preview it. If you don't see a Style you want, click the More button to expand the gallery and then select a Style. There are several benefits of using styles in Word. The main reasons are time saving, and a consistent professional look to your proposal document. Other top reasons include easy generation of a Table of Contents using built-in heading styles, cascading changes throughout the document when you make one change to a style, and the ability to use Outline View and Navigation. But it's not just headings and fonts.

Automating captions for figures and tables

If you're writing a long document that contains lots of tables, figures or illustrations (for example, a proposal or report), using Word's 'Insert Caption' tool helps you format, number and list them more efficiently. Word can add captions automatically as you insert tables or other objects such as Figures or Citations.

Deepen your knowledge to work more efficiently

You can also do much, much more with styles if you seek out software-applicable help or training materials. It is worthwhile spending time mastering these powerful software tools.

Appendix 2:

Sample Consultancy information and Practitioner Personnel Pages

BerLoki Consulting

BerLoki Consulting provides Project Management of financial systems implementations. It has supported the implementation of over 50 instances of different financial systems. Established in Norway in 1985, it now has offices all over the world.

Key Staff

Sven Herderdahl is the senior partner of BerLoki Consulting with 40 years experience in financial systems. Sven holds a PhD in IT from Harvard.

Alice Marckson is the Senior Business Analyst on the project holding a Masters of IT from MIT (US) and is a CPA.

Eva Atlasson will Project Manage your implementation. She holds a Master of Science from Oslo U..

Marc Shilohn is the Chief Financial Analyst. He has worked on 22 financial systems across the world and holds an MBA from LSE.

Each of our expert staff have years of experience in the implementation of financial systems across the globe. The four leaders listed above will each run teams to ensure the success of the project and the satisfaction of our worldwide clients. Together they have over 75 years of experience.

Endnotes

33. This can occur in areas such as political, environment and psychosocial change.

34. A letter of intent is a document declaring the preliminary commitment of one party to do business with another. A memorandum of understanding (MOU) is a document that describes the broad outlines of an agreement that two or more parties have reached. The primary difference between the two is that a letter of intent is not binding, whereas a memorandum of understanding is considered binding.

35. This list of tips was generated in Bing Chat and draws on a number of sources including 11 Tips To Improve Your Business Writing (With Examples) | Indeed.com

36. The five whys (5 whys) method explores the underlying cause-and-effect of particular problems to determine the root cause of a defect or a problem by successively asking the question "Why?". The number '5' here comes from the anecdotal observation that five iterations of asking why is usually sufficient to reveal the root cause. However, in some cases, it may take more or fewer whys, depending on the depth of the root cause.

37. If you use footnotes, insert footnote is found under the References tab in Word.

38. This section draws on Global Services' excellent blog Five Quick Tips for Winning Proposal Graphics - Global Services (globalservicesinc.com).

39. This tried-and-true model was originally the 'Gold Triangle' proposed in 1964. Leavitt, H. J. (1964). Applied organisation change in industry: structural, technical and human approaches.

40. This website provides a dizzying array of professional templates from www.visme.com/templates/proposals

Chapter 9 - Presentations: How to Create an Influential 'Pitch'

Chapter guide

In this chapter, we focus on presentation techniques for when you are pitching your proposal to the client. The presentation pitch is a logical next step after you have completed your proposal.

The principles and techniques we cover in this chapter can apply to any business situation. The important fact to remember is that when presenting, you - your BA team, or your consulting firm - are on show. Presentations are also targeted business communications (see Chapter 7 intro and section 7.4). So, this chapter has two objectives: 1) to outline how to develop a client centred presentation slide deck and 2) to build your competence and confidence as a presenter.

In one form or another, 'pitching' your ideas and solutions happens in all business communications. But pitches become particularly important when presenting in a professional situation, especially a meeting with a prospective client or a continuing client looking to re-engage you.

Professional presenting requires a skill set that is part of a practitioner's communication core competency (see Chapter 2). This competency is made up of planning, designing and engaging the audience when delivering the presentation. To achieve the chapter objectives, we cover:

- Planning and preparation;
- Creating your materials;
- Your professional image; and,
- Presenting with influence.

Introduction to Presenting

It is inevitable that you and your practitioner colleagues will be called upon to speak about a particular topic to a group, be it large or small. This can occur from the beginning of your career.

We know that the thought of speaking to a group can fill inexperienced and even experienced people with dread. But as with all professional skills, planning, preparation, and practice are the key to building confidence and competence!

Apart from your proposal, a presentation is a packaged summary of your research and ideas. That package must be all about the client as well as telling a clear, concise story about your solutions to their challenges and their value, while also telling a lot about who you are.

Great ideas wrapped in a mediocre presentation are like diamonds wrapped in old newspapers — bad packaging makes people question the value of what's being delivered.

Consultants and BAs need to 'sell' their advice, ideas, and expertise to clients. This is your 'product'. So, think about how to plan and package your pitch message to achieve a communication outcome and objective – every time!

What is a 'pitch'?

In a business context, a 'pitch' refers to presenting business ideas to another party such as potential or existing customers or project sponsors. The goal of a business pitch is to pique your listener's interest in the opportunities and solutions you are presenting. The outcome you need is for the client to decide, preferably in your favour. This outcome commonly concludes in one of three ways and is identifiable from the feedback you receive at the time. For example:

1. ***'Great, let's move to the next step.'*** This is a clear signal of the need to progress getting a contract or Letter of Intent in place and take the first step of moving to project kick-off. The client has decided to invest in the project you are proposing. This is a red-hot response.
2. ***'You're on the right track.'*** Here the client needs more information or detail or a different approach or solution. You need to determine what more they need, or where you are missing the mark to move forward with the client. This is a warm response.
3. ***'Thanks, but no thanks.'*** This may be couched in several different terms or excuses. Essentially something has not worked, and you may well have lost the opportunity. This is a cold response or 'oh darn, what do we need to do to improve our pitch?'.

Whether you get a red-hot, warm or cold response it's also helpful to try to target your pitch to best suit what you know about the client, and what motivates them. Each of the multiple possible pitch types has slightly different objectives.

Types of Pitches

These depend on where you are in the consulting lifecycle. For example, you could be planning:

- An *engagement pitch* to a group of executives or key stakeholders. This can happen before, at the beginning of, or during the lifecycle;
- A *service pitch* to a client or industry group. This usually happens during the lifecycle, or after completion if there is any remediation or additional work required.
- An *invited speech* or *conference paper presentation*. This is not part of the lifecycle but can trigger contact from potential clients who like what you are presenting and the values you or your firm stand for.

No matter the type, a presentation should always be tailored to the client or audience's needs and goals, their interest in your topic and their technical ability to understand what you are talking about.

It's important to keep your pitch brief and, as with your proposal, tell a client-centred story. Include just enough information about you or your firm, and how your past experiences and expertise make you uniquely qualified for the project.

Presenting in different situations

If the purpose of the presentation is an **engagement pitch** to a closed audience of client personnel, then the objective is very clear. Your presentation must be work-winning!

If the purpose of the presentation is a **service pitch**, again to a closed audience of client personnel, then the objective needs to be clarified. Here you return to many of your Dialogue / Diagnose techniques to establish the need, any underlying or hidden causes, and agree next steps and outcomes with the client. Be sure to check your project to establish whether what is being asked of you is within scope, or whether there is any danger of scope creep or scope leap happening (see Chapter 8).

If, on the other hand, you are presenting to an **industry group**, then there may be one or more people in the audience who are potential clients. They are listening carefully to your message because it resonates with a problem or opportunity they are facing in their business.

Remember that in all three of these scenarios, what you are giving is not a 'talk', it is a presentation. These potential clients are not only listening to you, but also watching you, viewing your supporting materials and judging your professionalism. They are connecting with you in three ways: logically, emotionally and ethically. As already covered, this means applying logos, pathos and ethos to engage the widest possible audience.

Feel the fear and do a great job anyway!

We have no doubt that most people reading this have needed, at some point, to stand in front of people and talk about something. This may have happened at work, but it could also have occurred at school, university, or perhaps at a social function like a wedding.

Some people love to present. They portray their character and ideas in a natural manner and approachable way. Others find it painful and frightening, a necessary evil.

You won't learn to present by reading this book. But you will learn techniques to practice.

No matter the circumstances, if you feel nervous or shy about presenting, our advice is:

- **Plan** and prepare carefully. Knowing your material and being sure that it is targeted to the audience goes a long way to reducing nerves
- **Breathe** - learn the power of taking a breath before you say anything. A deep breath in and out through the nose is a trick even the most seasoned pros use. It calms the nerves, and provides the oxygen your brain needs to support you in getting started
- **Practice** - find a safe environment, practise your craft, and take guidance from a seasoned professional or trusted colleague.

Organisations such as Rostrum and Toastmasters provide guidance and training in all types of public speaking. The purpose of presentation training is to take the presenter through three stages: Awareness, Self-Awareness (through practice and feedback), and finally Self-Correction.

After teaching presentation skills for many years, we have found it takes about six to eight '5-minute talks', usually in groups, with positive constructive evaluation (based on the techniques covered in this chapter) to substantially improve one's public speaking skills. However, let's not lose sight of the reason you are there.

The outcome of a consulting presentation is for the presenter to positively influence an audience using reference materials. So, breaking it down there are four main elements at hand to consider: planning and preparation, the audience, the material, and the presenter.

Planning and Preparation

Never underestimate the power of great communication. A well-crafted communication can help you land the job of your dreams, win a pitch, attract investors to back your idea, ensure you get to work on BA projects that match your skills and career goals, or elevate your stature within your organisation. To be a top presenter requires planning and preparation. Remember, great leaders inspire their followers with only words.

Never 'wing it' – your lack of preparation will be very clear to the client, especially if you are in a competitive situation. It is all about the three Ps – Plan, Prepare and Practice.

Planning a Presentation Event

In many ways the communication planning we have already covered in previous chapters is applicable to planning a pitch presentation. The seven steps to planning a meeting can be very useful here.

Create a Presentation Plan

A presentation plan is a detailed running sheet of the presentation. It's like a presentation agenda, providing a scaffold for how you will run the presentation to ensure you stay on track and on time.

Download or create a presentation checklist or run-sheet template and use one every time. (See Appendix 3 at the end of this chapter.)

Your run sheet brings forward your initial planning around the audience and their preferences. Note the following:

- Presentation logistics - how much time you have; who will attend (if a meeting); date and location what resources you need - projectors, handouts, computers, hand-notes, automatic slide changers, flipcharts, internet access etc.;
- Presentation audience, outcomes and objectives;
- Key points / main discussion areas for each objective
- Who is presenting (when presenting in a group), time allocated for each person's section of the slide deck; and
- How much time allocated to intermittent discussion periods and question time.

Get Feedback to determine whether your Plan is Feasible

An experienced presenter should be able to review your presentation plan and determine whether it is feasible. For example, trying to run through even 25 detailed slides in one hour including discussion, would probably confuse and bewilder your client, and does not provide realistic time for dialogue. You can practise your timings against your draft run-sheet and adjust as necessary to ensure a smooth outcome.

Taking less time is often okay. Going over time means the possibility of the client cutting short your presentation stopping you from important messages in your summary and conclusion. This type of preparation, therefore, needs a risk mitigation strategy for your communication planning. During the presentation, you might opt to have a team member keep you on track by employing low-key signals. If you're presenting solo, set a timer alarm on your phone – a quiet one. A haptic alarm (vibration) on a smart watch is ideal for this.

The Audience - who are you pitching to?

Here, we suggest you refer back to Chapter 5, 'Meetings' as the preparation for targeting your audience and tailoring your message is very similar. In this chapter, we suggest a deeper 'stakeholder analysis' approach.

- Who will attend? Who needs to be in the room?
- What do you know about them?
- What are their likely needs, interests in, and ability to understand the subject matter of your presentation?
- Is the decision-maker amongst them? If not, should the meeting be postponed until they are available?
- Who else (from a wider stakeholder perspective) should be in the room.

As you can see, these are questions relevant to a stakeholder analysis. As Molinsky and Tan[41] suggest in their article , *'First, figure out who holds the power to implement [or progress] your idea.'*

Before you pitch your idea, ask: Who has the power to decide whether (or not) our recommendations will be implemented, and what might they base their decision on? These are excellent foundation planning questions.

A quick review of stakeholders and who makes decisions

Some organisations have a clear, hierarchical structure, and are more likely to have a well-defined process around who needs to approve an idea before it is executed. Other organisations can be more challenging to navigate.

To conduct a stakeholder analysis, one of the most common approaches is a RACI matrix. This is useful because the acronym "RACI" stands for the four roles people usually play in relation to project decisions. Here's a simple breakdown:

- Responsible: the people who oversee completing outcomes, or tasks for reaching an objective.
- Accountable: the person who must sign off on the work of the responsible group - who gives final approval.
- Consulted: the people who need to give input to the group in doing the work.
- Informed: the people who need to be updated on the status of the project and made aware of the decisions that are made.

Creating a matrix will help you clarify key roles and responsibilities at each level of your client organisation and is also very useful in the communication planning of any type. Usually, the person you identify as "accountable" is the one who will ultimately say "yes" or "no" to your idea.

Be aware that it's rare for one person to have all the power in decision-making. Most commonly, decision-making is shared between the different leaders accountable for the project outcomes.

For example, let's say you have a fresh idea around how to engage a new audience for an IS implementation. It may be easiest (and fastest) to look for the person who drives the Information strategy, or the person in charge of Technology (depending on the type of project). Using the RACI matrix, you may discover that the Information / Data / Business Intelligence person makes the final decisions for data-related initiatives, but also relies heavily on specific members of their leadership team for input and considers technology and application impacts before making big decisions.

Whatever team, project, or division your idea falls under, get to know what leaders are involved in those areas of the client's business, and ask around to learn about what factors they consider when making choices. If you do not have access to this information, at a minimum, try exploring key people's LinkedIn profiles for clues about what might motivate the person.

Build a relationship with an internal advocate

Few early-career practitioners have the networks or experience to get their ideas immediately noticed by very senior people. Even if you identify the decision-maker, you may not get direct access to them. That's where an advocate can be invaluable. An advocate is someone who can champion your idea in high-level project meetings and discussions you may not be invited into.

The importance of this approach grows with the scope of the idea. If it's a simple idea with relatively low impacts (such as experimenting with a social media post or reaching out to a new client group), your advocate is more likely a middle level manager or technical specialist and may already have the direct power to put your idea into motion.

But if your idea is more disruptive (updating an old business system or implementing a new cloud platform to include AI), you will need both a technical advocate, as well as someone who has acquired the level of informal power that allows them to influence those who are formally in charge.

Here, your champion might be the senior data specialist or the head of Business Intelligence. They may not have direct project decision-making power, but they still have influence with the person who does because of their expertise.

It's all about ethos: building a foundation of trust with the right person or people. This will take time and will need to be developed over a series of engagements or projects where you prove your ability to pitch good ideas, provide evidence for the ideas' merit, and consistently follow through on promises and tasks. You need your advocate to respect you as a professional, and believe you are credible if they are to be your champion.

Do your homework. Study and analyse your audience and/or advocate, their career highlights, their management style, their preferences, to increase the odds of producing work they are aligned with and proud of. When they speak, listen with intention, and don't be afraid to ask questions.

Always stress-test your ideas first. This process will allow you to create a more robust and thorough pitch with fewer holes and logic gaps. Get feedback on your planned pitch from colleagues, your advocate or a decision-maker if you have access. You want to test the feasibility and understandability of your pitch with people whose work might be directly impacted.

Contingency plan for questions you might be asked

Questions are the guideposts to successful engagement. Throughout this discussion, it is a given that you know your subject matter. Planning for contingencies, those 'what if the client asks these questions,' moments, is good practice. All questions are 'good' questions: let your audience know this.

Plan answers for a range of possible questions so that you can respond in a positive professional way, irrespective of whether they are obvious, attacking, stupid or contrary. Be prepared to listen actively with interest and acknowledge the question and the person who asks it.

If unsure of the intent or meaning of the question, ask if you can clarify or explore the questioner's purpose or topic to avoid giving an irrelevant answer. Use the LAER technique described earlier in the book. Then, and only then, should you provide a response. If unsure, check that you have answered the query properly.

> **Example**: 'Thanks for your point, Ken. Help me understand why that is important to you.' Or,
> 'May I please check that I'm on the right track?', (then reframe the point back in your own words).

When completing your contingency questions, try to anticipate questions - get help from your colleagues or team.

If, during the meeting, you don't know the answer, say so and get back to them at a later stage - this provides an opportunity to have another conversation with the client. If presenting as a group, this might give you an opportunity to redirect the question to one of your colleagues.

Plan the focus of your materials

In this section we add to your knowledge about targeting your audience, and focus on designing your presentation to their needs,interests in your topic and ability to understand what you are presenting.

Design to target your audience

The reason you are presenting in the first place is to influence the audience towards a favourable outcome for both the client and the practitioner.

If the presentation is being conducted as part of an engagement meeting, for a more effective outcome, we suggest that two-way communication is better than one-way communication.

Design the presentation as a dialogue to clarify and agree points between the parties but be careful not to prolong the presentation and risk running out of time before you can finish communicating and discussing your key messages. Plan in enough time so that your audience can provide you with feedback through questions, discussion, and body language.

Align and focus what you are trying to say

You have already identified your audience and the type of presentation type. Here's where we suggest, if necessary, you can revert to all the work you have done so far in completing your canvas and writing your proposal. Much if not all the information you need will be there.

The art and skill of turning this information into a 'pitch deck' i.e., the materials you need to present to the client is to review (if necessary) and target your materials based on:

- The client's core concerns, issues, problems, or opportunities;
- The client's ultimate goal and how this aligns with and contributes to their strategy or business plan;
- Any intermediate objectives or states that must be achieved before achieving the final goal; and,
- Any benefits, through your actions and expertise, you can bring to your client to address their core concern / opportunity and assist in reaching their ultimate goal.

Once you have refreshed the alignment focus and relevance of what you need to communicate, you can determine how you are going to get your messages across.

How are you going to say it?

Here is where you consider what style, or means will communicate your messages in the most effective way?

Check your client's logos, ethos or pathos orientation:

Some clients like to rely on solid facts to make decisions. 'Give me the numbers!' they say. These can be facts about the issues, facts about what would happen if the client did nothing or facts about the solution. These clients need a logos approach.

Some clients like to see examples of where your methods have worked before. You will need to reference past assignments or other sources, to give them some comfort that what has worked in the past will work for them in the future. But remember that all clients see themselves as different and special, so you must acknowledge this when providing your examples. These are your ethos orientated customers – they want to know the ways in which you are trustworthy.

Some clients are visionary and keep their eye on the distant prize. Knowing the benefits and goals they seek, and communicating how your actions will provide these benefits and goals, will light a path for them into a possible future state. These are your pathos clients.

Many clients are decision-makers who need a mix of logos, pathos, and ethos. So, be aware: your audience will probably have a combination of these styles. If you are not sure what style will be most effective, then include elements of all the styles within your presentation.

Once you get to know the clients better, you can narrow your style and determine your pitch strategy to create the maximum influence on the decision-maker(s).

Do nothing can be a useful option to include

You may also need to provide them with options from which to choose. A do-nothing option is often revealing and should be considered along with action-focused options. The do-nothing option can potentially create risks for the client, making them aware that they must take action.Now you have identified the focus of your presentation, you're ready to pull everything together.

Plan to influence with your materials

In this section, we provide practical tips about how to optimize your presentation delivery, starting with your props and then moving to your slide deck.

Influencing with your props

Let's start with what to avoid! A common audience comment reflects their frustration with a poorly designed and delivered presentation. "I could have read the slides more quickly by myself and not sat through that boring presentation."

Presenters who read the content of projected slides are not presenting effectively. They can be considered unnecessary and time-wasting. Better presenters enhance the points projected to the audience by speaking around them, adding extra information or contextual stories. Here's how top presenters achieve this. They:

- Minimize the points on the slides. There are all sorts of rules such as a maximum of points (usually five to seven) and even the number of words (some say five or six) but use your judgement depending on the prospective audience;
- Avoid putting lengthy quotes or reams of information on a slide – it's just annoying to the audience; and,

- Provide readable sized print and diagrams to avoid anyone in the audience struggling to read what is in the presentation. This advice is particularly pertinent if you are presenting online – when you share a screen on say Zoom, and present a slide, it will be reduced in size considerably. Keep this in mind.

Consider other props

Slides as handouts: If your slide set is full of detailed information, some presenters consider sending or printing slide sets out before they present, to give your audience a chance to read ahead. The disadvantage of this is that it is revealing your story before you can present it and so the presentation is less 'fresh'. It also means the audience will potentially follow along the printed slide deck rather than concentrating on the person presenting. Good presenters want the focus on them so they can influence with their presentation style. Sending out slides beforehand also creates an opportunity for clients to develop wrong impressions because they can't clarify the points through asking questions when they are reading them. On balance, best not to do this unless absolutely necessary.

A **brochure**: Alternatively, you may want the audience to review it at a later stage. In this case, print and distribute, or send at the end. In this case, you can either print the slides or create a 'take away' in brochure form.

Build a diagram as you go to increase your credibility: Modern presentation software allows us to build complex diagrams step-by-step on a project screen. If the diagram is central to your communication, then we suggest you draw it on a whiteboard or flipchart as you unfold the details during the presentation. You see, when you draw the diagram live, it demonstrates that you know it intimately; it is coming from your body of expertise and not (perhaps) from someone else. This technique can help to increase your credibility with the audience.

The ultimate presentation is the **unscripted talk**. By applying good structure and flow techniques, a presenter can communicate three to five important points very effectively in a short presentation without the use of projected slides. The unscripted talk demonstrates high levels of skill in presenting and communication and high expertise in their topical area and finally, a lot of credibility. Senior politicians and newsreaders hide their speaking props using hidden tele-prompters. Movie, television and play actors learn their lines by heart to create greater believability. Imagine if any of these people read their lines from a visible script!

Checks and balances in planning slide deck design

Because slide decks are personal expressions of creativity, we won't dwell on their design. Our advice for slide presentations is to make them pertinent and interesting.

If building your deck in PowerPoint and other modern software, use a design template / theme and make use of the 'design suggestions' function. Do check the outcome though, as while this can provide a great theme, our experience has been there can be small fonts or other less effective treatment of your material.

- Diagrams and appropriate pictures should balance out information, making it easier to digest; and,
- Be careful not to use combinations of colour that cannot be read by a colour-blind person e.g. some people cannot distinguish red from green. No-one will ever declare they are colour-blind!

To keep the flow, know your material and practice. Use prompts on the slides, hand-notes or your memory so that you can start talking about the next slide as it appears on the screen or just before.

If presenting in a group, plan to have someone else change your slides for you; make sure they are practised in timing the slide changes - you shouldn't have to ask for a slide change - make it seem synchronous and prepared.

Use props to create interest - don't depend on slide sets alone. For example, flip charts, whiteboards, models and handouts can inject more interest during your presentation.

Plan for both in person and online delivery!

Because a huge portion of today's workforce now works completely remotely or in hybrid roles, it is essential you know how to present in person and online at the same time.

In many ways you're planning for a fully online or hybrid delivery needs to be even more meticulous, regardless of which platform you and your team members have selected to use. Maybe it's with Google Meet, Zoom, or Microsoft Teams; whichever software you're using for online meetings, it's important to focus on your presentation skills, your body language, your communication style, and the content of your slides. To begin with, you will need a presentation plan.

Presentation Plan

When you create a presentation plan or run-sheet, use your meeting agenda to design this - to guide the timing and sequence of your presentation. Consider the following when creating your plan:

- What are your meeting goals and objectives?
- What is the total time available?
- What is the maximum time available for presenting, allowing time for introductions, agreeing the agenda etc?
- What are the key messages for each section?
- How can you best allocate the available time?
- Who will deliver each section?

Top Tip: If multiple people are presenting, make sure the opening and closing presenters are confident and well prepared - often the same person. The closing presenter needs to be able to summarize key points made during the presentation clearly and succinctly. They also need to be able to include any agreements or next steps made / discussed with the client during the presentation.

Other considerations for your presentation should include:

1. Find out your client's technology preferences and send a link to their preferred meeting platform in your meeting invitation;
2. Remember to ask the audience's permission to record your presentation – include this in your agenda / run sheet;
3. Plan to be brief and keep slides simple;
4. Plan for interactivity and variety: Audiences tend to lose attention after about 10 minutes of hearing from the same presenter. If there is more than 10 minutes of content, try to break up sections by changing presenters or interactive activities to keep your audience engaged if available and appropriate. There are many interactivity tools embedded into platforms such as Teams (for example, polls, and short quizzes,). Alternatively, ask the audience for their opinions via chat;
5. Make sure the meeting room has a strong, reliable internet connection: plan to take a multi-connector just in case there are any issues connecting you to the audio-visual equipment;
6. Practice - do a technology check before the meeting to ensure that your microphone, camera, and any materials you would like to share are working properly;
7. On the day, ahead of the meeting, close all applications you are not using - keep any you need to switch to open - and practice screen sharing;

8. Arrive or go online at least 15 minutes ahead of the presentation to allow time to set up and check that everything is working. If necessary, ask for help from local tech support if you have any issues.

Once the presentation has started:

- If you are online, keep eye contact with the camera
- Speak with a strong, clear voice
- If you are not presenting, pay attention with eyes to the camera: mute your microphone but do not turn off your video.
- If you are screen sharing be aware that your slides or other materials will be smaller on the user's screens – small fonts become smaller, particularly in diagrams.
- Have someone available to deal with technical issues and to field email/text questions; and,
- Ask pointed questions to avoid too many people answering at once.

What is the purpose of your presentation?

- Identify what you're trying to achieve with the presentation. What are the outcomes (purpose) you want from the meeting? (Is it to test ideas and obtain feedback or is it further along – are you pitching your solutions and seeking a decision to proceed?); and,
- What are the communication objectives. Is it to test an idea or solution and obtain feedback? Is it to win the work or persuade a project team to follow a recommended course of action?

Depending on the type and purpose of the meeting, you may have already sent a calendar invitation to the client to set the meeting up (see chapter 5) and should have indicated the intended purpose and outcomes sought from the meeting. Align your communication outcome and objectives with the meeting purpose, and the identified preferences of your target audience.

Next, we cover the art of presenting your materials.

Your presentation roadmap

In this section we suggest creating a speaking outline based on your outcomes, goals and objectives to ensure you deliver appropriate content. Creating an outline will help you gather your thoughts and organise the content you want to deliver. If your presentation is not well organised your audience may have difficulty understanding your content, and you will be less likely to accomplish your goal. Remember that audience members will not have a written manuscript to refer to if they get lost during your presentation.

Create a structured presentation roadmap!

Create a Presentation Structure

Structure refers to the overall framework and makeup of the presentation - what material is in each part and how to order the material. Think about creating a professional presentation as you might create a short film or infomercial. To do this, imagine that you are the film director - break the presentation into acts to structure it.

Here we use 'acts' as an example of how to structure your presentation:

- **Act 1:** The Introduction indicates why you are there, and the practitioner's appreciation of the problem. (Open discussion, outline purpose, grab attention).
- **Act 2:** Body of the presentation: Approach, option(s) and benefits of options.
- **Act 3:** Conclusion: Agreements, call to action, client feedback sought, and wrap!

Act 1: Introduction

Your opening is one of the most important parts of any presentation for:

- Creating attention – get their attention with a statement, quote, startling statistic, story, etc. Establishing credibility – tell the audience why you are credible to speak on this topic (education, experience etc.).
- Being relevant – tell the audience why this topic is important to them.
- Leading out with purpose– tell the audience what your presentation is about and what you hope to accomplish.
- Ensuring your overall purpose is expressed as a value proposition[42] you might even draw on APV (Attribute, Purpose, Value) if appropriate.

Make sure that if you are presenting in a team, that you have your most experienced speaker deliver a confident, compelling opening. Opening is an art and a skill.

The Art of the Opening Line

Knowing how to start a presentation is crucial: if you fail to capture the audience's attention right away, your entire presentation can flop. Few listeners will stick with you to the end and retain what you have told if you don't master the art of how to 'open'.

If you are very nervous, the best way is to start by taking a deep breath, while at the same time, making sincere, friendly eye contact with your audience. Next, make sure you have crafted and practiced an opening sentence or two so that your breath has time to settle your nerves.

After you have said 'good morning / afternoon / evening', the best way to start nearly all presentations is to take a pathos approach. Appeal to and invoke certain emotions in your audience – curiosity, surprise, fear, or good-old amusement. It is always about the right opening, depending on your audience and what you judge might work best with them. [If you ever get the urge to start a presentation with a joke, then it had better work because if it doesn't you have just established your poor taste and reduced your credibility. Our advice - don't do it.]

For example, a client with a 'clunky' website. Here is an opening line.

> **Example**: "Good morning, everyone. (pause)
> You, your team, and your customers have lived with a slow, unreliable website for two years. Imagine how good it will feel when you switch up to a new, high functioning site? (pause)
> The purpose of our meeting today is to outline how to get from your past clunky software to best practice systems in your industry. My name is ... and I will be ... (summarising the presentation objective)."

Note how you introduce your topic with a strong pathos opening, before introducing yourself.

Other tips for starting a presentation effectively include exuding confidence, dropping the pleasantries, and going straight to the purpose and agenda. Alternatively, outlining your expertise, beginning with a realistic promise, or perhaps falling back on a relevant quote or a pop culture reference. Here are some additional techniques:

Act 2: The Body of your Presentation

As a general rule, for a 20-minute presentation you should not have any more than one or two goals.

Referring to your presentation plan, bring forward or create key messages for your goals and each objective. Limit your objectives and therefore your central messages to three or four and build your presentation around these key points. Here are some tips for creating the main body of your presentation:

- Review your presentation purpose / goal and objectives
- Identify main points and sub-points for each objective – each main point should include information that supports the purpose / goals.
- Identify and include important, relevant facts and data from your background research. This supports building logos and pathos, and enhances your credibility (ethos)
- Balance each main point: i.e. spend roughly the same amount of time on each main point.
- Include transitions (segues) that help the listeners understand how the ideas relate to one another. (Segues are explained later.)

At the beginning of each section introduce the purpose of the section and at the end, summarize central messages at the end and as you go through the material, then segue. Don't wander off on side-tracks - people want you to get to the point. Similarly, humor should be sparingly used, as some people find overuse annoying and unprofessional.Good flow and logic combined with skillful delivery creates a favorable outcome for your firm or BA team. So, next you need to plan how to plan for a successful conclusion.

Act 3: Conclusion

The conclusion of your presentation is not merely a formality; it is a powerful tool that can significantly impact audience engagement and retention. Think of your conclusion as the grand finale of a performance — it should leave your audience with a sense of closure and a clear understanding of the main messages you aimed to convey.

The final moments of your presentation should not only reinforce the information shared, but also leave a memorable imprint on the minds of your listeners. A well-crafted conclusion has the potential to resonate with your audience long after the presentation ends. You're looking for 'Wow'!It's in the final slides of your presentation that you can share the crucial information that the audience was looking for, be it contact information, your final offer or the key takeaways from your presentation.

Not only that, if you expect your audience to take a desired action after your presentation is over, it's the last section of your presentation which has the potential to motivate them toward it. A specific call-to-action is a statement where you ask the client what outcome you would like them to do.

Example: "Please consider our proposal! " **[Call to action]**
"It will benefit your firm by ...." **[Why they should act]**
"Your current issue is impacting your firm (in this way) and continues to do so" **[Why they should act NOW!]**

In general, your conclusion and close should be clear and concise and include:

1. Value proposition restatement – remind the audience of your presentation topic, value and benefits.
2. Main point review – remind the audience of your main points (in the order in which they appeared in your presentation).
3. Summary of any key points or agreements made by the client during the presentation.
4. Clincher statement – leave the audience with something to think about regarding your presentation.
5. Powerful closing statement of call to action.
6. Final slide with contact details.

Prepare questions ahead to ensure you achieve your goals and objectives and to fill any awkward silence at the end when you ask the client a question or for feedback.

Things to Avoid

There are many examples of things a competent, confident presenter learns to avoid at the end of a professional presentation. Build your skills through awareness of the pitfalls, and by seeking feedback from a trusted colleague.

There's always something to learn by observing a skilled presenter, but don't fall into the trap of comparing yourself, especially if you are just starting out. Rather, observe what they do: how they present, what techniques they use, and also, what they don't do.

Overloading the Conclusion

Avoid overwhelming your audience with additional details. Don't be tempted to introduce new information in the conclusion, unless you specifically including a summary of an agreement or key point from your client, made during the presentation. Instead, focus on reinforcing the key points you've already covered, leaving a lasting impression without introducing cognitive overload.

Ending Abruptly

Conclude your presentation deliberately and avoid abrupt endings. An abrupt finish may leave your audience feeling disoriented and can detract from the impact you aim to create. Instead, create a memorable ending with a clincher statement and call to action then pause for at least 10 seconds. This ensures that your audience recognizes the conclusion and has a moment to absorb the final thoughts.

Using Clichés or Generic Statements

Steer clear of clichés and generic statements in your conclusion. Instead of defaulting to common phrases like "Thank you for your attention," strive for authenticity. Craft a closing statement that aligns with your presentation's unique content and leaves a distinctive impression. Craft your final slide carefully.

Overly Complex Language

Using overly complex language in the conclusion can create confusion and diminish the impact of your message. Keep your language clear, concise, and accessible to ensure your audience grasps your final thoughts. This is particularly important if not everyone is technology savvy, or if you have people in the room whose first language may not be the same as yours.

Lack of Enthusiasm

Concluding with a lack of enthusiasm can leave your audience uninspired. Infuse energy into your delivery, emphasising the importance of your key messages and leaving a positive lasting impression[43].

Using a three-act approach will help you provide structure and flow. Appeal to the logos (logic), pathos (emotion) and ethos (ethics) of your audience, remembering your presentation is also a call to action! You want the audience to make a decision to act at the end of your presentation. So, make sure you end with a question or call to action.

Now we turn our attention to you as a presenter.

The Art of Presenting with Confidence

We know from experience that presenting with confidence requires careful preparation as well as a good knowledge of the role of the presenter as an influencer. Our number 1 tip?

Top Tip: Practice your presentation! We strongly recommend practicing your pitch aloud until you feel confident and comfortable. Often, if you have written your presentation, when saying it out loud you might find you stumble over words or phrases. Repeat these phrases to create 'muscle memory' until they are clear. Also, if a section / word doesn't sound right, change it in your practice session.

Prepare a culturally appropriate communication

In today's diverse workplace, communication issues can quickly take on an added dimension of complexity when dealing with people of a culture different from yours. Table 9-1 provides some ideas.

Even if there is no language barrier, cross-cultural communication is an important consideration. Every culture has its own set of values, and assumptions when it comes to face-to-face interactions. This means cultural norms can sometimes make getting your point across quite achallenge. Worse, the challenge may be something you are completely unaware of. This is why planning to communicate and understanding who will be present is so important.

Table 9-1 Cultural communication considerations

Area	Considerations
Understand etiquette	Many cultures have specific etiquette around the way they communicate, especially in formal settings. For example, many cultures expect a degree of formality at the beginning of communication between individuals. Every culture has its own specific way of indicating this formality: Some have protocols for starting a meeting; others use language formally such as 'Herr' and 'Frau' in Germany; ways of greeting formally such as the Māori Hongi; or, protocols around who speaks first etc. Be aware and don't make the mistake of jumping straight to first name terms, until you receive a cue from the other person to do so.
Avoid slang and informal language	All languages have a comprehensive range of slang, idioms and sayings. Your audience may understand the individual words you have said, but not the context or the meaning. As a result, you could end up confusing them or at worst, offending them. It also pays to avoid colloquialisms and swearing or more casual language as these can also cause confusion or offence.

Area	Considerations
Speak slowly and clearly	Even if English is the common language in a cross-cultural situation, do not speak at your normal conversational speed. Watching your pace and speak clearly, pronouncing words properly. Break your sentences into short, definable sections and give your listener time to translate and digest your words as you go if English is their second language. But don't slow down too much as exaggerating this might seem patronizing! This suggestion also applies to people speaking in their second language, as even if they are fluent, their delivery might be heavily accented and challenging to follow.
Keep it simple	Too many consultants hide behind important-sounding language, jargon, and technical terms. Please stop it! In a cross-cultural conversation, there's no need to make it harder. Keep it simple. Two syllable words are much easier to understand than three syllable words, and one syllable words are better than two syllable words. Say 'Please do this as soon as you can', rather than 'Please do this at your earliest convenience.'
Listen Actively	Active listening is a very effective way to improve cross cultural communication, and to show respect. Restate, reframe or summarise to check your understanding, and ask frequent questions. This helps build rapport and ensures that important information doesn't get missed or misunderstood.
Talk in concise sound bites	When people are speaking English as their second language it's better to talk to them in short exchanges rather than delivering a long monologue that might be difficult for them to follow.
Be careful with humor	Many cultures take business very seriously and believe in always behaving professionally and following protocols. Consequently, they may not appreciate the use of humor and jokes in a business context. Without awareness, your quip or joke could be deeply offensive.
Avoid closed questions	Don't phrase a question that needs a 'yes' or 'no' answer. In many cultures it is difficult or embarrassing to answer in the negative, so you will always get a 'yes' even if the real answer is 'no'. Ask open-ended questions that require information as a response instead.

The presentation is often 'where the rubber meets the road' But the heart of a good pitch is the quality of your materials, starting with targeting your audience.

Let's consider some of the influencing techniques used by seasoned presenters.

Presenting with influence

Before you have uttered your first word, you have already created an impression, often a first impression. As Greg's old mentor Bryn used to say:

"You don't get a second chance to make a first impression."

You need to pay attention to some subtle but important aspects of a presentation: cultural awareness, dress and grooming, stance, hands, eyes and voice. Know how to use each of these to influence your audience.

Dress and grooming

This is not an area on which we will dwell. However, your dress and grooming are an important part of your presentation. The important thing is that it is appropriate for the situation. Many believe that if you are 'expert' enough then people will forgive your dress and grooming issues. Not everyone is so forgiving. We are not here to give fashion advice but, as a general rule, we suggest you dress up a little, and more formally than is necessary.

A few years ago, there was a practice of attempting to mimic the dress of your clients. We suggest this can lead to a confusing corporate image and would recommend that you set a corporate or team standard of dress for such occasions and keep to this standard.

While times have changed and dress standards are no longer as formal as they used to be, if presenting, people will take greater notice of, and pay more attention to, someone who is well groomed and professionally dressed. Pay attention to details – clean shoes for example!

Next, we provide insights into influencing through the way you present.

Influencing with your Eyes

When you make eye contact with a person in the audience, you open up a path of direct communication.

From the audience member's point of view, you are no longer addressing the group, you are addressing them personally. We like to call this presentation technique: narrowcasting.

Eye contact is a way of demonstrating your honesty and openness. Throughout the ages, cultures have alluded to eyes being a window to the soul. By making open eye contact with as many of the audience as possible, you are maximizing personal connections and projecting your integrity at the same time. Hiding your eyes behind sunglasses is very disconcerting.

In his book, "The Power of Eye Contact", Michael Ellsberg[44] describes how Bill Clinton used eye contact to influence a nation. When he talked to someone either in a group or individually, he gave them his undivided attention through continuous eye contact.

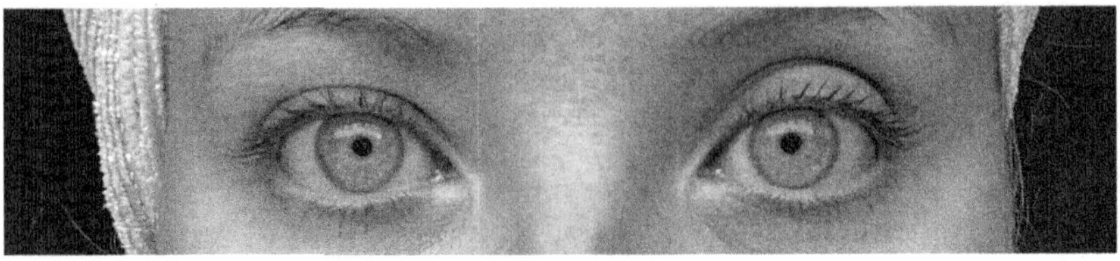

When presenting, you should consider what you are saying and to whom it might be important. If in a small group of identified clients, an experienced presenter will present a particular point to a particular person in the group using directed eye contact and other narrowcasting techniques.

> **Example**: When presenting on negotiation techniques at a large IT infrastructure provider in India, Greg was talking about the technique of bringing an independent senior figure with a high profile into a negotiation, to break a deadlock. While making this point, he made eye contact with the most senior person in the room (second-in-charge of the organisation) thereby acknowledging their power and influence.

By making eye contact with the audience, you can gauge their reaction to your presentation and vary it if necessary. If their eyes are 'glazing over' or even worse, closing, then it is time to change presentation strategy. One way to do this is to throw a question to a senior figure in the audience. Employees always pay attention to the boss. Or, if possible, ask your audience to discuss or do something (discuss something among themselves) to re¬invigorate their attention.

Combining eye contact with a directed hand gesture, a step forward and direct front-on stance, from the centre-front of your presentation area narrows the communication target even further. We will talk about all of these techniques as the chapter progresses.

Influencing with your Voice

This is a lifelong learning exercise. Mastering your own voice in presentations (and life in general) takes awareness and practice. Let's start with the basics:

Speak clearly and don't mumble. Watch your tendency to fade at the end of a sentence creating an inaudible moment – a drop off at the end of your sentence. Speak loudly enough so that everyone in the room can hear you - start with a sound check if necessary.

Remember to speak to your audience and not to a whiteboard or screen.

Inject variety into your voice. This creates tonal interest. First, there is volume. After ensuring that everything you say can be heard by everyone who needs to hear, then you can play a little with volume. One interesting technique is the loud whisper. A leading TV financial reporter would always give his market report in a loud whisper, creating the impression that he was telling you a secret.

The second variation is ***pace***. Nervous presenters, who want to deliver and get out as quickly as possible, tend to speed up leaving the audience unable to absorb the information and discern important points. However, used properly, pace can help with emphasis. Vary your pace, slowing down to communicate the important ideas. While not necessarily effective for all audiences, speaking slightly quicker on a technical topic can create an impression of expertise.

Master the art of the pause - stop altogether. In other words, pause intentionally for effect. You know you have an audience's attentionwhen you can prolong a pause and there is silence throughout.

Try it out. Just after you deliver a key or summary message - pause and let the point sink in with the audience. Try the contemplative pause, stopping for a moment to reflect or consider what you are about to say. Try the 'ponder' pause – ask a pertinent question then pause, stopping for a moment for your audience to reflect or consider. Embrace the power of the pause!

Vary your pitch. Pitch is the rise and fall of your speaking register. Normally you would lower your pitch at the end of a sentence after raising it during or at the beginning of a sentence. When asking a question, or making an assertion, you raise it at the end rather than lowering it.

Raising your pitch at the end of a sentence is how the listener determines that a statement is actually a question. For example, try saying "You understand this point" first lowering your pitch at the end, then raising it, to see the difference.

You can increase your pitch variation in sentences by being more intentional in your phrasing. Using phrases lets you raise and lower your pitch more often. Listen to a top television reporter as they do their 'walk to the camera'. They deliver their message in phrases, not sentences, emphasizing particular words with pitch variation, by placing variations at particular parts of the phrase.

Tone is a more difficult variant. A good example of a tone change is when a newsreader changes topic from say, the death of a famous person (serious tone) to a light¬ hearted story of baby ducks crossing the road (humorous tone). Tonal variation reflects the different parts of your character (gentleness, aggression, humour) and helps to maintain interest. Lack of variation is called a monotone and can result in a deadly boring presentation.

Using filler words. Now it is time to tackle some difficult presentation issues. First, we must talk about the generic filler: um or ah. If you are going to present professionally these ums have got to go. They are very distracting and annoying. Next time you are listening to someone present, start counting their ums and ahs over a period of 15-20 seconds. Multiply this figure to calculate the presenter's ***um-rate per minute***. Too often this can be up to 20 or so ums per minute.

The best technique to overcome the ums is to substitute it with a pause. Overcoming the ums normally requires assistance from others who agree to alert you to their presence, until you become self-aware enough to feel an enough to feel an 'um' coming and substitute it with silence.

A hidden variation to the um is when a person uses a particular word to fill the space until they decide what their next phrase is going to be. A common word in the teenage vernacular is 'like'. I have heard teenagers recount a story and use up to 20 'likes' per minute. My training response is to ask them to continue without using 'like'. They slow down and put together much more cohesive sentences.

Another favourite filler word is 'actually'. This is a grown-up version of 'like'. Another is 'ok', an attempt to gauge whether the audience has understood / agreed with the previous point or to signal a change of topic. These filler words are also common, distracting the audience from the message you are trying so hard to communicate.

Influencing with your Hands

Apart from your voice and perhaps your eyes, your hands are the next most expressive parts of your body. If you are wondering what to do with your hands, the default position is to keep them by your side in as relaxed a manner as your temperament allows.

Don't hide your hands: Putting one or both of your hands in your pockets can give the impression that you are hiding something. Holding your hands behind your back is okay if you are in the army, but otherwise it is better to keep them on show. Variations on hand hiding include hitching fingers or thumbs into belts or loops and arm folding.

Use your hands purposefully to emphasize certain points: The best presenters use their hands to paint a visual picture of what they are speaking about. Good singers and entertainers do this as a matter of course. Most politicians use their hands well. Gestures can be categorized into include-exclude, emphasis, directional and picture building.

Include-Exclude Gestures

Some common gestures include the palms-out: opening your arms and specifically, your palms (should be up), to the audience - this embraces them and includes them in your presentation. Prime ministers and presidents use this gesture all the time when addressing their 'fellow country men and women'.

Asking the audience a question is an inclusive act and so the arms out palms-up position can be used.

Folding your arms has the opposite effect. You are excluding the audience - creating a barrier between you and them. When presenting in a group with non-speakers at the side of the staging area, it is not unusual to see the non-speakers folding their arms. They are saying "I am not part of this. Keep me out of it". If you are part of a presentation team, then you are contributing to an impression on the audience. A bunch of practitioners in suits with their arms folded can look intimidating, a little bit like bodyguards ready to shoot the first person who asks a question.

Other profile-widening gestures that can be intimidating include the hands-on-hips and the thumbs-in-belt positions. These are best avoided.

Emphasis Gestures

A common emphasis gesture is the hand-chop. The hand-chop is the preferred gesture of orators. A variation is the double-hand-chop, where the hands are facing parallel to each other and act in unison.

Another emphasis gesture is the finger-jab or finger-point. This gesture should be used very carefully, as some cultures are sensitive to pointing gestures. So, the direction of the finger-jab should be directed downwards, preferably at an object, and certainly not at a person.

Borrowing from church hand-signals, some speakers adopt the 'prayer-hands' gesture, palms together pointing generally upwards. This can emphasise thoughtfulness and sincerity in the point you are from prayer-hands to palms-out is very church-like, and can be powerful but should be used sparingly.

There are so many emphasis gestures (e.g. thumbs-up, A-OK, stop-sign etc.), so it is impossible to list them all. These are very important in presentations. We encourage you to observe others and build your emphasis gesture repertoire.

Directional Gestures

While travelling overseas, have you asked directions and received them in a language with which we were not overly familiar? I learnt to ask people with a cane, who would often respond by waving their cane in accordance with the lefts and rights that I needed to take to reach my destination. I would count their gestures and set off in search of another person with a cane or hopefully good hand gestures.Directional hand gestures are well known to all and most famously used by air stewards to indicate the restrooms and exits during the pre-flight demonstration. Just like aeroplane etiquette, when clients are on your site, it is good manners to indicate emergency exits and restrooms. Our advice is to use the complete arm and hand and avoid finger-pointing or thumb gestures when indicating directions, just as airline stewards do.

Building Gestures

Superior presenters will build a picture with their hands. Using techniques from mime artists they will outline shapes, mimic recognizable actions and paint the air with interesting contours and profiles. To be effective, the picture building gesture must match the words or concept you are talking about at that particular moment.

For example, if talking about integrating two information systems you might bring your hands together and interlock your fingers. Consider what gesture you might use when talking about the 'fast pace of technology', 'environmental chaos' or 'changing the goalposts'.

You can be creative in painting your visual picture and generate a lot of energy and attention from the audience. Remember, however, that overuse of gestures can divert the attention of the audience away from your message. Don't overdo it! Usually, the bigger the venue, the more people, the grander your hand / arm gestures can be.

Influencing with your Stance

Often overlooked, the stance is another important aspect in the presentation toolkit. Unless there is a good reason, you should never sit down while you are presenting, unless it is an informal setting with amaximum audience of three.

You should stand so that you are reasonably steady, upright, authoritative and facing your audience. Some presenters favour the right side or the left side of the room. So, their natural stance turns them slightly away from part of the audience for most of the presentation. Be careful that you do not present to one side of the room, only to find your decision-maker is on the other side. Some presenters will face the projected screen for a great deal of the presentation. Let's discuss this further.

Many presenters employ projected slides to support their intended message to the audience. They also use them as speaking points - reminders of what to say and when. This necessitates constantly turning to the screen to see what to say next. This means that the speaker is constantly reinforcing that the message is contained in the slides.

The question becomes: What or who is the definitive source of the message? The answer must always be the presenter!

Ensure that you don't cross your feet or lean on one leg (usually associated with the single hand in the pocket stance). Swaying and rocking can be very distracting and in severe cases cause sea-sickness.

When asked a question you should lean forward (indicating your interest) and focus your full attention on the questioner. Keep your stance directed at the questioner showing you have their full attention.

Stand Still or Move Around?

Now we come to another big question! Stay still or pace? Staying still is very authoritative and of course necessary when you are speaking from a podium. Moving around injects energy but too much and it becomes a distraction. In a large space you may have to walk around between your props. Most consulting presentations are done in a smaller venue such as a boardroom and so moving about tends to be limited.

Using a podium can be helpful for holding notes and controlling a screen presentation, but it tends to hide most of the speaker, perhaps restricting your hand movements (podium speakers tend to hold it with one or both hands) and restricting your stance. However, it keeps you still and so helps with portraying authority. Nervous speakers like podiums because it gives them something solid to hold while they are presenting. Or they can hide behind them. Watch out because podiums enable you to tap and rock, movements that are distracting. Avoid these.

When standing behind a broad, opaque podium, all you can see is the speaker's head and shoulders. This can have the odd effect of over emphasizing your hand movements. My advice is to come out from behind the podium, if possible, and stand fully in front of your audience. This way you can use the full range of presentation influencing techniques.

Using your Stage Properly

When presenting standing up you are effectively on a stage and there are techniques that will professionalize your presentation. In Figure 9-1 the sections of a stage are listed. There may or may not be a podium. If you use a podium, that is fine, but it may also be restrictive. Let us imagine that there is no podium. How and when do you use the different sections of a stage in your presentation.

When talking to your slides you will either be Stage Left or Stage Right between Centre and Upstage. If you are controlling the slides yourself, ideally the laptop that is controlling them is placed on a small table in front of you so you don't have to turn around to check that that right slide is showing. And you can refer to the contents if necessary. Using a remote control to change slides creates a smoother look or having a colleague change the slides for you is even better. In that case, try and avoid saying "next slide" - rather use a small hand signal so that the slide change can happen while you are talking.

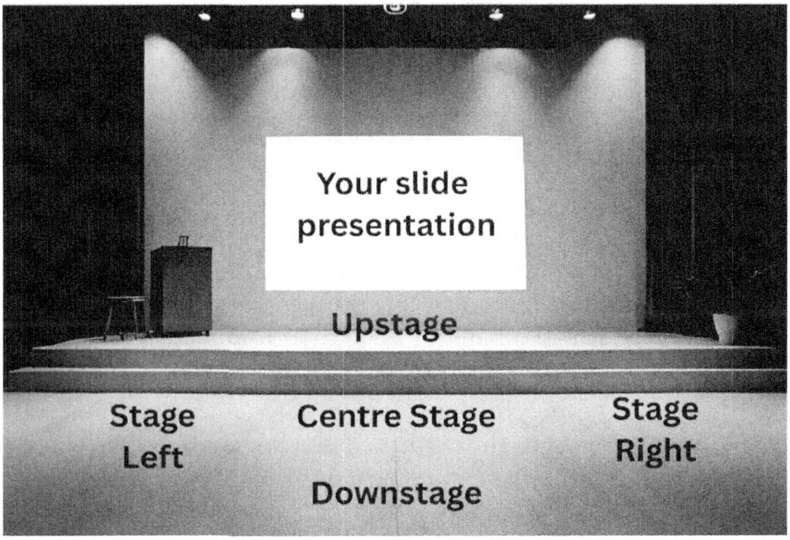

Figure 9-1 Sections of a stage

By staying Stage Left or Right you are placing the emphasis on the slide. If you want to move the focus back to you as a speaker move to Centre Stage - for actors this is where they want to be to draw attention to themselves. The further Upstage Left or Right you are, the more you are taking focus off yourself and putting the focus on the slides. When you want to emphasise a point you move Downstage and more Centre Stage. Similarly, if someone asks you a question you move Down Stage / Centre Stage. When answering the question, you 'narrowcast' (directly look into the eyes of the questioner, lean forward a little and direct the answer to the person who asked the question. You might adopt a more open stance with an open single-handed gesture i.e. as if you were offering them a 'helping hand'.

Similarly, when you open the floor for questions, you stand a little more Upstage and Centre Stage so as not to be less intimidating and 'forward'. You adopt an open-handed position to make questions more welcoming. If the question is on one of your slides, find the slide and move to Left or Right Stage so the audience can see the information requested. Then move back to Centre Stage to take back control of the dialogue.

When you are on stage, your position will move the focus from you as the presenter to the slides and back again. The steps in Figure 9-1 are just to emphasise Upstage and Downstage. You will almost always be on a flat surface. Use the stage, your stance, hands, eyes and voice to enhance the presentation. And now we will discuss a few more techniques and considerations.

Presenting the Material

This section provides general advice on presenting the material. Let's start with four advisories around behaving appropriately:

Advisory 1: Be professional: be careful not to be critical of current or past events within the company, because you may be presenting to those who brought about those events.

Advisory 2: Be respectful of other's time: your presentation materials should be long enough to cover the subject but short enough to be interesting.

Advisory 3: Be prepared to present in person and virtually for all presentations.

Advisory 4: Be respectful: do not swear or use inappropriate, offensive words or concepts. Be sensitive to contemporary social practices e.g. do not start your presentation with "Ladies and Gentlemen" as you may offend those who identify as neither.

But first, let's look at the art of creating flow.

The Art of using Segues to create Flow

Your audience will pay attention so long as your message is relevant to them, and as long as you know where you are going. So, pay a lot of attention to structure (covered earlier in this chapter) and flow.

Flow is the art of connecting one section or point to the next. The art of connection is dependent on your use of segues. A segue is a phrase or sentence that relates one point to the next, thereby creating flow. So, the segue between Act 1 and 2 in the example could be:

> **Example**: "Now that we have discussed and agreed our understanding of the issues you are facing, let us now turn to some options to mitigate or eliminate these issues".

A segue guides the listener through the logic of the presentation structure. As well as connecting forward with a segue, you can also connect backward - linking your current point to prior points made in the presentation, or better still, the discussion with the client. Segues also provide a signal to the next speaker that it is their turn.

Example: "Having now covered our approach to addressing your issue, my colleague Atlas Mac will address the technical infrastructure that we will be using."

Dealing with presentation anxiety

Almost everyone experiences some level of speech anxiety when delivering a presentation. Effective presenters are those who use that energy to help them in their efforts.

Consider the following when managing your speech anxiety before and/or during your presentation:

- Practice helps lessen speech anxiety.
- Don't let negative self-talk undermine your efforts. Instead, turn those negative messages – like "I'm going to embarrass myself" or "I'm going to fall" – into positive messages – like "I'm going to be successful" and "I am poised and self-confident.
- Visualise your success.
- Remember to breathe. If you take a few deep breaths before starting your presentation, it will oxygenate your brain and calm your nervous system giving you more focus.
- Pretend you're confident.
- Remember that your audience wants you to be successful.
- Drink water prior to delivering your presentation to avoid a dry mouth/throat..
- Remember that the audience will likely not notice your anxiety.

Whether you are a university or college student or a working professional, the more you prepare and practice and the more experience you have delivering presentations, the more effective you will be.

Chapter Summary

Pitch presentations are a very important aspect of a consultant and business analyst's professional skills. The outcome that practitioners are seeking is to influence the client towards engaging their services or including them in a project team.

Clear, well-paced and interesting delivery, without distracting mannerisms, will maximize your chances of success.

The art of designing, delivering and ending a powerful, professional presentation is a skill that evolves with practice and creativity. Embrace the challenge, experiment with various techniques, and tailor your conclusions to resonate with your audience. By doing so, you'll elevate your presentation skills and ensure that your every slide leaves a lasting imprint on your clients' minds.

In the next chapter we tackle how practitioners deal with change.

Endnotes

41. Molinsky, A. and Tan, J. (2021) How To Get Your Big Ideas Noticed by the Right People Harvard Business Review https://hbr.org/2021/04/how-to-get-your-big-ideas-noticed-by-the-right-people

42. Your value proposition is the core of your presentation. It is the statement that summarizes why your offer is valuable, relevant, and unique for your client. It should answer three questions: What problem do you solve? How do you solve it better than anyone else? And what client benefits do you deliver? To craft a compelling value proposition, use clear and concise language, emphasize the benefits over the features. Your goal is to create the basis to quantify your value with evidence in the main body of your presentation.

43. Some material in this section is based on https://presentationexperts.co.uk/a-guide-to-crafting-powerful-endings-inpresentations/

44. Ellsberg, M. (2010) The Power of Eye Contact Harper Collins. 9780061782213

Chapter 10 - Advanced Negotiation Techniques

Chapter guide

At some point in your career, you will have to negotiate with a client, senior leader, supplier or other party. You may be negotiating for yourself or on behalf of another party, such as your firm or your client. This chapter will teach you some principles and techniques to assist you in this process. If you master some or all of these techniques, then you will be able to employ them to your advantage, spot others using them, and understand the overall negotiation process a lot better. So long as there is equal power between the two parties negotiating, the better negotiator will generally have the advantage.

In this chapter, we cover:

- A definition of negotiation
- How to use engagement skills to build your negotiation competencies
- Planning and preparation to negotiate
- More ways to persuade using logos, pathos and ethos
- How to consider negotiation positions and offers.

Introduction to Negotiation

First, let's consider exactly what we mean by negotiation.

Definition: A negotiation is a dialogue between two parties, each of whom wants something from the other. It is a process during which the parties consider alternatives and aim to reach mutual agreement, usually around a set of interrelated issues.

Practitioners can use the logos-pathos-ethos model to assist them in understanding the dynamics of this process. But first we should have a close look at this definition, to see what might create advantage for the practitioner during this process. We will describe each part of our definition and explore it in depth.

De-composing the Definition of Negotiation

'Definition...a dialogue between two or more parties...'

This is a communication exercise that requires clarity of speech. If verbal communication is not your strength, you can't quite get your ideas out clearly, or trip up in your speech, then perhaps someone else can talk on your behalf during a complex negotiation. It is very common for parties to use professional negotiators or lawyers to lead a negotiation because they can normally communicate well and carefully. Our experience, however, is that most practitioners are normally well-spoken, intelligent individuals, and when given the right tools and frameworks, become sharp and competent negotiators.

Negotiation uses many of your Engagement Skills

Many of the skills and techniques discussed in Chapter 4 on Engagement apply directly to negotiation. This is because the engagement process is a negotiation. The techniques of discovery and the elicitation of requirements are also useful skills in the negotiation room. Practitioners have many useful skills to bring to the negotiating table, once they realize how to employ them.

Other skills from requirements elicitation, such as questioning, reflecting the requirements back to the other party, analysis and synthesis of the discussions, and attention to detail are all useful negotiation tools.

Use Logos, Pathos, and Ethos

Creating a better rationale, based on the facts elicited from the other party, helps practitioners to enhance their argument to their own advantage. Having the right, or a better argument is the logos tactic in a negotiation. Most amateurs believe that a better argument will win the day. They are normally frustrated to find out that this is mostly wrong. In negotiation, pathos and ethos are equally important and very powerful.

Practitioners with experience also realise during requirements elicitation that the way they present themselves to the other party (i.e. in a friendly and professional manner), will get better results. The positive relationship you build with the other party helps to open the communication channels, thus improving your ability to understand and empathise (not necessarily agree) with the other party's positions. [A position is the offering or stance of one party on a particular issue.] Creating a positive relationship is a pathos tactic.

Realizing that pathos is as equally important as logos in negotiation will make you a better negotiator. First of all, it is people who make decisions in negotiations, not machines, and people are driven by their instinctive emotional responses and behaviours. Most successful salespeople know that customers will buy products and services from people they like. In negotiation, the principle is the same. You are more likely to gain concessions from the other party if they like you.

Another realisation that assists in understanding the other party and their decisions, is that sometimes the attitude or position taken by that party is based on an emotional pretext.

The following example demonstrates the importance of emotional positions and closely held values in peoples' decision-making processes.

> Here's an example: Some years ago, the father of a friend helped paint Greg's house. The painter – we'll call him Bob - was a retiree from Bristol in England, so Greg asked him to paint all the tricky bits on his old house. Before Bob agreed to taking on the job, he asked Greg a question or two. "Do you follow football?" he asked, referring to soccer.
>
> Greg told him that he enjoyed watching the odd game but didn't follow it closely. Bob then asked whether Greg preferred any particular team from Bristol, the city in which he was born, schooled, worked, married and raised a family, one of whom emigrated to Australia.
>
> Greg answered that he had heard of the Bristol 'Spurs' but did not follow them. This was the right answer. Bob said that if Greg had indicated any preference at all for this team, he would not have taken the job. He was a Bristol 'City' fan!

So, here was a strongly held pathos - emotional position that had nothing whatever to do with painting the house but could have terminated our painting arrangement. There is no logic (logos) in this; no essence of fair play (ethos), just emotion (pathos). He simply would not have done the job, and no amount of logical argument or ethical propositioning would have changed his mind. From a cultural viewpoint, this type of attiture is probably accepted in regional England, but totally foreign in urban Australia. And that is why it didn't make sense to Greg at the time. Reflecting on it, however, he realised it was just another example of emotion-based decision-making.

> **Top Tip:** Once you realise that you can't win over an emotional position (pathos) with logical argument (logos), you have taken a step forward in your negotiation skill set.

The next consideration about this dialogue is that most people will negotiate in an ethical manner. IS professionals are normally smart and educated with considerable skills. They will negotiate fairly; stay true to their word (e.g. when they have agreed to a position, term or condition, they won't go back on their word); and, make fair and reasonable offers and concessions. If you find the other party unethical in their dealings, then consider your future business dealings with this party as uncertain and risky. If you perceive a party to be untrustworthy during a negotiation, ask yourself "do you really want to be in business with these people?"

'Definition…each of whom wants something from the other.'

Each party has something to offer in the exchange of value and benefit that is being negotiated. While the parties are negotiating and the deal is still open, it is reasonable to assume that the party on the other side of the table wants what the IS consultant has to offer. The negotiation is normally centred around an exchange of the client's money for the IS consultant's services, but both parties need to derive value. This could be a very superficial analysis of the situation – there may be other factors at play.

Know what you're trying to Achieve

When entering a negotiation, if you don't know what you are trying to achieve - i.e. what you want - then how will you know when you have got it? Let us expand a little.

From a practitioner's view, perhaps the person or team will gain experience in a new industry; be working with a new client and a promise of further work; gain significant profile by association with a new client; gain experience in a new field or with a specific software package, process or method; or, gain a foothold in a new market, country or region.

This additional value or benefit, if realised by the practitioner, could be very valuable. If the client also realizes it, then they can use this to gain more concessions from the practitioner. The questions for practitioners are therefore:

- Do you know what additional value might be gained from engaging with this client?
- Is it of value to you, your firm or your team or can you ignore this additional value, i.e. not give any concessions to the potential client for these extra benefits?

From the client's view. Similarly, using the example of an engagement negotiation: Does the client understand the additional benefits you may bring to the engagement such as lower risk, quality methods, tried and tested frameworks, individual and unique expertise, a network of associates who can provide advice, trustworthiness, a partnership approach, warranties over the work and a myriad of other benefits. The one question for the practitioner is:

Do you really know what your client wants?

For their Firm? For Themself?

Sometimes the person on the other side of the desk really wants to be a consultant themselves! We have seen this happen a few times. After the conclusion of a large engagement negotiation or selection process, one of the client personnel is hired by the consulting firm.

Is this ethical? No. Did it influence the outcome of the negotiation? Well, only the people involved will really know the answer to that question. This is an example of one alternative bargaining chip that can occur in negotiation.

'Definition...a process during which the parties consider alternatives...'

As each party moves towards the outcome that they want from the negotiation, each must give and take to reach a mutual agreement. This normally involves the consideration of different alternative solutions, which may be as simple as a change in the charge-out rate of a consultant, or a complex combination of different positions, terms and conditions associated with the deal.

Negotiating parties can view the process as a positive, shared problem-solving exercise or a battle between two opposing camps that ultimately ends with one party being the winner and the other a loser.

The style of negotiation will often drive the types of alternatives offered and considered. We will talk about this a little later in the chapter. The style of the two parties will also determine whether an agreement is reached and how it is reached.

'Definition... to reaching mutual agreement.'

The aim is always to reach an agreement that satisfies both parties. It is inevitable that both parties may not end up with all the outcomes that they would have preferred, but nevertheless each party will hopefully end up with a satisfactory result. When mutual agreement is reached, the negotiation is concluded.

'Definition...conclude around a set of interrelated issues'

When a negotiation is a simple exchange e.g. a simple product is exchanged for money, the process is often very quick. As the product or service becomes more complex, the issues overlap and impact on each other.

Often the negotiators are grouping or trading off sets of issues during the process. This increases the complexity of the negotiation and requires one of two things:

- a person who can keep and juggle several issues in their mind; or,
- very careful note taking.

The best negotiators are usually very bright with an eye for detail, exactly the profile of an IS consultant.

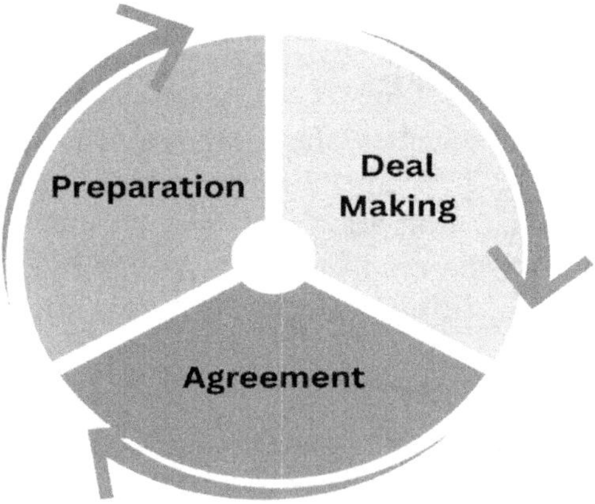

Figure 10-1 Elements of Negotiation

We have spent a little time talking about what negotiation is because each of these attributes become important during the process. Once again, we have tried to create a scaffold for understanding the negotiation process that is consistent with the way the practitioners view the world: steps, structure, attributes - in other words, a framework. There are three basic phases in the negotiation lifecycle: Preparation, Deal-making, and Agreement as shown in Figure 10-1.

These three phases all take place within a logical, emotional, ethical, and sometimes mythical or imagined environment.

Preparation

Before starting preparation, it is helpful to understand that there are two main types of negotiators.

The first type is a confident, experienced person who strongly believes in their negotiation skills but is often untrained. Sometimes, this negotiator's idea of preparation is to think about a couple of issues while they are travelling to the negotiation site.

The second type has pursued knowledge in the art of negotiation, tested and practised that knowledge in the negotiation room and so prepares for the negotiation carefully (perhaps talking through their strategy with someone else beforehand). Once you are trained in these techniques, you will learn to recognise them in others. When you recognise that the other party is trained, you need to be a little more careful.

Unless there is a power imbalance between the two parties, the second negotiator will usually prevail. A power imbalance occurs when one party does not have to give away any concessions during a negotiation e.g. when you sign up for a mobile phone contract you either accept the terms and conditions and price or you don't get the service.

If, however, you are a large government department negotiating to buy thousands of mobile phone services in a competitive market, the power between the two parties is more evenly balanced and the terms, conditions and price become negotiable.

Under this scenario, you want to be the second type of negotiator, skilled and well prepared. Here are some things to think about when in the preparation phase.

Know who you're negotiating with

An essential part of preparation that is useful in the room (i.e. in the face-to-face negotiation meeting) is personal information about the other parties. Personal facts about the other negotiators will help you identify their motivations, understand their style and create 'common ground' to help build and sustain good relations. People who like you will more likely engage you and will generally treat you better in their dealings with you.

Prepare for the negotiation to Fail

Without wanting to sound negative, the first consideration a negotiator should have is what to do should the negotiation fail. This is not an invitation to a self-pity session, but rather a realistic look at alternative paths you and your firm may take. Of course, you really want the deal to go through; but at any cost?As a practitioner, there will often be limits to your financial and ethical positions, which you probably do not want to cross. If your normal charge-out rate is $1000 a day, can you really accept $500 and still pay the rent, your overheads, your employees and yourself? Are you willing to write a report for a client that does not reflect the real situation or outcome thereby putting your reputation at risk? Will you implement a system that you know won't work for the client? Will you execute a project when you have no expertise in the area?

> **Top Tip:** In your preparation for any negotiation, you must prepare and set out the lines that you will not cross.

Crossing these lines will create unacceptable risk to your financial health, integrity, and reputation. It doesn't really matter what expertise you have gained, what methods and frameworks you have developed or what experience you have accrued, because without a healthy financial position, integrity, and a good reputation, you are headed for failure.

If the negotiation is not about engagement, but rather is an issue during the execution of a project (such as scope creep), you will still have to decide what to do if the dialogue breaks down irretrievably. Such an outcome is often foreseen in the contract for services or engagement letter and set out in clear terms. Usually, a client and consultant will only enter serious talks with the expectation that there will be an active outcome.

Again, we stress that this is not about negativity, but rather about protecting yourself and your firm should the relationship with the client break down. If you haven't started the project, then you should think about what alternatives you have should the project / engagement not go ahead (e.g. there are other clients to win - check the pipeline report). If you have started the project, this is your exit strategy.

Winning at all costs

When some people enter the negotiation room their emotion and ego overtake logic. They want to "win" at any cost. If they don't "win" it is a personal affront associated with a negative emotional response. Think of it as a temporary uncontrollable addiction. An example is the person at an auction who will keep bidding until they win the item, spending far beyond their budget. This intense emotion also affects negotiators with poor self-control. A person who believes their negotiation skills exceed the others' risk becoming aggressive, assuming fixed positions and failing to give concessions even when they are reasonable. As the negotiation progresses, their need to close the deal intensifies and poor decisions are made, driven by pathos. Be aware of this behaviour.

Practitioners with poor negotiating skills will concentrate on the fees as the single bargaining chip, offering discounts to clients to get the job. A wily client, who senses emotion creeping into the consultant's offering, will drive the fees lower, perhaps beyond what the consultant can afford. Again, knowing the logos limits of your bargaining (e.g. fees, scope, time, risk etc.) and having the discipline to stick to them can save you from poor pathos-driven decisions.

Confidence and Expectations

Related to winning at all costs is the notion of confidence. Some negotiators develop unrealistic expectations of the results of a negotiation dialogue and this expectation will help determine their level of confidence.

If a practitioner lacks confidence in the negotiation dialogue for any reason, this may lead to undervaluing their service value and driving down fee expectations. A lack of confidence can lead to desperate attempts to win the deal, even when such desperation is not warranted. Sharp clients will sense this desperation and use it to negotiate a better deal for themselves.

Conversely, too much confidence about the expectations of the deal can lead to poor negotiation outcomes because the negotiator won't consider reasonable trade-offs. Faced with a trained negotiator, the overconfident deal-maker will become frustrated and more competitive. They will reduce the dialogue to a win-lose game, make irrational decisions and overlook alternative multi-issue deals. A lack of confidence or too much confidence drives emotional responses when logical responses are required. The deal may be lost entirely if a negotiator loses control of their emotions.

A negotiator must remain open-minded about the outcome, flexible to alternative ways forward and self-aware of responses based on emotion rather than logic and ethics.

Consider your positions

All IS consulting firms must adopt a set of principles to guide them in their working life with clients. Such principles include the behaviour of the consultants, ethical practices, fee policy, work-life balance, quality of work, image and appearance, availability, reliability and the professional conduct of a firm's affairs. These principles will assist consultants in the firm (and teams of BAs) to adopt positions prior to entering a negotiation dialogue.

To prepare for a negotiation, an IS Consultant should consider the issues that may arise and adopt positions about these issues. Some examples of issues include minimum daily rates for consultants, time and scope considerations, risk appetite, access to senior client personnel, and senior management support.

If more than one person is involved in the negotiation from the practitioner side, then these positions are best agreed beforehand. A wily client will pick up on disagreements between the practitioner personnel (in-fighting) and use them to their advantage.

This is not to suggest that your positions won't change during the negotiation process; on the contrary, you may give concessions in return for other advantages and benefits. If you don't have a starting point, however, the other party may define it for you.

To prepare your positions (e.g. time to complete the engagement), you may seek information from the client about their situation and issues.

Deal-making

A negotiation is a dialogue between two parties, each of whom want something from the other. It is a process during which the parties consider alternatives and aim to reach mutual agreement, usually around a set of interrelated issues.

During the dialogue, information is exchanged (logos), emotions arise or are generated by the information exchange (pathos) and ethical behaviours are expressed or implied (ethos). In the room we also encounter behaviours and positions based on mythical tradition or simply not based on anything (muthos).

During the dialogue, the two parties exchange information with each other to assist in establishing their position or change the other's position. The more you know about the issue at hand, the better logical argument you can put to the other party.

For example, when negotiating a telecommunication contract both parties knew the telecommunications company (telco) had issues with their billing system. The telco would frequently undercharge clients because certain activities were batched into the billing system and not aligned with the monthly billing cycle. Their position was that the undercharged amounts should attract small interest charges. This position is logically and ethically very fair, easy for the telco to defend and difficult to argue against. We knew that their billing system had been configured to automatically apply these interest charges.

You see, the thing about big telco contracts for large organisations is that you are dealing with thousands of small bills that aggregate into one big bill, so the process must be automated otherwise it would be too expensive to manually adjust the undercharges. We knew from talking to telco software programmers that there was no functionality to automate overcharging events. So, in the rare instance that a telco overcharged, the system could not automatically calculate interest owed to the client.

Using logic and ethics (the sense of fair play- if you do it to me, I should be able to do it to you) we anticipated that they would charge us interest on underpayments if they would pay the same interest rate on overpayments. This is a fair, logical and ethical position to balance their original position on underpayments and therefore difficult to argue against. They agreed. We then played the 'information' card and asked: "Can your system do this?"

The telco lead negotiator was a salesperson who responded with a quick "yes thinking this was a (logical) feature of their system. So, we then asked the lead negotiator and their technical support people to check this, which they were happy to do thinking that such a feature would be there for sure. We moved on to other issues and positions. The next day, the telco team came back to the negotiating room to inform us that their system did not automatically deduct interest from overcharging and that overcharging was a rare event "so it wouldn't affect us much". They went on to say that undercharging was common and still wanted to charge interest on the undercharges.

We held our position easily because it was fair and logical, so eventually they had to drop the interest on undercharging. This little piece of information about their billing system saved our client a lot of money. Since both parties behaved fairly throughout the contract, it was concluded in a very friendly and cooperative manner. Each believed they got a good deal.

Most negotiation occurs superficially without an awareness of technique. Good technique is about the presentation of information to support your range of positions. Having prepared thoroughly, you should have your 'information house in order'. If you don't, and the other party is well informed and prepared, then get ready to be outwitted, usually as a result of the other party's better logos position.

Positions – working towards agreement

During the deal-making process, each party will establish positions, sometimes called anchors as shown in Figure 10-2. An anchor is a point from which negotiators add or subtract. People create anchors based on past information, industry standards or just by making them up!

Most people rely on anchors to orient themselves in the negotiation. Once the anchors are set, they judge decisions and trade-offs in relation to these anchors. But remember, these anchors may just be based on a whim. When the positions vary, the range of negotiation is established. These positions are easily understood with a single-issue negotiation.

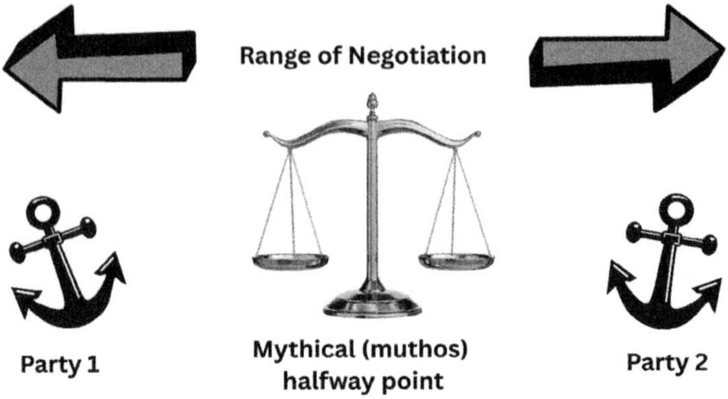

Figure 10-2 Anchors and negotiation range

Consider the following example...anchors. But remember, these anchors may just be based on a whim. When the positions vary, the range of negotiation is established. These positions are easily understood with a single-issue negotiation.

Consider the following example...

> **Example**: Party 1 may want to charge $10,000 for a project. Party 2 may only want to pay $8,000. Each is flexible and willing to change their positions. So, Party 1 increases their position to $8,200 and Party 2 reduces their position to $9,500. The process continues until neither party wants to budge from their position, or agreement is reached.

Commonly, one party will suggest they compromise on a half-way point. Apart from the ethical sense of fairness, this half-way point is a mythical point arising from a traditional process of settling and deal-making. Every time you move your position you also move this mythical half-way point.

Consider the bids in Table 10-1. In this negotiation, the two parties are heading towards a mythical half-way point of $8,750, a probable ending point for the deal. Party 2 is doing a little better by bidding in smaller increments.

This is a suggested strategy. Make your increments small and bid them slowly. A fast, large incremental bid indicates that you are prepared to change more. A slow, small incremental bid signals an unwillingness to move too much from your position.

Table 10-1 Example of single-issue price bids

Party 1 Offer	Party 2 Offer	Mythical Halfway Point
$10,000	$8,000	$9,000
$9,500	$8,200	$8,850
$9,100	$8,400	$8,750
$9,000	$8,500	$8,750

Walking Away

Without a pre-decided walk away price, you can agree to taking on a consulting project that will result in a loss to the firm. A good negotiator in the other party can sometimes take you below your walk away price with arguments such as the promise of better work to come or how valuable this experience will be to you. Don't take the bait. If they promise you future work, you can suggest that this is included in the contract – expect this suggestion to be declined.

If you decide on a walk away position (for any reason e.g., the job is too big or outside your experience,) then you need to have in mind what you will do if you do walk away. You see, if you don't really have an alternative then you may be trapped into taking any offer on the table. A sharp negotiator could pick up on this and use it to drive the price and other conditions down to a detrimental level.

When you reach that walk away point, politely tell the prospective client that you can't do the job under those conditions, and you will cease the negotiation. Don't bluff. Walk away because it is the right thing to do. Perhaps the client will reconsider their position if they really want you on the job. Furthermore, if the client successfully manages to negotiate with a competitor for a lower (what you consider to be a walk-away) price, often the project is doomed for failure because the competitor cannot provide the service at below cost or they cut the quality of the services and inevitably major issues arise. Even if you walk away, tell the client, should any issues arise between your competitor and the client, you are quite willing to re-open the negotiations.

Top Tip: In your preparation you will have decided what your 'walk away' position will be on price and other issues.

Fixed Pie vs. Expanding Pie

A fixed pie negotiation has a single issue such as price. Many negotiations are about single issues – these can create a Win-Lose outcome. If you are in a fixed pie negotiation and you are unhappy about the way it is going, then try expanding the pie. In other words, introduce another issue. If the client wants to force down the price on a consulting project, you can counter in several ways:

- Reducing the seniority / experience of the team [There is an old consulting saying: "If you pay peanuts, you get monkeys"].
- Reducing the scope of the project - normally the scope would be reduced by deleting activities at the end of the project, so that the client can request these once they see the benefits of those activities.

Sometimes a change in the terms and conditions can give the consultant some flexibility e.g., right to pull out of the project at any time. The more complex the agreement, the more issues you have to play with in the expanding pie.

One positive way to expand the pie is to inject variable performance-based objectives e.g. a percentage of revenues. Here's an example:

> **Example**: Airports normally charge airlines a fixed fee for landing their aircraft. A local airport wanted to attract more airlines and greater traffic so instead of fixing their landing fee they based it on the number of passengers on the plane. This was an incentive for more airlines to fly to that destination, building their business on the introduction of the new route. As the airline built their business, passenger numbers increased and so did the landing fees.

By changing the way you look at the deal, innovating with new ideas and approaches, and questioning the logic of 'conventional wisdom', you can create better deals in partnership with your clients.

The Flexible Pie

Sometimes you might be negotiating in a context that you are not sure about; that is, you don't have experience with the other side's view on the variables in the expanding pie. Best if I give you an example.

Example: A colleague of mine was offered a senior role at a European firm. He was to head up a subsidiary and was asked by the CEO to put forward a proposed compensation package. He prepared for this negotiation by looking at similar compensation packages but did not have information on what that particular company paid their executives. So he developed a list of all the components of a compensation package: Salary, Equity / Vesting Schedule, Revenue Share, Bonus Scheme, Benefits, Relocation Expenses, Accommodation Support and Travel Tier (1 - First Class, 2 - Business Class, 3 - Premium Economy, 4 - Economy). He then created his starting position. When he engaged in the negotiation, whenever they reduced one component he negotiated an increase in another component. Ultimately they gave him what he wanted because they recognised his skill in negotiation was going to be an enormous benefit for their firm.

Recording what has been Agreed

One issue with complex negotiations involving multiple issues is recording what has been agreed. Once an issue has been agreed upon, it should be noted in the minutes or the draft agreement. Because issues can be interrelated, the other party might want to come back and amend an agreed issue (i.e., change their mind).

Once this issue is 'undone', all associated bargains are back on the table (revert to their previously 'un-agreed' state). Most negotiators understand this, but some unethical or inexperienced negotiators think it is okay to undo part of the arrangement but still keep the benefits they gained. This is not okay. Good notetaking will assist you in assuring the ethos of the exchange.

Remember, a negotiation is about the exchange of value between parties. When each believes that the value they receive from the deal is beneficial, then agreement can be a pleasant and simple affair.

A good negotiator will sense the value offered to the other party depending on the responses. If a negotiator senses that a particular part of the deal holds a lot of value to the other party, they will increase the quantum of the trade-off.

For example, if there is no alternative - the client wants a particular piece of software written and needs it very quickly, they may not have time to scour the market. The practitioner could be opportunistic and charge an outrageous amount for this, but ordinarily ethos would prevail. It would not be the time, however, to offer a reduced fee rate either!

Preparing First Offers

Who makes the first offer? It depends. Sometimes it is appropriate for the consultant to make the first offer (e.g. on fees, risk, time, quality). Sometimes you want the client to make the first offer (e.g. scope). Just as for buying a house, your first offer should not be ridiculous. It should be ambitious but discussable.

You must be able to explain it using an APV (Attribute-Purpose-Value) statement. It should be based on industry norms, and you should have prepared the basis for the first offer in your preparation. If the other side are competent negotiators, they will also be prepared. The important point is to: ask for what you want; use Anchors; and, be observant – watch for 'flinches'. We explain these three useful techniques next.

Ask for what you want!

The other side might just say YES! Of course, you may have lingering doubts that you could have gotten more out of the deal. You may not have really understood the value exchange in the deal. It is a learning experience, and you should remember that you just got what you wanted!

Use Anchors

A starting offer is a position. If the other party does not agree with the starting offer, then a counteroffer is extended. These two positions are the anchors, and they define the range of the negotiation. In a single-issue negotiation this is a linear range. In a multiple-issue negotiation, it produces a multi-dimensional range where agreement will occur somewhere in an area of outcomes.

If you 'split the difference' between two anchors thereby reaching some half-way point, the final figure is quite meaningless. It seems fair but may not be to one of the parties. Again, this can be used as a technique to take you beyond a walk away position if the other anchor is very low (or high depending on the issue) compared to yours. The 'fairness' of the mythical half-way point is difficult to argue against because of the ethos implied. Just remember this can be used as a negotiation technique by an experienced trader.

Watch for 'Flinches'

Sometimes the other party can flinch or wince when an anchor / position is put on the table. In other words, the other party reacts to the anchor in some physical way. Seeing the flinch, the party setting the anchor moves it, usually to the advantage of the party that flinched. A flinch can prevent an anchor from taking hold, forcing a new anchor to be quickly established. A change of anchors reduces or increases the range of the negotiation and subsequently moves the mythical half-way point (where a lot of people end up). Rather than reacting to a flinch, the negotiator should take the opportunity to explain the anchor and why it was set in that position. A flinch is a negotiation technique that works well on inexperienced negotiators.

The way that people sometimes react to a flinch is to change their position prior to a counter-position being put forward e.g. a consultant offers to do a project for $5,000. The client flinches. Without any further discussion, the consultant reduces the fee by $500.

Negotiation is an Exchange of Information

During the trading process to get to a deal, you are constantly exchanging information. Knowledge is power, so gaining information about the other party's issues, positions, business, industry, and objectives provides you with an understanding of what they want, but more importantly, what they value. The more you know about what they really value, the greater the value you can extract from the deal.

Information is gained through research, but often the best understanding of value is gained through direct questioning. The other party will be doing the same, so trade question for questioon and use LAER (Listen, Acknowledge, Explore, Respond) to really understand their issues and interests. Focus on these issues and interests rather than their positions.

It is these interests and issues, logically or emotionally held values and mythical or ethical stances that underlie their positions and anchors. If you want them to move their anchor on an issue, then you really need to be able to frame your argument correctly using your knowledge of their values.

> **Top Tip:** Again we note it is almost impossible to argue by logic (logos) against a position that is held emotionally (pathos) or ethically (ethos). Similarly, it is hard to defend a mythical (muthos) anchor using logos.

Something to avoid and also watch out for is what is called a 'drum roll'.

Watch out for the 'Drum-Roll'

A drum roll is an indication that the following statement is important. When one party does a drum roll, the other party knows that an important point is about to be made - an issue or position of great value. A drum roll could be blatant such as "It is important that ... you start on Monday".Another indicator of a drum roll is a pause, followed by a very serious and direct specific closed question such as "Is Dan M on the team?" Assuming they are asking this because they want Dan on the team (rather than making sure he won't be), you immediately know that Dan can be charged out at full rate. An alternative way of asking this is an open question such as "Who will be on the team?" This might avoid the drum roll.

Avoiding drum rolls is mostly done by not emphasizing important points or issues that you require. Include these points in the normal course of conversation without bringing the other party's attention to their importance for you. This forms part of your concession strategy.

Concessions

It is normal for both parties to give some concessions to the other party during the negotiation. Concessions are positions, issues, or anchors that you give up in the exchange process. For example, you may give up the right to put inexperienced consultants on the project, or to charge accommodation for consultants you are flying in because you don't have the expertise locally. In the preparation stage and during the deal-making, you will decide what concessions you may give the other party and what their order of importance could be. They will be doing the same.

Some negotiators create a position of false value using the drum roll technique. For example, if you insist the car you are buying must be red and the dealer doesn't have any red ones left (a point you know in advance), by conceding on the colour the dealer might concede on the price. As you can see, good preparation, good research, probing questions and superior negotiation techniques can provide advantages.

Offers

When bargaining, it is normal for trading to consist of offers and counteroffers. All offers are signals as well as anchors. If the first offer is made and the anchor holds, then counter offers can be signals of eagerness. Counter offers that are too large or too quick create the impression that you will make further concessions. Offers based on small increments with increasing pauses create an impression that you won't move too far away from your anchor. Remember, to combat an anchor that is not moving, you need to understand the underlying values and issues. If that doesn't work, you can try expanding the pie. And if all else fails, you might take a break or try to bring in a mutually respected third party to break the deadlock. If the deal still continues to be unsatisfactory, then you might have to walk away.

Bidding Strategies

When bidding i.e. negotiating a position or making an offer, make sure you are not negotiating with yourself. Sometimes an inexperienced negotiator will put a position forward and instantly lose confidence in that position. Before the other party has time to respond they reduce their position. People who are 'big talkers' - those who cannot cope with long silences in conversations - are prone to this. The other party might be considering the offer in a positive way. Before they can respond or agree, the 'big talker' has made a better offer to them.

We are talking about two techniques here. The first is that a party should avoid making new proposals until the current proposal / issue / anchor is fully discussed. Examine it carefully using LAER. If it is a complex and interrelated set of positions, you can ask for a point-by-point response. Lawyers will do this regularly when negotiating.

The second technique is the slow response mentioned earlier. By simply taking your time, you can extract a concession from an inexperienced negotiator. Greg's father, an experienced sales executive, used to say to him:

"To have control, first you must exercise self-control"

Wise words that are best put into practice by detailed preparation including identifying and mitigating risk.

Risk

Different parties react differently to risk in accordance with their risk profile or appetite. If they have a large risk appetite, they will be open to innovative and uncertain approaches. If they have a small risk appetite, then they will be security conscious. If dealing with a client with a lesser risk appetite, you may want to consider breaking the project into smaller parts or phases.

At the end of each phase, offer a decision point to the client as to whether they want to continue with the project. Also, creating variable performance and payment deals can accommodate a wide range of risk profiles. It is not unusual to overestimate or underestimate risk in an information systems or digital transformation project.

> **Top Tip:** AInformation is the key to influencing the risk views of the other party. Prepare well!

Agreement

To reach a final agreement, you will have to close the negotiation and close the deal. Use the close types described in Chapter 4.

With engagements, you will need to document the scope and conditions of the project. Work through every part of the agreement and make sure you understand all the points. Should you both become aware of flaws or terms, which have been left out of the document, include them. The other party might suggest they are minor and don't need to be included. Perhaps they don't want these specific terms and conditions in the agreement.

It is reasonable to include any term or condition that you think is important. If the deal is large or complex, you should probably have a legal representative look it over.

Nibbles

Once the deal is done, watch out for nibbles. Nibbles are small extensions of work or little changes to scope, personnel etc. requested by one party after the deal has been concluded. Nibbles are often requested during the celebratory period directly after the deal has been sealed. Experienced negotiators know that people are prone to agree to nibbles during the post-signing euphoria, when goodwill is at its peak. The response to a nibble is to reopen the negotiation.

Personalities

Many negotiation books and articles concentrate on the personalities of the people involved in the bargaining.

Personality types are compared and analysed. These include such types as the aggressive, passive, and comedic. We are not going to address these types other than to say it is our belief that personality is not as important as the techniques that people use. If an aggressive person uses anger to dominate a negotiation, then consider your ongoing relationship with them during the conduct of the consulting engagement. Is this really a person that you want to deal with? Does their power match their aggression? Do they have rights and entitlements that allow them to dictate terms aggressively? It is better to recognise the technique than try and make a decision based on the other party's personality What is their game plan? We consider some of these concepts in the next section.

Game Plans

A game plan is a series of techniques or 'moves' that negotiators use to improve their outcome. Game plans tend to be based on power, rights and interests. A question to consider is:

"Who has the most power in this negotiation?"

If the power imbalance is very large, then the weaker party will always have to submit to the more powerful party's terms and conditions. Similarly, each party will have certain rights under legislation or regulation. Or perhaps you claim rights under an umbrella of ethical principles or general fairness. The question is, when can you claim these rights?

When power positions and rights positions are fairly equal, concessions and value propositions will be traded. In Table 11-2 and 11-3 are some common negotiation techniques with which one party tries to gain an advantage over another party. It is important to be aware of moves and countermoves, so that you can react to the other party's technique in an appropriate way.

Table 10-2 Negotiation Moves

Move	Description
Disapproving or Criticising Style	Judgement or criticism of the style of the other party e.g. "You are over-reacting"; "That is a bullying statement.
Making a Threat	Suggesting some aggressive act or danger that will make you give a further concession.
Disapproving or Criticising Style	Judgement or criticism of the style of the other party e.g. "You are over-reacting"; "That is a bullying statement.
Making a Threat	Suggesting some aggressive act or danger that will make you give a further concession.
Challenging Competence	One party challenges the expertise, qualifications or competence of the other party to establish greater power.
Humiliate ideas	An antagonistic approach towards issues or positions put forward by the other party in an aggressive way to reduce the value of the proposition.

A 'move' is when one party uses a technique to gain an advantage in the negotiation. A 'counter move' is a technique to either reduce that advantage or deflect the technique. Some 'moves' have the intention to shock, catch you 'off guard' or put you 'off balance' and so create a power imbalance. Rather than react as expected, a professional negotiator will remain calm and recognise the 'move' as a negotiation technique. The 'moves' come in all different types. We present some example moves in Table 10-2.

As you can see, there are a wide range of moves to make as well as be aware of. It is also important to understand some basic counter moves. We demonstrate some counter-moves in Table 10-3.

Table 10-3 Negotiation Counter Moves

Counter-move	Description
Name and shame	Demonstrating that you are aware of the move e.g., "I could sue you for that remark," or "We all know you would not do that!"
Interrupt	Taking a break can interrupt the logical and emotional flow of a negotiation.
Question	"How would you answer if someone else asked you that question?" or "Help me understand why that's important to you."
Correct	Provide an alternative explanation or add additional research or facts.
Change tack	Shift the focus to another point or change to a power or rights debate.

Recognising a move and using a counter move takes practice. It is common for parties to just react to a move. Moves are made by professional negotiators to put the other party off balance. Or they could be made by amateurs who lack the ability to develop a good relationship. To react with a counter move in an effective manner, you have to recognise the move. The following example shows the effectiveness of dealing with a move properly.

Example:
"You are getting too emotional about this issue" [The other party is criticizing your style]

"No, I am not!" [this counter could spiral unproductively and is not recommended] rather...

"I care about this issue a lot." [You logically support your position]

"Lets focus on the problem not my reaction." [You are countering their technique by changing tack]

"Why would you say such a thing?" [Questioning with potential for name and shame].

These techniques are powerful tools and take practice. After a while they come naturally and you get a sense of calm and control in a negotiation context. There are lots of little negotiations in real life that will give you opportunities to try these techniques.

Chapter Summary

There are many general techniques that you can use to gain advantage in the negotiation process. The important things to remember are the three phases: preparation, deal-making and agreement. Each of these phases has specific considerations and techniques.

Negotiation happens at two levels. The first level deals with the content; you need knowledge of the issues and the objectives that you want to achieve. The second level deals with the strategy and techniques employed by the negotiators. Most people only operate at the first level. Hopefully this chapter has given you some tools, so that you can operate at the second level and become a more skilled negotiator.

Chapter 11 - Practical Considerations for Dealing with Change

Chapter guide

In this chapter, we cover a range of practical change situations that IS consultants and BAs will encounter. Our focus is on a combination of change situations that practitioners will encounter almost daily – People, Process and Technology change.

We introduce change within the context of the consulting lifecycle phases and concentrate on how practitioners can increase the likelihood of change succeeding. In this chapter we cover:

- Reactions to change such as the stages of grief
- How to increase the likelihood of change success
- Change models – how to identify and use the right model for the job
- Change considerations during the IS Consulting lifecycle
- Four steps for dealing with change
- The importance of governance in successful change.

Introduction to Change

In Chapter 1 we established the environment in which Information System Consultants and Business Analysts work. In Chapter 2, we established that the principal outcome of information systems consulting projects is organisational change. IS consultants and BAs build a better and brighter future for their clients through invention, improvement or development i.e. change of business processes, systems and technologies.

For some in the client firm, the change is welcome, necessary for survival and competitiveness. For others it is not welcome, unnecessary, scary and an anathema.

For Example: For the last 30 years, enterprise systems have been dominating the computer software marketplace, creating some of the largest software companies in the world. Many of these systems were initially implemented in the late 1990s and early 2000s and are so large and complex that replacement is almost impossible. However, change to these legacy systems needs to be a scheduled part of maintenance and ongoing investment. Otherwise, their existence creates massive technical debt

In reality, thousands and thousands of people around the world make their living from being expert in keeping these legacy systems and processes running, particularly within their firm or industry. Replacing these with new software or a cloud platform threatens to make their expertise almost worthless. How do you think these people feel, and how can you best transition to the new system in a positive and planned way?

Large and complex business processes and systems need real expertise to operate and maintain. It takes years of training, experience and expertise to master such complexity. This requires all the knowledge, skills and experience (competencies) of working with a Systems Thinking mindset as covered in Chapter 2.

Dealing With vs Managing Change

We are not keen on the term 'Change Management'. It suggests that by using specific management techniques, executives can monitor and control the emotions of their workforce throughout a change event.

We prefer the term 'dealing with change' because in certain cases, the sense of loss (of the AS-IS situation) is very real to the individual, and this loss can be recognised, but not always reconciled.

In many ways this is reflected in a phenomenon called systems separation anxiety.

Systems Separation Anxiety

When an information systems person does a job well, like any other, they are satisfied. They feel fulfilled, proud of their skill, achievements and proficiency.

As highlighted in the previous example, skilled technicians identify with their skillset and, to varying extents, can appropriate the technology. Appropriation means to connect with their specific technology skills as part of their identity. It becomes part of them and a source of self-esteem.

There are plenty of examples: try taking a 'Mac' devotee into a Windows environment; or, suggesting a MOODLE person move to a Teams for Education platform; or, that a LINUX buff shifts to a fully Windows environment; or, a V8 petrol-head shifts to a TESLA... you get the picture!

People, Process, Data and Technology are at the heart of Information Systems change. To plan to 'wrench' the technology away from someone who has appropriated it is like taking away a part of their life; it ceases their interactions with a familiar world. To change a system or process with which a person strongly identifies, is like moving them to a foreign country. They don't speak the language; everything is different, and they are not sure what to do. They experience loss; loss of familiarity, loss of fluency; loss of part of their identity.

Change requires careful planning and skillful execution: applying logos, pathos and ethos is a good place to start.

Logos, Pathos and Ethos – Reactions Differ

Professional practitioners always plan to treat people affected by changed circumstances with respect and care. The reaction to change for those not affected can be a logical one (logos) - 'it needs to be done so we can maintain our competitive advantage in our markets'. The reaction to change for those who are affected can be emotional (pathos). The emotions vary over the change period. Preparing for this emotional rollercoaster and dealing with it as best as one can, reduces the general organisational stress that can arise when change is inevitable.

Logos often doesn't work very well. And logos is what people often receive in organisational settings.

Here are some examples of (largely management) views we have encountered over the years:

> **Example**: "Once they get used to the new system, they will love it. It fixes all the problems of the old system" (logos response)
> "I don't know why everyone is so down on this change. They need to get over it!" (ignoring pathos)
> "A bit of training will fix things up. Besides, they should be welcoming a new and exciting system!" (logos response and potentially getting the pathos response very wrong)

Part of a practitioner's role is to help the client understand these different reactions and to convince them of the wisdom of investing in building change capability into the project to overcome and deal with the stages people move through from an emotional perspective.

Stages of Grief

Another good starting point is understanding the stages people move through when confronted with change. Here it is useful to compare the reaction of some to change to the death of a friend or acquaintance. While people get used to the person's absence over time, the fact remains that all interaction with that person has ceased forever and many experience the change through the stages of grief.

In 1969, Swiss Psychiatrist Elisabeth Kubler-Ross[45] studied terminally ill patients and derived five stages of grief through which people pass. Her influential book, 'On Death and Dying' has informed multiple change approaches, research models and other practices. She extended this research to other situations including relationship breakups, loss of job, incarceration, personal loss and further catastrophes. These stages are commonly cited and may be familiar.

The stages of grief Kubler-Ross identified (as shown in Table 11-1) remain useful and informative when considered in the context of a major information systems change.

Helping your client understand and plan how to deal with change requires a good working knowledge of a wide range of possible change approaches to increase the chance of success.

Table 11-1 Adapted from Kubler-Ross's 5 Stages of Grief

Stage	Explanation
Denial	In this stage the person is trying to block the reality of the situation, refusing to accept the situation. At this stage they mainly believe that the change or course of events may not necessarily occur.
Anger	Once the person realizes that denial is futile, they can become angry with others (or themselves) for the situation in which they find themselves. In this state, dealing with these people requires skilled and sensitive handling and can be challenging.
Bargaining	People will try to negotiate or bargain for a 'better' outcome to achieve an escape-path from their situation. This is a sign of moving towards acceptance, but they are not there yet.
Depression	During this stage, affected employees can become sullen, cynical and communicate less. They can become uncooperative, even disruptive in subtle and undermining ways. This stage is marked by sadness and fear of an uncertain future. This can be, however, the start of acceptance of that unknown future.
Acceptance	Employees realize that they can't resist the inevitable and they begin to accept it. They are showing signs of coming to terms with the change.

Increasing the Likelihood of Change Success

According to change research conducted by Prosci, ignoring the people side of change can have dire consequences. Failing to analyse change impacts and plan for the implementation, adoption and usage of a new system, process or technical solution, risks increased costs and unrealized expectations.

Cost escalation can arise from poor requirements analysis which in turn can lead to costs associated with 'redesigning, reworking, revisiting, redoing, retraining, rescoping'[46], and in some cases, pulling back. Any of these unintended outcomes can lead to unrealized expectations, even project failure.

To a very significant extent, change is about people and change leadership capability. Failing to plan for and lead the people side of change contributes to greater absenteeism and attrition, reduced productivity, lower morale, and disengaged employees. In addition, customers and other key stakeholders can also feel the impacts. Dealing with change helps you mitigate these sometimes mission-critical risks.

Change can impact processes, systems, technology, tools, job roles, accountabilities, workflows, mindsets, behaviours, customers, suppliers and ultimately strategic success or failure.

Each change impacts different groups within your client organisation differently. In our experience, the most important steps to helping a client deal with a proposed change starts with determining two things:

- The likely People, Process, Data and Technological impacts of the change proposed; and,
- The client organisation, business unit or team's change capability – how mature are they in this regard?

We already covered change impact analysis in Chapter 7 Impacts to be managed. Gauging your client's change capability maturity will help you identify and recommend an appropriate change model and approach. It will also help you identify and manage risk. Impact Analysis can also determine your Approach, as described in Chapter 7).

Change Maturity Analysis

Change models provide a framework for analysing and measuring an organisation's maturity and can help you identify and prioritise areas for improvement.

Maturity analysis refers to the process of assessing an organisation's level of maturity in a particular area, such as change, technical or governance capability. This can be done using a maturity model, which is a framework for measuring a company's maturity. Usually, these models divide maturity into levels or stages as the basis of maturity assessment.

Assessing Organisational Maturity

The first step in assessing the organisation's maturity is to choose a maturity model that is relevant to the client situation and specific to the type of changes you need to evaluate. For example, technical, people or process change, strategic change, or capability change.

There are many different maturity models available online, each focusing on a different area of organisational capability. Some common examples include the Capability Maturity Model Integration (CMMI) for software development; the Organisational Project Management Maturity Model (OPM3) for project management; and the Prosci Change Management Maturity Model for change management.

Once company leaders understand their current organisational maturity, they are more likely to support parallel capability development towards a higher maturity level and embrace a recommended model. Many commonly available maturity models provide tools and resources to help you assess the organisation's maturity, including questionnaires or self-assessment templates to help you gather the information you need to evaluate the organisation's capabilities and determine its current level of maturity.

Levels of Maturity

The specific levels of organisational maturity vary depending on the maturity model being used. However, most maturity models divide maturity into several levels or stages, with each level representing a higher degree of maturity.

For example, the Prosci Change Management Maturity Model has five (5) levels, ranging from no change management to organisational competency. Each level involves more attention and management of the people side of change. Levels are:

1. Ad Hoc or Absent Change Management
2. Change Management on Isolated Projects
3. Multiple Projects with Change Management
4. Organisational Standards for Change Management
5. Organisational Competency in Change Management

Similarly, the Capability Maturity Model Integration (CMMI) for software development has five levels of maturity:

- Initial
- Managed
- Defined

- Quantitatively Managed
- Optimizing.

These two examples clearly illustrate the usefulness of helping your client see where their capabilities lie and where these will help or hinder change achievement. These insights are also useful when considering an appropriate model for change.

Using the right Change Model

A skilled practitioner will work with the client to identify which model or combination of models will help manage risk and increase the chances of delivering the expected change outcome. There are multiple proven change models. However, not all models are created equal. Many are designed for large-scale organisational changes while others are better used for smaller business transitions. In Table 11-2 we showcase some common change models, highlighting the type of change circumstances that best suits each model. Once you have selected a model, you can use or modify its criteria to evaluate your client organisation's current capabilities and determine which level of the model best describes their current state of maturity. Another check practitioners can make is to consider change during the different phases of the IS Consulting Lifecycle.

Table 11-2 Sample of change models and their uses

Model Example	Uses
ADKAR	This is a good model to use in conjunction with strategic change models as it builds management and employee buy in. **ADKAR** is an acronym for the five stages an individual experiences when going through change and the need to create: 1. **Awareness**: of change necessity 2. **Desire**: enthusiasm for the change 3. **Knowledge**: individuals know what to expect and what you expect of them in the change process 4. **Ability**: employees have the training they require to carry out the changes 5. **Reinforcement**: ensure employees have everything necessary to keep these changes ADKAR focuses on starting a discussion with employees about the reasons why changes are necessary. It values clear instructions about how to implement changes and what employees can expect. It also allows employees to participate in the process which helps them feel valued.

Model Example	Uses
People, Process, Data and Technology	Commonly only referred to as the PPT (People, Process and Technology) model, this is a good base change model for IS consultants and BAs alike, especially when data analysis and business intelligence requirements are added in. This model is versatile, as it can be used for small-and large-scale change.
Kotter's 8-step change model	John Kotter's eight step change model is another that is useful when the people aspects of change are a key success factor (or barrier / risk). The eight steps of Kotter's model are: 1. Creating a sense of urgency 2. Building strong coalitions 3. Forming strategic visions 4. Getting everyone involved 5. Enabling action by removing obstacles 6. Generating short-term achievements 7. Sustaining the changes 8. Instituting the changes The model ensures that employees understand why change is necessary and can be useful if employee resistance is anticipated. The framework helps build trust and encourages teamwork. By setting out clear objectives, it can bring staff together to support each other as a team.
McKinsey 7-S	This is a complex model which is useful for difficult transitions involving strategic change with impacts across the whole organisation. The seven 'S's are: strategy, structure, systems, shared values, style, staff and skills. The seven elements represent each part of an organisation's processes, from the employees to company culture. According to the model, strategy, structure and system are the 'hard elements' which are easier to control. Shared values such as staff, style and skills make up the 'soft elements', which are more cultural and difficult to change.

Change during the IS Consulting / BA Lifecycle

Depending on which change model is most appropriate to your client situation, it is also useful to consider change during the stages of the IS Consulting Lifecycle. Increasing familiarity with a new information system provides stakeholders with a better understanding of how it will be employed in their context.

During the Dialogue / Diagnose and Plan / Design stage of a systems development or configuration project, users are often asked to provide input into the new design. This process provides some 'buy-in' by the stakeholders into the new system. But this process is frequently flawed.

Without a full understanding of the new architecture and its capabilities, users are not yet able to maximize the design of the new system. Considering how best to deal with the impacts of change during these two phases will provide useful insights when preparing your change approach and when preparing communications associated with change (see section 10-5).

Equally, change impact or change performance analysis conducted during the perform stage, or during the 'making the change 'sticky" stages of the lifecycle (covered later in this chapter), requires careful analysis. Here, both impact and urgency analysis can be useful.

Alternatively, the practitioner may need to return to the Dialogue / Diagnose phase to identify and mitigate root causes or risks.

Watch for Suboptimal Approaches

Rather than create and redefine new business processes, there can be a tendency to want to recreate existing processes within the new technical architecture.

Such suboptimal behaviour is commonly accepted, even asked for by clients because it reduces the organisational knowledge stress on the broader population of users. The knowledge stress, in this case, transfers to the technical team, who are responsible for configuration, extensions, program changes and other modifications. "Leave the radical process changes to the next iteration" is a sentiment often heard in client firms.

As the users and stakeholders become familiar with the new systems, often through actual use after go-live, they realise its capabilities and start to suggest changes and modifications. This is a true sign of acceptance within the client firm. Before this acceptance starts to take hold, however, there are challenges for the IS consultant.

These challenges can be more easily understood by returning to Kubler-Ross's work (as shown in Figure 11-1) and understanding the emotional (pathos) implications when dealing with the stages of change.

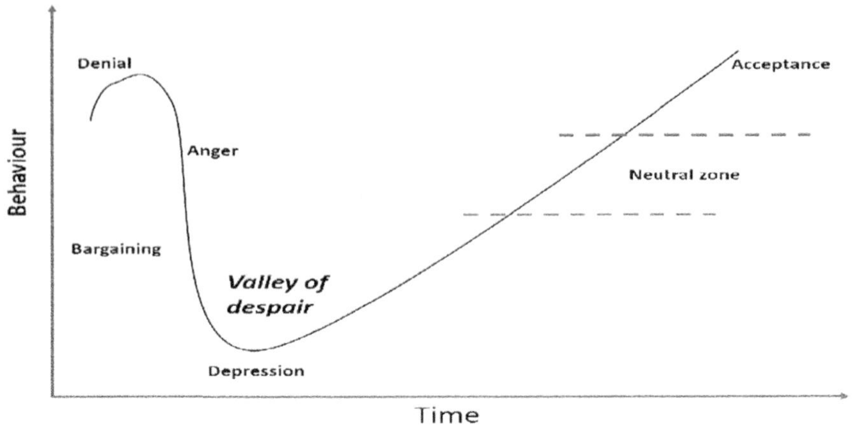

Figure 11-1 The Valley of Despair

Emotional challenges have characteristic behaviours, most of which lay within the common phenomenon of reduced or low morale. Low morale can impact affected and unaffected client staff, around the bargaining and depression stages of grief, and is sometimes referred to as entering the 'Valley of Despair'.

As people emerge from the valley of despair, they enter a neutral zone, where they may make the change towards a positive view of the future. During this period, IS consultants should try to communicate the vision of a future life beyond the 'go-live' point.

One problem often faced by IS Consultants is that by this time, having completed the implementation and passed the go-live and initial support stages, they have exited the organisation. So, the change issues arising later are blamed on the consultants' prior activities. Building a change strategy into the assignment in the post-implementation stage can alleviate this issue.

While Kubler-Ross's work has been accepted by many, it has also been challenged. Some research has shown that, overall, staff in organisations can be reasonably adaptable and adhere to the program of change.

For this to occur, staff must perceive that management is across the situation, support the change and communicate regularly to staff. Look at any list of reasons for project failure and you will find the entry 'lack of executive commitment'.

Not all client staff will experience these stages of grief, but some certainly will. If those affected strongly are vocal or influential amongst their peers, then their change issues must be dealt with effectively. Irrespective of the numbers affected, it is good practice to deal with the change associated with information systems projects.

Once you understand the client organisation's change capability and maturity, and how they might move through the stages of change, you are better placed to craft and recommend an approach that will most likely deliver the promised change outcomes.

Next, we suggest four practical steps for dealing with change.

Four steps to Dealing with Change

In this section, (see Figure 11-2) we briefly consider four activities that assist a client organisation deal with change. These four activities are to Prepare, Communicate, Address the Knowledge Gaps and Make the Change 'sticky'.

Preparing for Change

The initial phases will likely follow a project planning approach. You are planning the project and you are planning a change implementation. Change

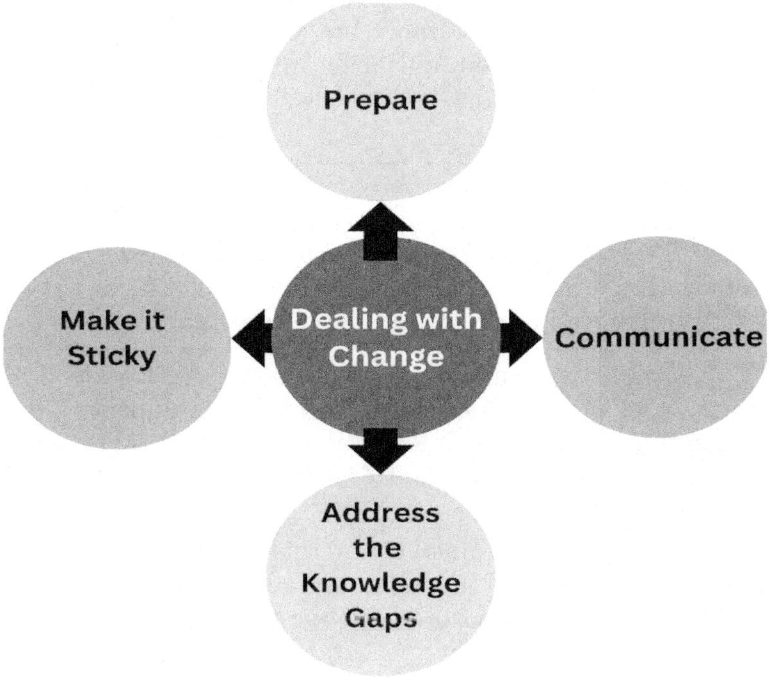

Figure 11-2 Four ways to deal with change

arising from Information Systems does not usually appear overnight.Prior to their execution, decisions are made to either buy or develop software and to change or rearrange processes. Consequently, news of the change will generally precede the change itself. This provides an opportunity for the client, usually in conjunction with their consultant or BA, to take control of the communication channels in a proactive manner.

In (the loop) versus Out (of the loop) Groups

Once the first communications are made, a new division in the client firm can arise. The first group in this division is the 'in' group, who took part in the decision-making and should mostly be committed to the change. The 'out' group includes the remaining staffand external stakeholders, upon whom the effects of the decision will be dispensed, and who have little control or power over that decision. Since consultants and / or BAs are always part of the 'in' group, emotional reactions can be directed towards them as well as to the executive decision-making group.

Conventional change wisdom suggests bringing the wider organisation into the conversation about the forthcoming change preferably in both the Dialogue / Diagnose and Plan/Design phases. This is good practice, allowing the client executive and consulting team to further gauge reactions and the readiness of the organisation to change. Involvement and engagement will then inform a decision about how much change can occur without major negative impacts.

> **Top Tip:** Remember, the role of an IS consultant and BA is to affect beneficial organisational change through information systems. If the change looks like it might not be beneficial, because the client firm is not ready or capable, it is in the interests of all parties to consider alternative paths to the required outcomes.

During IS projects, typical actions to include stakeholders in the change process include: meetings; co-design workshops; information or briefing sessions; printed or electronic information sheets; and, other communication channels such as chat forums, and Teams or Zoom briefings or forums for remote staff.

Strategies, such as the creation of an internal client team that works with the consultants, merely extend the 'in' group and further identify and perhaps solidify the 'out' group. To extend the 'in' group as widely as possible, the client executive must explain the reasons for change and measure the effectiveness of these communications.

Preparing to Communicate

Communication planning needs to include an engagement plan targeted at identified key people. It will also include project communication (governance reporting) as well as suggestions for pre- and post-implementation communications such as management and staff briefings and opportunities for consultation or co-design. This ensures your approach deals with the change at all levels, and at the appropriate time throughout the whole process. It is important that change communication is carefully planned and controlled. If there are no plans or controls, if a change event is 'leaked' to the staff, rumours can develop with incorrect information, fuelling stress and uncertainty.

As already discussed, decisions around new or changed information systems arrangements can impact the morale of staff (e.g. outsourcing schemes where job changes and job losses are common).

The planned and deliberate timing of announcements regarding these plans can reduce uncertainty, thereby avoiding rumours and other channels of misinformation. Planned and managed briefings, engagement forums and communications contribute to greater buy-in and smoother changes in the organisation.

> **Top Tip:** When determining what you will communicate consider the risks involved in the change process at the same time. (see Table 11-3)

A risk assessment that considers all affected segments will provide some indication of what information needs to be disseminated to each segment.

As well as a risk assessment, practitioners should consider the impacts of the people, process or technology change for each target audience or segment and refer to or initiate any required maturity or capability analyses.

By conducting impact, capability and maturity analyses and understanding the effects of the change on the individual parts of the organisation, practitioners can craft targeted messages, design workshop and consultation events, improved vision statements and craft relevant future-state messages.

Creating a Communications Plan

In this section we return to communication planning, this time with an emphasis on change communication planning - Table 10-3. This table looks at each stage of the lifecycle and provides an overview of the objective (what) examples of interventions you might use (how) and the timing of these (when) as well as who to target.

To complete a change communication plan, review Table 8-4 'Considerations for reporting and governance' to refresh your knowledge about how to target your plan.

Then consider the following tips to build you knowledge:

1. Identify your key audiences, **WHO** and **HOW** – their needs in terms of what messages, medium type, frequency and volume / level of detail;
2. Align the **WHAT** aspects of your plan with the project plan and key milestones, from the perspective of both the focus of key messages as well as the timing, ensuring that you have a pre-launch phase at the beginning as per Table 10-3;
3. Craft communication objectives for each audience, and medium type. Important messages can be targeted at specific segments, packaged in an appropriate way and delivered with maximum impact. It is important to communicate at the right time using the right medium.
4. **WHEN** - Schedule the following: Launch events and consultation or co-design workshops; the creation of briefing packs for senior leaders, managers and team leaders for key phases of the project; and, project reports and governance communications to align with the project plan **REVIEW** - chedule to elicit feedback about project communications (applicable to large scale change projects) as well as identify communications expectations for post-implementation review.

The main point to remember is that implementing a technical change is just a matter of effort. But organisations are not technical artifacts, they are made up of people who respond to change in different ways. Communication is the way new ideas and new processes are disseminated to people. Get the communication right, and you will find that dealing with the change is simpler and easier.

Crafting different Message Types

An important step in dealing with change is having the client executives, managers and team leaders communicate the rationale behind the change to the stakeholders. Research suggests that most people want to hear significant work-related news, face-to-face from their immediate manager or supervisor[47]. Always start with creating communication objectives for every topic and audience.

Table 11-3 Change Communication Plan

Stages	Who	What	How	When
Post-decision to proceed	Board, senior leaders, managers and supervisors; project sponsor and leader	Clear understanding of the different audiences; identified needs, and preferred methods and media type and timing of communication; clear understanding of timing and frequency	Method of delivery: Multimedia; risk registers; Management and team leader briefings; staff consultation forums; co-design workshops; face to face meetings; open door and 'brown-bag' lunch time sessions; meetings with key stakeholders and key customers; intranet Q&A and project progress site; new user champion examples; videos; newsletters; project updates and reporting; governance reporting.	Timing to coincide with project milestones and target segment needs; to coincide with senior leader reporting and compliance require -ments; to meet identified staff expectations of timing, frequency and medium; to inform decision-making; To support agile project processes; to register risk, monitor and mitigate.
Dialogue / Diagnose	Senior leaders, managers and practitioners			
Plan / Design	Senior leaders, managers and practitioners			
Perform	Senior leaders, managers and project team			
Post Project	Senior leaders, managers, project team and senior consultant or BA			

Creating Compelling Views of the Future for each Segment

Part of creating the appetite for change is helping stakeholder segments understand what the post-change future holds. Each stakeholder segment will experience a different future, so a single vision is not sufficient.

The client executive needs to craft a vision for every segment, not just the employees or users of the new systems. These visions should entice stakeholders to want to see the change happen, to arouse their curiosity about the outcomes. In some cases, this means creating a sense of urgency.

Using Rationales

Rationales can either be positive: 'the company will be a better place because of these new processes and systems' or negative: 'if we don't do this change, the company will be worse off, and this will impact on you, our employees, as well as our customers and other stakeholders'. Crafting a suite of messages to the stakeholder segments, with the rationale behind the change, will keep the communication channel control within the client executive team. Rationale messages might take the form of stories.

Using Stories

Stories can be a powerful communication form. Effectively, they bundle facts, reasons and logic (logos) into an emotional package (pathos). Stories can draw on the ethos of the firm and address the emotional responses of the stakeholders, who are the ones dealing with the change. Reasons for change are important to the internal processing of change by employees. Wrapping these reasons into an emotionally charged story can help their journey towards acceptance.

Crafting Briefings for Managers and Supervisors

Practitioners can help in this regard by creating a set of messages for each stakeholder group. By helping them prepare and present materials, stories, videos and rationales, they assist in helping to explain to their people why this change will be good for the organisation and for them, or alternatively, why not changing will be detrimental.

Creating Contingency Messages

While strong leadership from the client executive and their visible backing for the change is important, practitioners should be wary of the employees who do not back the proposed changes. Weakness in the desire for change at the top allows naysayers in the middle and the bottom of the organisation to flourish. Creating a vision and contingency messages about a shared future and the benefits for all stakeholders, with a suitable sense of urgency, will assist the client executive to drive the change within and outside the organisation. Remember, any customers or suppliers affected by systems change are important stakeholders and the change on them also needs to be managed professionally.

Addressing the Knowledge Gaps

As discussed earlier, the grief that may arise from changed systems and processes is often linked to the existing knowledge a person or team has about the current systems and processes. These people identify with these systems and processes because they know them; know what to do when things go awry; know how to manage them under awkward or uncertain conditions; know how to make them 'sing'. A new process or system requires a familiarisation process, generally achieved with education and training. From our many years' experience in IS, knowledge management and education, we can attest to the three stages of employee development during an IS change event or process. These comprise a three-step process as set out in Figure 11-3:

- Knowledge transfer from experts (internal and external) to a growing number of users;
- Evidence that new knowledge and competence and confidence in the use of the new systems, process or technology is growing and people are using these as intended; and,
- Evidence that there is strong uptake, few if any consequences of an old system, process or technology being turned off and emerging evidence of advanced users and champions.

By the time the third phase has been reached, the new approach has become part of culture – 'and how the organisation conducts its work. The knowledge has been transferred into the organisation.

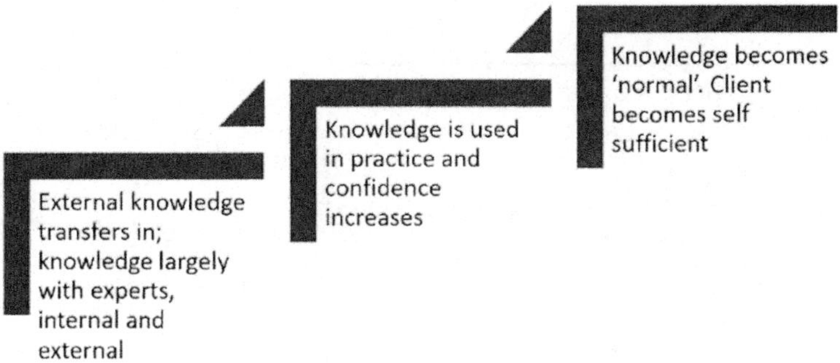

Figure 11-3 Steps in Client Knowledge Acquisition

By the time the third phase has been reached, the new approach has become part of culture – 'and how the organisation conducts its work. The knowledge has been transferred into the organisation.

Knowledge Transfer into the Organisation

A new system is designed with the assistance of (external) IS consultants. BAs in particular work with clients to identify user requirements and use-cases. Both consultants and BAs identify needs and configure or build the system or process in a co-creation partnership.

Knowledge about the new system or process usually emanates from external sources; typically, consultants, trainers or other lead users. Knowledge and process 'cheat sheets' can be embedded into knowledge bases on an intranet where help and content can be searchable.

Information Systems consultants bring their external product, service and system knowledge in and combine it with the client knowledge during the change project.

Another strategy for Knowledge Transfer to the organisation is to hire personnel from outside the client or place consultants in the client organisation on a variable cost, fixed-term contract basis.

Practical Application by the New Users and Stakeholders

During test phases or after go-live, users and stakeholders become familiar with the system and work with external knowledge sources who provide support or guidance.

As mentioned previously, the beginning of this phase can be very difficult (during the 'Valley of Despair' shown in Figure 11-1) as new users grapple to familiarize themselves with the change and create new personal routines that grow into a body of expertise.

> **Top Tip:** Always ask external suppliers to provide detailed product information and access to training manuals, online help and training materials. You can save a lot of time and money by using or modifying existing materials developed by suppliers. Quality, accessible learning materials are essential for maximising knowledge transfer, and for moving the organisation into confident and competent users of a new system.

Knowledge Self-Sufficiency

Over time users become less dependent on external sources of expertise and become self-sufficient users of the new systems and processes. In a mature knowledge organisation, users frequently interact with each other to solve problems, run internal training on systems / processes. Some client firms create a searchable knowledge base to assist their support processes.

A word of warning. Systems projects can often run overtime, also affecting the budget. Training is a late phase in a systems project and becomes an easy budget item to reduce. The timing of training also becomes problematic if the project runs overtime.

Ensure that training is executed as closely as possible to go-live, to reduce the gap between Knowledge Transfer and the opportunity for Practical Application.

Making the Change 'Sticky'

Unlike some other types of organisational change, systems changes are generally replacing an old product or process with a new one. There is little opportunity for client personnel to go back to using the old system, unless it is a pure process change.

Access to the old system is either restricted or not technically available. If it is an entirely new system that automates a manual process, then the risk of reversion exists. The practitioner should examine ways to make the new system or process 'sticky' with a focus on what will work for the specific organisation, division and/or team.

'Sticky' change is visible when three areas of agreed value or improvement are evident:

1. Improved performance;
2. Improved individual performance; and,
3. Improved change capability e.g., identified areas of knowledge or skills gaps, or change leadership capabilities have measurably improved.

Measures of Improved Performance

These measures will differ for each project because they are associated with the project achieving the desired outcomes, outputs, goals and objectives, the OOGOs agreed from the proposal and embedded into the guiding contract (consultants) or statement of intent (BAs). These Measurable Organisation Value (MOV) metrics focus on whether or not the project or initiative delivered what was expected. While most are pure MOV, some can also represent User Calculated Value (UCV) or Client Calculated Value

(CCV). Here are some examples of performance metrics:

- Adherence to project contract, project plan and KPI achievement – simple MOV measures such as on time, in full, within budget, or those measures that directly align with a governance metric from the organisation's strategy or current business plan.
- Performance improvements – % improvements from the current state to the desired outcome - classic MOV!
- Business and change capability – these are commonly CCV or UCV measures of satisfaction with leadership and management of the change process.
- Benefit realization and ROI - can be either CCV or MOV.
- Quality of execution – degree of knowledge transfer; usability and user experience measures - CCV or UCV measures.

Measures of Individual Performance

These UCV and CCV measures indicate the extent of confidence in the outcome, (e.g. competence and knowledge transfer) and comfort (confidence and satisfaction) of individuals impacted by the change process and outcomes. Measures identify where employees are in the change process and how they are progressing.

Individual performance metrics can be used flexibly to determine individual employee or individual team or business unit performance improvements associated with the change, and include:

- Awareness and understanding of the change
- Employee engagement, buy-in and participation measures
- Adoption, and utilization evaluation
- Compliance and adherence evaluation
- Competency, proficiency and confidence measures, and observations of behavioural change
- System generated issue, compliance and error logs
- Service and help desk issue, compliance and error logs and calls and requests for support
- Employee satisfaction surveys – especially if a benchmark survey was conducted before project kick-off

Measures of change capability improvement

Regardless of the type of change, all structured change management initiatives rely on the capability of the senior leaders, managers, supervisors and employees to embrace and make the agreed change, and to make it 'sticky' to achieve the desired ROI. It is also useful to consider measuring the success of the change plan and activities conducted throughout the process. According to comprehensive global research on digital leadership conducted by MIT Sloan and Capgemini[48] investing in a combination of the right resources (e.g., financial and technological) as well as leadership capability development produced significant improvements in profitability, market capitalization and revenue generation in all types of organisation, and within all industry sectors – no exceptions. This seminal research did not specify the change processes used. However, we suggest that measures associated with improved organisation and individual performance can provide both UCV and CCV indicators of change process and MOV measures of overall program success.

A strategy-matching mix of incentives and disincentives, promotional materials and commitment by the client's senior leaders and managers will enhance 'stickiness'. Celebrating step achievements along the way is a common tactic to keep momentum going during a systems project.

The Role of Governance in making Change 'Sticky'

There's a saying that has been around for decades:

'What gets measured, is what gets done'.

This saying suggests that if those responsible and accountable for projects also have an expectation of measurement and reporting (i.e., project governance as well as corporate governance oversight of large-scale projects) then the probability of a project being delivered as agreed becomes higher.

Scheduled measurement and reporting helps to keep managers, supervisors and practitioners focused on what you're trying to achieve.

Without governance oversight, the OOGOs, milestones, measures, and standards are no longer kept front of mind and therefore risk being side-lined in preference for business as usual.

Expectations of governance starts with senior leader focus and clear expectations.

There are three areas of governance oversight. You are looking for governance structures, processes and relational mechanisms[49]:

- Governance structures - clear roles, responsibilities and accountabilities, Board, Senior leaders, technical specialists, external suppliers and project team;
- Governance processes - proposal and contract quality, planned project OOGOs, reporting and communication type and frequency, risk registers; and,
- Governance relational mechanisms - effective meetings, problem-solving and performance coaching, consultation and co-design approaches and well targeted communications at all levels.

Each of these three areas can also be used to test maturity and to cross-check for measurable value and its achievement. Planning for and measuring the success of these capabilities will increase the chance of lasting, 'sticky' change and the expected Return on Investment (ROI).

Chapter Summary

New systems, technology and processes can affect all parts of a business operation from organisational structures and governance processes to staff productivity and morale. New jobs and roles are often created, requiring new skills and perhaps new attitudes.

In modern organisations, innovation and change is needed to maintain relevant and competitive. Systems changes are accelerating as AI, cloud platforms and automated systems pervade all aspects of client operations and management. IS consultants and BAs have a large role in this innovation and rapid transformation.

Often, during the engagement phase, IS consultants and BAs challenge their clients to experiment and reach out beyond their comfort zone. Consequently, it is their role to return them to their comfort zone, to a state where knowledge transfer builds capability –competence and confidence - at the end of a systems- or process-driven change.

There are four change management considerations that IS consultants and BAs should attend to in assisting their clients deal with the change associated with systems and process projects. These are:

- Preparation;
- Communication;
- Addressing knowledge gaps; and,
- Making change 'sticky'.

Bringing the outcomes, outputs, goals and objectives into how each project is measured and monitored (governed) will not only increase the chances of project success, your personal, team or your consulting firm's credibility and reputation are likely enhanced.

In an information systems project, success is mainly based on getting the people on board with the change.

In the next chapter we cover negotiation.

Endnotes

45. Kubler-Ross, E. (1969). On death and dying (Vol. 1). New York: Macmillan.

46. Why Change Management (prosci.com)

47.Larkin, T. J., & Larkin, S. (1996). Reaching and changing frontline employees. Harvard Business Review, 74(3), 95-104.

48.Westerman, G., Tannou, M., Bonnet, D., Ferraris, P., & McAfee, A. (2012). The digital advantage: How digital leaders outperform their peers in every industry.https://ide.mit.edu/wp-content/uploads/2016/04/TheDigitalAdvantage.pdf

49. De Haes, S., & Van Grembergen, W. (2015). Enterprise Governance of IT: Achieving Alignment and Value (Second edition).

Springer.

Book Conclusion

This concludes our practice guide covering many of the activities and capabilities of IS Consultants and Business Analysts. We hope you've found it informative and useful.

In this book we have looked at the consulting lifecycle, engagement, proposals and using a business canvas to prepare them, presentations, client meetings, negotiation and change. The lens we often use has three important elements: logos, pathos and ethos – logic, emotion and ethics.

Using this lens helps make you aware that the systems-change you are trying to influence others to adopt relies on decisions made by people and ultimately affects a wide range of people.

Everyone has their own history of experiences that shape their reactions to change, information, arguments and attempts to influence their decisions. The approaches we suggest in this book consider these histories of experience by making you aware of them and by providing practical, enabling techniques that address important consulting elements in a holistic way.

We urge you to use these techniques in your professional practice.

Notes

Printed in Dunstable, United Kingdom

91342616R00188